FOR THE NEXT GENERATION

The **U**rban **M**inistry **I**nstitute's

MENTOR MANUAL

Third Edition

TŪMI
is a ministry of

WORLD IMPACT
TRANSFORMING COMMUNITIES TOGETHER

TUMI Press
3701 East 13th Street North
Wichita, Kansas 67208

Table of Contents

7 | Preface

Section I: Understanding The Urban Ministry Institute

13 | Our Parent Organization: World Impact, Inc.

18 | Our Purpose and Ministry Objectives:
Equipping Leaders for the Urban Church

21 | The Vision of The Urban Ministry Institute

23 | Of Whose Spirit Are We? A Primer on Why We Seek
to Retrieve the Great Tradition for the City Church

30 | Sacred Roots and the *Capstone Curriculum*

35 | The *Capstone Curriculum* Overview

38 | The *Foundations for Ministry Series*

41 | Our Certificate and Diploma Programs

43 | MAP Course and Process for Diploma Students

44 | The Nicene Creed and Its Role in Leadership Development

49 | Dealing with Theological Diversity: Holding Fast the Good

Section II: Understanding the Role of the Mentor

57 | The Profile of a TUMI Mentor

63 | The Mentor and Cultural Contextualization

66 | Our Pedagogical Approach to Lessons:
Contact, Content, Connection

68 | The Case for Case Studies

74 | Literacy and Language Issues: Helping Students Succeed

78 | Reading Standards

80 | TUMI Course Credit and Accreditation

Section III: Understanding the Essentials of Class Administration

85	Managing the Class Schedule
87	Studying and Planning: Your Personal Preparation
88	Preparing Class Paperwork
92	Readying Your Facilities and Classroom
94	Assigning, Recording and Processing Student Grades
98	Wrapping Up Final Details

Section IV: Understanding the Mechanics of Class Instruction

101	Leading a *Capstone Curriculum* or *Foundations for Ministry Series* Class Session
112	Handling Projects and Student Assignments
120	Dealing with Difficulties in the Classroom

Appendix

127	*Appendix 1* Our Distinctives: Advancing the Kingdom of God among the Urban Poor
134	*Appendix 2* The Key Components of "In-Context" Theological Education
136	*Appendix 3* Overview of the *Capstone Curriculum* and Summary Objectives
139	*Appendix 4* Teaching Objectives for the *Capstone Curriculum*, by Module
237	*Appendix 5* Professor's Guide
240	*Appendix 6* Fast Facts on the *Capstone Curriculum*

241   *Appendix 7*
Comparing the Scripture Memorization Lists in the
Capstone Curriculum and *Master the Bible System*

245   *Appendix 8*
Ways to Schedule Your Training Programs

246   *Appendix 9*
Sample Weekly Class Schedule

247   *Appendix 10*
Sample Course Schedule

249   *Appendix 11*
The Three-Step Model

250   *Appendix 12*
The Exegetical Project:
Using the Three-Step Model to Exegete Scripture

252   *Appendix 13*
Documenting Your Work:
A Guide to Help You Give Credit Where Credit Is Due

256   *Appendix 14*
Sample Student Information Sheet

257   *Appendix 15*
Sample Attendance Record Sheet

258   *Appendix 16*
Sample Reading Assignment Handout

260   *Appendix 17*
Sample Reading Completion Sheet

262   *Appendix 18*
Sample Grade Recording Sheet

263   *Appendix 19*
TUMI Grade Scale

264   *Appendix 20*
Scripture Memory Grading Form

265   *Appendix 21*
       Proctoring

266   *Appendix 22*
       World Impact's Affirmation of Faith Statement

268   *Appendix 23*
       Creedal Theology as a Blueprint for Discipleship and
       Leadership: A Time-tested Criterion for Equipping New
       Believers and Developing Indigenous Leaders

281   *Appendix 24*
       There Is a River: Identifying the Streams of
       a Revitalized Christian Community in the City

282   *Appendix 25*
       The Nicene Creed

283   *Appendix 26*
       The Nicene Creed with Biblical Support

285   *Appendix 27*
       We Believe: Confession of the Nicene Creed (Common Meter)

286   *Appendix 28*
       We Believe: Confession of the Nicene Creed (8.7.8.7. Meter)

287   *Appendix 29*
       The Apostles' and Nicene Creed Bibliography

290   *Appendix 30*
       An Abridged Bibliography on Becoming
       an Effective Mentor and Teacher

291   *Appendix 31*
       At-a-Glance Responsibilities Checklist
       for Site Coordinators and Mentors

296   *Appendix 32*
       The Role of Women in Ministry

300   *Appendix 33*
       Capstone Student Educational Learning Hours

303   *Appendix 34*
       Mentor Sign-off Form

Preface

Greetings in Christ! On behalf of all of us here at the Institute, we welcome you to your role as Mentor of one of our classes! What a privilege it is to be able to partner with you as you join us in mentoring others at our satellite of *The Urban Ministry Institute*. We are confident that as you share with others your experience in ministry and knowledge of God's Word, God will use you to enrich and equip them to bear fruit for the Kingdom. Christ himself has promised to bless you as you lead and share with your students your skill, prayer, and experience.

We have designed this Mentor's Manual to help you fulfill your ministry with us with excellence and creativity. Your role as a Mentor is critical to the overall success of your students' educational preparation. We trust the Lord that through your study of this manual you will come to better understand how you can best provide your church leaders with quality theological and ministry education.

Our vision for facilitating servant leadership development is rooted in a burden to raise up a generation of men and women outfitted by their knowledge of Scripture, energized by the power of the Holy Spirit, and burdened to serve the broken and the poor in the city. Given the numbers immigrating to cities, the diverse populations yet to be evaluated among the urban unreached, we surmise that we may need in excess of 500,000 pastor-shepherds in the next decade. Your interest in equipping leaders with the Word of God is a direct answer to the prayers of his people who for years have sought his blessing upon the millions of unreached peoples in the cities of the world. Our prayer as a ministry is that God will multiply your efforts and equipping in such a way that laborers are raised up for the urban harvest. Your contribution is critical to this effort.

Surprisingly, you will see from the argument within this manual that we do not view ourselves primarily as an educational institution but rather as a network dedicated to equipping and training leaders who serve the under-served in the city. Whether you are a site coordinator, mentor, or volunteer this is essential to both understand and embrace. Of course, it is far easier to use the categories and paradigms of the academy as you establish an educational training center; missions, however, tends to be seen as a more practical, pragmatic kind of activity. TUMI was born in the cradle of a zealous mission organization dedicated to planting churches among the poor in the cities of America. We were born with a burden to flesh out the universal priesthood, with a missionally informed perspective that every mature disciple of Christ has gifts and opportunities that can make a difference if we release them to serve.

Unfortunately, seminary education is simply too inaccessible for many in the city. It costs too much, it is usually offered far from city environments, and it is made of up highly technical, esoteric curriculums designed for specialists and not for disciplers. Furthermore, we may tend to see seminary education as a privilege only for those considering the call of the clergy, or the academically gifted or qualified, or for those who have the background and resources to afford it. While we cherish the workers that traditional seminary education has produced for the Church, we are convinced that we must train thousands more workers for the urban harvest. We can only do this if we keep this mandate clear, and not become distracted by traditional issues and arguments of the postmodern seminary academy.

I am thankful to God for the amazingly qualified and humble team that makes up our TUMI National staff. They are all capable urban missionaries and educators, mentors extraordinaire, and some of them contributed greatly to both the content and form of this updated manual. Their ideas were practical, helpful, and theologically and pedagogically wise, and we are deeply grateful for their thinking and suggestions. Special thanks to TUMI National staff who contributed to this revision: Andrew Lee, Ryan Carter, Rich Esselstrom, and Hank Voss. These men are capable and remarkable, and their contribution to this manual has been herculean, and above that, their friendship in the Gospel is highly prized.

We are unequivocal in our confidence that our Mentors are the difference makers in the equipping strategy of the Institute, not only encouraging the students in their walk with Christ, but also deeply enhancing the ways they comprehend and apply the truths of each module. Through your diligent prayer and facilitation, your students will meet their educational and spiritual objectives, understand the truths offered in each audio or video lesson, and apply them in their own unique ministry context. We are convinced that your diligent preparation will make a real difference in the lives of your students, shaping them spiritually and helping them fulfill their role in kingdom advancement.

Make certain, then, that you carefully study this manual, consult our website for further discussion and resources, and interact with your Site Coordinator regarding any questions or concerns that may arise as you engage this material. Your diligence will make all the difference in the lives of the dear saints of God who will be identified, equipped, and released for ministry through your training.

Again, thank you for your interest and your desire to serve God's people by teaching the Word of God. May God richly bless you as you equip others on behalf of the Kingdom of God!

Anticipating God using you in a marvelous way,

Rev. Dr. Don L. Davis

Section I

Understanding The Urban Ministry Institute

Our Parent Organization: World Impact, Inc.

World Impact, Inc., TUMI's parent ministry, is an interdenominational missions organization committed to facilitating church-planting movements by evangelizing, equipping, and empowering the unchurched urban poor.

Evangelism: Everything we say and do that reveals the love of God to our neighbors.

Equipping: Training urban disciples to live a healthy Christian life and to make new disciples.

Empowerment: Indigenously led church-based ministries transforming communities together.

Purpose Statement
Our Purpose is to honor and glorify God and delight in Him among the unchurched urban poor by knowing God and making Him known.

Mission Statement
As a Christian missions organization, we are committed to facilitating church planting movements by evangelizing, equipping, and empowering America's urban poor.

Vision Statement
Our vision is to recruit, empower, and release urban leaders who will plant churches and launch indigenous church planting movements.

Global Ends Statement
The empowered urban poor advancing God's Kingdom in every city through the local church.

Tag Line
Transforming Communities Together

OUR FOCUS AREA: EMPOWERING INDIGENOUS URBAN CHRISTIAN LEADERS

We advance God's Kingdom through the local church, *empowering indigenous urban Christian leaders* through several leadership initiatives:

- TUMI
- Associates
- Leadership retreats (SIAFU)
- Evangel School of Urban Church Planting
- Urban Church Associations (UCAs)
- Urban Christian Education: Christian Schools
- Incarceration to Incorporation (I2I)

Our Ministry Model
You can do it; we can help.

History of World Impact

World Impact is a Christian missions organization committed to planting churches among America's unchurched urban poor.

Dr. Keith Phillips, Founder and President of World Impact

Keith is the third child of Frank and Velma Phillips. Keith's father, a veterinarian, organized some of Billy Graham's first crusades and was a co-founder of Youth for Christ and World Vision. He was instrumental in bringing Korean War orphans to the United States (this later became the Holt Adoption Agency). As a freshman at UCLA, Keith began directing Youth for Christ clubs in the inner city of Los Angeles.

The Inception of World Impact

In 1965, Keith Phillips began a Bible club for children in Jordan Downs Federal Housing Project in Watts (Los Angeles). Before long, neighboring housing projects asked him to expand his ministry into their communities.

As a result of speaking at BIOLA's Chapel, 300 students signed up to help Keith. Soon, college students from Azusa Pacific University, Life Bible College, Pepperdine, USC and UCLA joined this outreach.

Our Growth over the Years

Our initial thrust was to children living in federal housing projects; hundreds accepted Christ. Soon, career missionaries moved into the inner city to make disciples and expanded our outreach to teenagers and adults.

- World Impact was incorporated in March, 1971.

- By 1972, we had opened ministries in Los Angeles, Wichita, Portland, Omaha and San Diego.

- In 1975, Keith wrote *They Dare to Love the Ghetto.*
- In 1976, World Impact began ministries in St. Louis and Newark, and moved into our National Headquarters in Los Angeles. World Impact of Canada was incorporated.

- In 1977, our Fresno ministry began.

- In 1981, Morning Star Ranch in Kansas established a two-year discipleship program for young men from the city. Keith wrote *The Making of a Disciple*.

- In 1982, we opened the Los Angeles Christian Elementary School, which emphasizes academic competence, Christ-like character and self-confidence to prepare our students for a lifetime of discipleship.

- In 1984, we started Inner City Enterprises, a job-training program which taught young people how to work.

- In 1985, Keith wrote *No Quick Fix*. World Impact started the Newark Christian School and thrift stores in several cities (Sonshine Shops). In Newark, we renovated abandoned row-houses and rented them to families involved with our ministry. Later, many of those families bought these homes.

- In 1986, the former St. Louis YMCA building was remodeled into a Ministry Center with the help of thousands of volunteers and inner-city workers. An 11-acre, 88-unit apartment complex (The Village) was acquired in Wichita for use as a worship center and the Good Samaritan Clinic. We acquired a 172-acre camp, THE OAKS, 65 miles north of Los Angeles and built a prayer chapel.

- In 1987, a 10,000-square-foot gymnasium was built for our Los Angeles ministry and Christian School.

- In 1988, Ministry Centers in Fresno and San Diego were acquired for worship and job training. Our Chester, Pennsylvania, ministry opened. We acquired a school building in Chester to start the Frederick Douglass Christian School. We started Saturday-night Celebrations across the country for urban believers.

Massive immigration took place in our cities during the 80s. Millions came in from Latin America and Asia. Our Los Angeles Celebration Church went from English speaking, to English and Spanish, to all Spanish. Fresno missionaries ministered to many Hmong, Vietnamese, and Cambodians.

Our Parent Organization: World Impact, Inc.

- The 1992 Los Angeles riots focused national attention on the inner city.

- In the 90s, we became a church-planting organization nationally. We trained other ministries to plant urban churches through The Crowns of Beauty Conferences, The School of Urban Church Planting and The Nehemiah Team.

- In 1991, we added a thirty-acre camp north of Scranton, Pennsylvania, Harmony Heart.

- In 1992, we opened ministries in Oakland and San Jose.

- In 1993, we opened ministries in San Francisco and Detroit.

- In 1994, the Watts Christian School opened.

- In 1995, we opened the Frederick Douglass Christian School. Churches were planted in Los Angeles, Wichita and Newark. Deer Creek Christian Camp in the Colorado Rockies was acquired and became World Impact's fourth camping ministry.

- In 1995 we began *The Urban Ministry Institute* (TUMI) in Wichita, Kansas, to provide theological education to urban leaders.

- In 1996, we celebrated our 25th year at Operation Jericho, a national staff conference on church planting. We began our Dallas ministry, published our Missionary Orientation Training Course for new staff orientation, and Keith wrote *Out of Ashes*.

- In 1999, the Crowns of Beauty Conference welcomed 1200 registrants from multiple countries. Second and third Conferences were held with similar results in 2001 and 2004.
- In 2000, we conducted our first week-long Church-Plant School for urban church-plant teams. We have since trained 32 teams.

- In 2001, initial TUMI satellite campuses were launched in three cities; the John Mark Curriculum was completed.

- In 2002, the first TUMI *Capstone* module was released.

- By 2004, we had planted twenty churches in eight World Impact cities, Hayford Hall was dedicated at THE OAKS, and we held our first Candidate Acceptance Program to screen and orient new World Impact missionaries.

- In 2005, the full 16-module set of *The Capstone Curriculum* was completed.

- In 2005, World Impact missionaries convened at THE OAKS for a WI-FI (World Impact Focus and Identity) Conference. We expanded TUMI's satellite program, which by 2010 reached 75 sites in 11 countries.

- In 2010, TUMI's *Capstone* Spanish translation was completed. Our efforts expanded beyond planting churches to equipping indigenous leaders to plant churches, with the vision of launching church-planting movements in the city.

For more information on our ministry and work in various locations across America, please contact us:

World Impact, Inc.
2001 South Vermont Ave
Los Angeles, CA 90007

323-735-1137
323-735-2576 fax
www.worldimpact.org
wiinfo@worldimpact.org

Our Parent Organization: World Impact, Inc.

Our Purpose: Equipping Leaders for the Urban Church

Our Purpose and Ministry Objectives: Equipping Leaders for the Urban Church

As a Mentor, you are partnering with us to invest in the lives of Christian leaders in the city. It is important to us that you fully understand our purpose. The following statement defines the essential reason that we exist.

> The Urban Ministry Institute is a training institution that exists to equip leaders for the urban church, especially among the poor, in order to advance the Kingdom of God.

Each part of this statement has profound importance to us.

To Equip Leaders

Although we live in a culture where leaders are often openly disrespected and the very idea of leadership is sometimes seen as oppressive and restrictive, we believe that leaders are of fundamental importance in all of human life. Nowhere is this more important than in the life of God's Church.

The Urban Ministry Institute (TUMI) exists to equip Church leaders who are serving and investing in others. These leaders may be pastors or lay leaders, men or women. They may be evangelists, missionaries, Sunday School teachers, worship leaders or those who visit the sick. The key is that they have a recognized ministry role in their church (formal or informal), that they have people toward whom they feel a leadership responsibility, and that they are called and motivated to invest in and equip others as disciples of Jesus Christ.

For the Urban Church

Half of the people alive today live in cities, and that number is constantly growing. This calls for a special focus on urban churches, especially in those areas which have historically been neglected, or have large concentrations of people who have not been reached with the Gospel of Christ.

Believing strongly that effective ministry cannot take place apart from the body of Christ, *The Urban Ministry Institute* is committed to enriching the life and outreach of urban congregations and their servant-leaders. All of our programs and materials are designed to equip men and women effectively to serve in the context of a local assembly. Applicants must be actively participating in a church body in order to be considered for acceptance in our programs. The key criteria for admission is the recommendation of their pastoral (or denominational) leadership.

Especially among the Poor

We believe that God has chosen those who are poor in the eyes of this world to be rich in faith and to inherit the Kingdom which he promised to those who love him (James 2.5). Whether you are rich, poor, or somewhere in between, we believe that Jesus has given all believers a theological mandate to prioritize the poor in their life and ministry.

By the year 2025, one out of every three people on the planet will live in urban poverty. We believe that God is raising up leaders who will go to the unreached millions among the urban poor both in America and around the world. More importantly, we believe that God is raising up dynamic leaders from among the urban poor who deserve access to quality theological education. As a Mentor, you have the high privilege of serving those leaders that God has called to be rich in faith and helping to equip them as they reach their cities with the Gospel of Christ and his Kingdom.

In Order to Advance the Kingdom of God

The Church of Jesus Christ is vitally important to God's will because it is the agent of the Kingdom of God, charged to function as salt and light in the midst of a decaying and corrupt world. We believe that we live "between the times" already experiencing the life of the in-breaking Kingdom of God, but still looking forward to the consummation of that Kingdom when Jesus returns and "every knee will bow and every tongue confess that Christ is Lord." "Between the times" the freedom, wholeness, and justice of the Kingdom of God is to be embodied and proclaimed by the Church. A church community is responsible to show visibly what the "Reign of God" looks like when it is embraced by people who acknowledge Christ's lordship. *The Urban Ministry Institute* is dedicated to helping churches make God's Kingdom visible in all the dimensions of Christian community life, and in its ministry to the needy in the city.

Our Ministry Objectives

In light of these commitments, *The Urban Ministry Institute* embraces the following ministry objectives:

Our Purpose: Equipping Leaders for the Urban Church

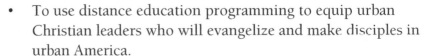

Our Purpose: Equipping
Leaders for the Urban Church

- To use distance education programming to equip urban Christian leaders who will evangelize and make disciples in urban America.
- To create a network of training centers in urban areas that can provide excellent and affordable ministry education that is sensitive to urban culture.
- To facilitate the multiplication of healthy, reproducing urban churches, especially among the poor.
- To promote and apply a biblical understanding of freedom, wholeness, and justice for the city.
- To provide a forum for discussion, research, and publication that compassionately addresses the aspirations and challenges of the city.
- To stimulate dialogue and cooperation among churches and urban ministries who seek to serve the city.

Program Goal: Wisdom

We believe that the end goal of Christian leadership training is wisdom. "Everything is permissible for me but not everything is beneficial" (1 Cor. 6.12). Therefore, those who train Christian leaders must, like Paul, "proclaim [Christ] admonishing and teaching everyone with all wisdom, so that we may present everyone perfect in Christ" (Col. 1.28).

Christian leadership training is intended to contribute to the formation of men and women who possess godly wisdom and Christ-like character. In helping to prepare these leaders, the goal of *The Urban Ministry Institute* is not just that they become "smarter" leaders. Our deepest prayer to God is that they might become wiser leaders, able to discern the leading of the Holy Spirit, to possess the mind of Christ, and to apply the teaching of the Scriptures in their own unique ministry context.

The Vision of The Urban Ministry Institute

Rev. Dr. Don L. Davis. © 2007. The Urban Ministry Institute

And the Lord answered me: "Write the vision; make it plain on tablets, so he may run who reads it. [3] For still the vision awaits its appointed time; it hastens to the end – it will not lie. If it seems slow, wait for it; it will surely come; it will not delay. [4] Behold, his soul is puffed up; it is not upright within him, but the righteous shall live by his faith."

~ Habakkuk 2.2-4 (ESV)

To Facilitate Pioneer Church Planting Movements among America's Unreached Urban Poor Communities

The Urban Ministry Institute is a ministry of World Impact, an interdenominational missions organization dedicated to evangelism, discipleship, and church planting among the urban poor in America. As World Impact's training and research center, TUMI seeks to generate and strategically facilitate dynamic, indigenous church planting movements among the poor to reach the unreached populations of America's inner cities.

In order to attain this purpose, we will help form strategic alliances between and among urban pastors, Christian workers, and missionaries, along with churches and denominations and other kingdom-minded organizations in order to trigger robust, evangelical pioneer church-planting movements in the city. It is our hope that these movements will multiply thousands of culturally conducive evangelical churches among America's urban poor. We intend to use generally our expertise on behalf of the churches in these movements in order that they might glorify God the Father in their Christ-centered identity and their Spirit-formed worship and community life. Our commitment is to help these urban congregations defend the historic orthodox faith in the context of urban culture, and engage in kingdom-oriented social justice and evangelical mission practically, where they live and minister.

To Equip Leaders Serving the Churches That Arise from Evangelical Church Planting Movements

Furthermore, we will strive to ensure that the leaders and congregations of these church-planting movements are equipped for effective urban ministry and empowered to affiliate with other leaders and churches in shared identity and purposeful association.

The Vision of The Urban Ministry Institute

We will strive to enable the leaders and churches arising from these movements to participate as active members of larger networks of healthy assemblies, where they can be encouraged in their common worship and discipleship and be enriched in dynamic and ongoing fellowship. We will facilitate the establishment of effective structures of godly oversight and stewardship which will protect them from schism and heresy and encourage them to collaborate together through strategic projects of giving, service, and mission.

To Spawn Aggressive New Church Planting Initiatives among the Poor in America and across the Globe

Finally, we will strive to see that the evangelical leaders and churches from these movements join together in explicit unity for the purpose of fulfilling the Great Commission among the urban poor in America, and wherever possible, around the world. Starting with the American unreached poor, we will challenge every Christian leader, urban church, and church-planting movement to collaborate and coordinate their gifts, efforts, and resources to advance the Gospel of Christ and his Kingdom to every urban poor community on earth. We will begin with our own Jerusalems and Judeas here in urban America, and hope to grow throughout this continent, and in our hemisphere.

Ultimately, we will seek to assist these same church-planting movements among America's urban poor to aggressively advance the Kingdom by rapidly multiplying similar church planting movements among the unreached urban poor of the mega-cities of the world, especially those recognized as Gateway cities within the 10/40 Window.

Of Whose Spirit Are We?
A Primer on Why We Seek to Retrieve the Great Tradition for the City Church
Rev. Dr. Don L. Davis

In theology and worship, in discipleship and outreach, nothing is more important than knowing your spiritual legacy, the roots of your spiritual ancestry, the proverbial Rock out of which you were dug.

In order to discern the origins of our own heritage, we need to do some spiritual genealogical work, as it were, to detect more precisely what constitutes the roots of our faith in Jesus Christ.

Like all believers worldwide, we who count ourselves as disciples of Jesus of Nazareth believe that in his incarnation the Kingdom of God has come to earth. While not fully consummated, the coming of the Word made flesh (John 1.14-18) into the world means that the long reign of the curse has been broken through the death, burial, and resurrection of Jesus Christ. As our Lord and Messiah, Jesus has set his people free from the oppression of the devil, the condemnation of the Law, and the power of sin and death. Because of this freedom Christ granted to the people of God, we may now explore and employ different forms of worship and service to God in the Church, provided of course that we remain faithful to the Gospel and well anchored in the apostolic tradition as expressed in the Holy Scriptures.

Throughout the history of the Church, Christians have expressed their liberty in Jesus to change, transform, abridge, or edit their respective structures, norms, and practices. Such freedom has been confirmed on the basis of the consent of the churches and their duly commissioned leaders, and always with a view to glorify God in Christ.

These expressions, whenever valid, have sought to recover in richer expression our full Christian heritage as guided by the Holy Spirit. Truly, our liberty in Christ permits us to follow our consciences as we express our worship and service in ways consistent with Scripture. All people of all cultures who follow Christ in obedience are obliged to express their love and affection towards God in ways consistent with their own custom and practice.

Without question, the work of God in Christ was accomplished on behalf of all the peoples of the world, and all creation itself. In tens of thousands of human cultures, the Good News of God's love in Christ has been communicated, embodied, and reproduced. In each culture where the Spirit has moved others to trust in Christ, believers learn and confess the one true faith, the Gospel of Jesus Christ, which has given birth to Christian salvation and communities from the ends of the earth throughout the world. This free expression and embodiment of Christ in culture is essential when members of a people group confess and obey Christ as Lord of all.

While the Gospel has freely been distributed through the world, it has not changed, and its basic message remains unaltered and unadulterated. No generation of believers is free to alter the message of the biblical vision of the Kingdom of God; that message is fixed and unchanging. However, we also gladly affirm that our Gospel-formed evangelical identity allows and demands that we do all we can to give full and fresh expression to the meaning of the Gospel of Jesus Christ in the context of our culture and community.

Today, the contemporary evangelical church finds itself impacted by and situated in an age of postmodernism, civil religion, hedonism, pragmatism, and egocentrism. These cultural winds of compromise and change all (to some degree) have influenced the worship and service of the body of Christ in our various traditions and cultural expressions of our faith. These challenges call for a new discovery and reappropriation of the faith once-for-all delivered to the people of God. To meet these threats and to take advantage of our present opportunities, we must seek to be transformed, renewed, and enlarged by the Christian Story in order to give truer witness to Christ and his kingdom reign.

One of the richest sources for transformation and a renewed faith and discipleship lies in our retrieval of the Great Tradition, i.e., those doctrines, practices, and structures employed by the ancient Church as it sought to give expression to the truth concerning Jesus Christ. The ancient Church's faith and practice serves as the authoritative source of all of our various Christian denominational practices.

In terms of time, the Great Tradition can be measured from the period between the time of Christ and the middle of the fifth century. This "tradition lying behind all particular Christian expressions" sought to faithfully articulate, express, and defend what the

Apostles passed down to us, and to embody its teaching, worship, discipleship, and experience. The Great Tradition both predates and is the source for our specific associational and denominational emphases, and represents the foundation of all valid contemporary Christian thought and practice. From the beginning, Christians have believed, adored, been formed by, and borne witness to the same Story outlined in the Scriptures. For us, the God who created, covenanted with Abraham, who redeemed Israel, and who was incarnated in the person of Christ, is truly the God of the Church, and of all believers in Jesus Christ.

Why ought we pay attention to the ancient Church? Are we involved in our own fresh attempt to rediscover "the New Testament Church practice" in such a way that jumps across the historical divide, and ignores how the Spirit has worked in the Church through the ages? No. Our attempt to understand our common roots is not a rejection of what the Holy Spirit has done and is doing in and through the Church in history. Rather, we are suggesting that rediscovering our common roots can allow us to find fresh, vital ways to both reaffirm our true spiritual identity and communicate the Gospel afresh to our neighbors today.

As a church passionately transformed by the presence of the risen Christ, the ancient undivided Church endured the challenges of schism, heresy, paganism, imperial domination, and societal immorality. They overcame the formidable attack of Gnostic deception (that ancient heresy which called into question the human nature of Christ), and withstood the advance of a number of vicious heresies all designed to undermine the Gospel's clarity and truth. The early Christians articulated a faith that summarized and defended the Apostles' teaching and established structures of worship that led its members (many of whom were poor and oppressed) into a living hope and the presence of Christ.

Beyond question, the ancient undivided Church was a Christ-centered community. Most of its councils and creeds had to do with his person, his work, and his authority among his people. Governing themselves according to a councillor vision of leaders who swore allegiance to the Lord Jesus, the ancient Church defined spirituality in terms of the people of God reliving, reenacting, and embodying the life and work of Jesus in the baptism into Christ (*catechumenate*), the rhythm of the Lord's Day celebration, practice of the Christian year, and a shared spirituality held in common among the churches.

Of Whose Spirit Are We?

Of Whose Spirit Are We?

Rather than succumbing to societal pressure, these believers lived a faith that enabled them to represent nobly the Kingdom of God in their time and lay a foundation and example for us to follow today.

Because of this, we are convinced that a critical retrieval of the Great Tradition can enhance our ability today to bear witness to the Kingdom in a troubled and lost society.

Let's be plain about our goals in this effort. Our retrieval of the Great Tradition does not naively assert that everything the early Church believed and practiced ought to be reproduced today, regardless of what they asserted or did. Furthermore, neither do we suggest that they were a perfect community. In our view it is wrongheaded and unbiblical to advocate a nostalgic return to simply repeat whatever they did in an ape-ish and unthinking fashion. That goes against both our biblical conviction that the Berean spirit is noble (who even vetted the teaching of Paul the Apostle over against the Scriptures, cf. Acts 17.11) and our Protestant heritage of being reformed and always reforming. Truly, our time is our time, and we cannot merely attempt to return to the "good old days" of pristine community. Like it or not, it has been over two thousand years since the Church of Jesus Christ was formed, and the Spirit of God has been active throughout that entire history, with all its speed bumps and bruises included.

Rather than seeking a nostalgic return, we desire to learn from the Great Tradition in order to meet our challenges in this pressing hour. I am convinced that the rediscovery of this Tradition can empower urban leaders and their congregations to withstand the temptations of our time and help them to maintain hope and courage in the face of societal and spiritual evil. Above all, embracing the Great Tradition can enable all of us who love Christ to reconnect with the historic origins of our faith and be transformed again by returning to the sacred roots of our spiritual source – the apostolic tradition canonically informed by Scripture, climaxing in the glorious person and work of our risen Lord Jesus. Retrieving the Great Tradition can empower us to affirm our past, live courageously in our present, and anticipate our future and the coming reign of God in Christ.

**We Do Not Live to Study, but Study to Live
and Bear Witness to the Living Christ in the City**

This Story of God in Christ is the fuel in the engine of authentic theological preparation and leadership development, and every satellite must confess what all Christians have confessed from the start. Jesus is Lord, to the glory of God the Father. The Story of God in Christ can greatly enhance your purpose and studies, enrich your worship, and re-calibrate your direction as you mentor students at your site.

Remind yourself and your students often that Jesus of Nazareth is the reason proper for all we do in Christian leadership education: to become like him as Elder, Chief Shepherd, and as the Bishop of our souls is the *raison d'etre*, the reason for our existence in leadership education. Nothing less than him will suffice; nothing more than him is needed. For us, Jesus is Lord of all.

For more information about *Sacred Roots*, visit our website: *www.tumi.org/sacredroots*

Of Whose Spirit Are We?

The Story of God: Our Sacred Roots

Rev. Dr. Don L. Davis

Of Whose Spirit Are We?

The Alpha and the Omega	Christus Victor	Come, Holy Spirit	Your Word Is Truth	The Great Confession	His Life in Us	Living in the Way	Reborn to Serve
The LORD God is the source, sustainer, and end of all things in the heavens and earth. All things were formed and exist by his will and for his eternal glory, the triune God, Father, Son, and Holy Spirit, Rom. 11.36.							
THE TRIUNE GOD'S UNFOLDING DRAMA — God's Self-Revelation in Creation, Israel, and Christ				THE CHURCH'S PARTICIPATION IN GOD'S UNFOLDING DRAMA — Fidelity to the Apostolic Witness to Christ and His Kingdom			
The Objective Foundation: The Sovereign Love of God — God's Narration of His Saving Work in Christ				The Subjective Practice: Salvation by Grace through Faith — The Redeemed's Joyous Response to God's Saving Work in Christ			
The Author of the Story	*The Champion of the Story*	*The Interpreter of the Story*	*The Testimony of the Story*	*The People of the Story*	*Re-enactment of the Story*	*Embodiment of the Story*	*Continuation of the Story*
The Father as Director	Jesus as Lead Actor	The Spirit as Narrator	Scripture as Script	As Saints, Confessors	As Worshipers, Ministers	As Followers, Sojourners	As Servants, Ambassadors
Christian Worldview	Communal Identity	Spiritual Experience	Biblical Authority	Orthodox Theology	Priestly Worship	Congregational Discipleship	Kingdom Witness
Theistic and Trinitarian Vision	Christ-centered Foundation	Spirit-Indwelt and -Filled Community	Canonical and Apostolic Witness	Ancient Creedal Affirmation of Faith	Weekly Gathering in Christian Assembly	Corporate, Ongoing Spiritual Formation	Active Agents of the Reign of God
Sovereign Willing	Messianic Representing	Divine Comforting	Inspired Testifying	Truthful Retelling	Joyful Excelling	Faithful Indwelling	Hopeful Compelling
Creator — True Maker of the Cosmos	Recapitulation — Typos and Fulfillment of the Covenant	Life-Giver — Regeneration and Adoption	Divine Inspiration — God-breathed Word	The Confession of Faith — Union with Christ	Song and Celebration — Historical Recitation	Pastoral Oversight — Shepherding the Flock	Explicit Unity — Love for the Saints
Owner — Sovereign Disposer of Creation	Revealer — Incarnation of the Word	Teacher — Illuminator of the Truth	Sacred History — Historical Record	Baptism into Christ — Communion of Saints	Homilies and Teachings — Prophetic Proclamation	Shared Spirituality — Common Journey through the Spiritual Disciplines	Radical Hospitality — Evidence of God's Kingdom Reign
Ruler — Blessed Controller of All Things	Redeemer — Reconciler of All Things	Helper — Endowment and the Power	Biblical Theology — Divine Commentary	The Rule of Faith — Apostles' Creed and Nicene Creed	The Lord's Supper — Dramatic Re-enactment	Embodiment — Anamnesis and Prolepsis through the Church Year	Extravagant Generosity — Good Works
Covenant Keeper — Faithful Promisor	Restorer — Christ, the Victor over the powers of evil	Guide — Divine Presence and Shekinah	Spiritual Food — Sustenance for the Journey	The Vincentian Canon — Ubiquity, antiquity, universality	Eschatological Foreshadowing — The Already/Not Yet	Effective Discipling — Spiritual Formation in the Believing Assembly	Evangelical Witness — Making Disciples of All People Groups

Sacred Roots and the Capstone Curriculum

Sacred Roots and the Capstone Curriculum

Sacred Roots: Retrieving the Great Tradition
*Capstone as the Foundation for Training Your Leaders
to Rediscover and Retell the Story That Spans the Ages –
Satellite Training Is Grounding Leaders in Christ Jesus!*

As a satellite of *The Urban Ministry Institute*, our consistent, fervent prayer for you and your students is that you would all be personally transformed by the powerful Story of Christ, and that all of you, being transformed by him through the Word and his people, would find new, effective ways to share that Story in the communities and churches you represent. However we tell it, demonstrate it, sing it, or share it, the truth of Jesus Christ remains for us the same, vital, and true confession held so dear since the time of the apostles, and continues to stir hearts and transform lives today.

Capstone was created to help you equip your students to understand, embrace, and defend our shared common faith, i.e., our *Sacred Roots*. Once understood and embodied, then we can train them to defend and contextualize our common faith in their churches and ministries. *Capstone* can enable our students to ground new believers in this essential biblical story of their new-found faith, and show them how to instruct maturing Christians to deepen their faith in the solid foundation that Christ's story represents.

Our desire is for you as Site Coordinator and Mentor to learn to show your students how they can benefit from hearing the story of Jesus told over and over again in the context of both private devotion and public worship. As you have treasured Christ and his salvation story for years, may he continue to transform you through it, deepening your own walk and revealing how you may fall in love with him afresh as you both retell and remember the Greatest Story ever told.

When all is said and done, when all quizzes and exams are taken, when all courses are completed, and diplomas awarded, only one thing really matters. That we have trained a new generation to claim as true and for themselves these simple but profound Gospel stories, OT salvation promises, and meaty theological affirmations of the Epistles which speak of an itinerant Jewish preacher who has forever changed history, turning it to the will of God.

As a Mentor of a satellite of the *Institute*, it is your task in all you do to point to this one common faith, this one grand tale of God's faithful love to us all in Jesus Christ. It still has the power to transform, and can remake the cities of our nation and our world, as the Spirit leads. This is your task, and this is your privilege.

As we mentor students in the always-everywhere-and-by-all tradition of the Church, we will have the honor of equipping God's leaders who will, God willing, continue on their work as equippers in the body of Christ. This task of training is universally applicable; all TUMI students, from whatever traditions they represent, can embody, guard, and instruct their congregations in the truth of Scripture, and thus prove their connection to that one people of God as defined by the Nicene Creed: God's "one, holy, catholic, and apostolic church."

Nothing will prepare you better for mentoring *Capstone* or *Foundations* courses than gaining a mastery of the ancient consensus of the Great Tradition, i.e., the historic orthodox teaching of the Church. For a more thorough understanding of *Sacred Roots*, please read *Sacred Roots: A Primer on Retrieving the Great Tradition*, by Dr. Don L. Davis. In this book, you will see that the Christian Faith is anchored on the person and work of Jesus of Nazareth, the Christ, whose incarnation, crucifixion, and resurrection forever changed the world. Between the years 100 and 500 C.E. those who believed in him grew from a small persecuted minority to a strong aggressive movement reaching far beyond the bounds of the Roman empire. The roots this era produced gave us our canon (the Scriptures), our worship, and our conviction (the major creed of the Church, and the central tenets of the Faith, especially regarding the doctrine of the Trinity and Christ). Dr. Davis suggests how we can renew our contemporary faith again, by rediscovering these roots, our *Sacred Roots*, by retrieving the Great Tradition of the Church that launched the Christian revolution.

For more information about Sacred Roots, visit our website: *www.tumi.org/sacredroots*

Sacred Roots and the Capstone Curriculum

Sacred Roots and the Capstone Curriculum

Capstone Overview

What has been believed everywhere, always, and by all.

~ Vincent of Lerins

The *Capstone Curriculum* is a 16-module training program, designed to be engaged at a seminary level, to serve as the most essential knowledge and skill learning necessary for effective urban ministry and church leadership. Based on an expanded and detailed discussion of the critical sections of the Nicene Creed, the *Capstone Curriculum* seeks to equip learners in the foundational truths of the Great Tradition of the Church. It was constructed to offer solid, historically orthodox, Christ-centered, biblical training to urban leaders that is both culturally sensitive and entirely affordable to those who normally would be excluded from training because of academic background or cultural distance.

The curriculum is organized around four departments or categories, Biblical Studies, Theology and Ethics, Christian Ministry, and Urban Mission. Each department contains four modules or courses, each with four lessons which contain the content of the material in a structured, systemic manner. Each module consists of a Mentor's Guide, a Student Workbook and DVD (two video discs containing four hours of video). Additionally, each module includes a full complement of training tools (case studies, quizzes and exams, exegetical and ministry projects, Scripture memorization assignments, and required and suggested supplementary textbooks).

The *Capstone Curriculum* is specifically structured to be used in a variety of formats, time frames, and teaching venues. As a complete training curriculum, it may be accessed through *The Urban Ministry Institute's* Satellite Certificate program. This curriculum provides a Christian leader all they need to be effective servant leaders in their family, church, and ministry contexts.

While each individual module in the *Capstone Curriculum* possesses its own unique set of learning objectives based on the theme and goals of the course, the following objectives are our "across-the-curriculum" objectives for the entire set. These objectives represent the pedagogical constellation of aims that every module and all modules seek to represent. In that sense they comprise the key, fundamental goals of the entire resource, and ought to be remembered and referred to regardless of the individual module under consideration.

- To ground emerging urban leaders in the Gospel of Christ, enabling them to know the basics of conversion and their own calling to salvation and leadership
- To root our students in the indispensability of the Church to serve as both agent and locus of the Kingdom, and for them to serve the church practically and specifically in the local assembly
- To equip urban leaders with the necessary study skills to study, apply, teach, preach, and minister the Word of God in the urban context, applying their learning in the context of their own personal lives and church ministries
- To challenge urban leaders to regularly memorize select portions of Scripture, and develop the discipline of review to retain and utilize texts both devotionally and in ministry
- To establish urban leaders in a Christ-centered vision of Scripture, and equip them in a Nicene-based, biblical theology that is congruent with the historic orthodox faith of the Great Tradition
- To provide a biblical foundation for both understanding and practicing Christian leadership in the context of the Church, with a special emphasis and appreciation for spiritual formation in urban communities, especially among the poor
- To train urban leaders to evangelize, disciple, plant, pastor, and minister within evangelical urban churches which will be spiritually vital, culturally conducive, and aggressively reproductive within the various people groups needing Christ in the city
- To encourage urban leaders to find practical, meaningful ways to promote justice and demonstrate mercy within broken and needy urban communities, and discover ways to display hospitality, generosity, and compassion in the places where they live and minister

The Elements of a *Capstone* Module
Each module consists of a Mentor's Guide, a Student Workbook and DVDs (two video discs containing four hours of video). Additionally, each module includes a full complement of training tools (case studies, quizzes and exams, exegetical and ministry

Sacred Roots and the Capstone Curriculum

projects, Scripture memorization assignments, and required and suggested supplementary textbooks).

For Our Satellites: Acquiring Additional DVDs or Mentor Guides
From time to time many of you will find it necessary to obtain additional copies of a Mentor's Guide or DVD. It goes without saying that circumstances will arise when you will need to obtain additional copies of either (e.g. sponsoring simultaneous classes at different venues, lost or misplaced copies of DVDs, etc.). We want to accommodate all such circumstances while, at the same time, protect TUMI's copyright on its own materials.

As you already know, we demand that each TUMI site purchase official copies of our curricula (visit *www.tumistore.org*). We do not allow unauthorized duplication of any of our TUMI curricula. No satellite is allowed to make copies of any of our resources without receiving permission directly from us here at TUMI National. Anyone found to be duplicating our materials without our express consent may jeopardize the status of their site! This policy safeguards the integrity of our content and helps us cover our expenses here in order to keep our prices as affordable as possible.

Sacred Roots and the Capstone Curriculum

The Capstone Curriculum Overview

The Capstone Curriculum: Developing Urban Christian Leaders for the Church and the Kingdom Matthew 21.42			
Biblical Studies (God) Matthew 4.4	**Theology and Ethics (Kingdom) Matthew 6.9-10**	**Christian Ministry (Church) Matthew 16.18-19**	**Urban Mission (World) Matthew 5.14-16**
Conversion and Calling	The Kingdom of God	Theology of the Church	Foundations for Christian Mission
Bible Interpretation	God the Father	Foundations of Christian Leadership	Evangelism and Spiritual Warfare
The Old Testament Witness to Christ and His Kingdom	God the Son	Practicing Christian Leadership	Focus on Reproduction
The New Testament Witness to Christ and His Kingdom	God the Holy Spirit	The Equipping Ministry	Doing Justice and Loving Mercy: Compassion Ministries

Terminology
- *The Capstone Curriculum:* The entire four-unit, sixteen-subject teaching program designed to develop urban Christian leadership for the Church and the Kingdom
- *Department Area:* Four subjects organized under the headings of either Biblical Studies, Theology and Ethics, Christian Ministry, or Urban Mission
- *Module:* One subject in a unit
- *Lesson:* An individual teaching presentation in a module
- *Segment:* A twenty-five minute video teaching normally used in a lesson

A *Capstone* Module
- Each module is divided into *four lessons*
- Each module is designed to be taught in *twelve classroom hours* surpassing the well-accepted "CEU" (Continuing Education Unit) standards
- Each module features *a Student Workbook, a Mentor's Guide, and two DVDs* (four hours of video)

The Capstone Curriculum Overview

Sample Lesson Outline (Three-Hour Lesson)
20 minutes - Attendance and Quiz
10 minutes - Mentor-led Contact section
25 minutes - First Video Segment
20 minutes - Student Question/Response
15 minutes - Break
25 minutes - Second Video Segment
20 minutes - Student Question/Response
45 minutes - Mentor-led Connection:
  • Student Application and Implications Discussion
  • Case Studies and Problems
  • Assignments
  • Ministry Projects
  • Counseling and Prayer

The *Capstone Curriculum* is designed to be used in a variety of formats, time frames, and venues. As a complete training curriculum, it may be accessed through *The Urban Ministry Institute's* Certificate program. As a modular program, the *Capstone Curriculum* may be taught as seminars, workshops, conferences, small groups, or various other applications.

The Capstone Curriculum
Developing Urban Christian Leaders for the Church and the Kingdom – Matthew 21.42

Biblical Studies *The Lord God • Matt. 4.4*		Theology and Ethics *The Kingdom • Matt. 6.9-10*		Christian Ministry *The Church • Matt. 16.18-19*		Urban Mission *The World • Matt. 5.14-16*	
1	Conversion and Calling	**2**	The Kingdom of God	**3**	Theology of the Church	**4**	Foundations for Christian Mission
	The Word That Creates The Word That Convicts The Word That Converts The Word That Calls		God's Reign Challenged God's Reign Inaugurated God's Reign Invading God's Reign Consummated		The Church Foreshadowed in God's Plan The Church at Worship The Church as Witness The Church at Work		The Vision and Biblical Foundation for Christian Mission I The Vision and Biblical Foundation for Christian Mission II Christian Mission and the City Christian Mission and the Poor
5	Bible Interpretation	**6**	God the Father	**7**	Foundations of Christian Leadership	**8**	Evangelism and Spiritual Warfare
	Biblical Inspiration: The Origins and Authority of the Bible Biblical Hermeneutics: The Three-Step Model Biblical Literature: Interpreting the Genres of the Bible Biblical Studies: Using Study Tools in Bible Study		Prolegomena: The Doctrine of God and the Advance of the Kingdom God as Creator: The Providence of God The Triune God: The Greatness of God God as Father: The Goodness of God		The Christian Leader as Deacon The Christian Leader as Elder The Christian Leader as Pastor The Christian Leader as Bishop		Spiritual Warfare: Binding of the Strong Man Evangelism: The Content of the Good News of the Kingdom Evangelism: Methods to Reach the Urban Community Follow-up and Incorporation
9	The Old Testament Witness to Christ and His Kingdom	**10**	God the Son	**11**	Practicing Christian Leadership	**12**	Focus on Reproduction
	The Promise Given The Promise Clarified The Promise Personalized The Promise Universalized		Jesus, Messiah and Lord of All: He Came Jesus, Messiah and Lord of All: He Lived Jesus, Messiah and Lord of All: He Died Jesus, Messiah and Lord of All: He Rose and Will Return		Effective Worship Leading: Worship, Word, and Sacrament Effective Christian Education: Incorporating, Parenting, and Discipling Effective Church Discipline: Exhorting, Rebuking, and Restoring Effective Counseling: Preparing, Caring, and Healing		Church Growth: Reproducing in Number and Quality Planting Urban Churches: Sowing Planting Urban Churches: Tending Planting Urban Churches: Reaping
13	The New Testament Witness to Christ and His Kingdom	**14**	God the Holy Spirit	**15**	The Equipping Ministry	**16**	Doing Justice and Loving Mercy: Compassion Ministries
	The Messiah Announced The Messiah Opposed The Messiah Revealed The Messiah Vindicated		The Person of the Holy Spirit The Prophetic Work of the Holy Spirit The Powerful Presence of the Holy Spirit I The Powerful Presence of the Holy Spirit II		The Ministry of Proclamation: Kerygma I The Ministry of Proclamation: Kerygma II The Ministry of Teaching: Didache I The Ministry of Teaching: Didache II		Let Justice Roll Down: The Vision and Theology of the Kingdom Doing Justice and Loving Mercy I: The Urban Congregation Doing Justice and Loving Mercy II: Urban Community and Neighborhood Doing Justice and Loving Mercy III: Society and World

The Capstone Curriculum Overview

The Foundations for Ministry Series

The faculty and staff of *The Urban Ministry Institute* are dedicated to providing urban churches and their leaders with the most affordable, biblically based, and culturally sensitive theological resources available. Our attention at our national headquarters concentrates on developing practical, biblical and user-friendly ministry tools for leaders in urban churches. We currently have a wide array of theological resources all of which have been designed with the needs and opportunities of urban church leaders in mind.

Two of our premier resources are our *Capstone Curriculum* and our *Foundations for Ministry Series*. Our *Foundations for Ministry Series* are materials drawn directly from courses which our professors have taught at our Wichita-based *Hope School of Ministry*. We have reformatted these courses for distance education use and are now making them available to urban churches and ministry training sites throughout the country.

Here at *The Urban Ministry Institute* we are dedicated to facilitating leadership development among urban churches, and intend to produce a wide variety of resources, events, and programs to help in this vision. Please check our website (*www.tumi.org*) for a complete listing of our current leadership development resources, as well as for updates on new and future resources that we will soon develop and make available for your use.

The topics and materials covered in our *Foundations for Ministry Series* courses are foundational to effective urban ministry and will prove invaluable to anyone seeking to equip leaders in their cities. These courses are self-directed studies created to help individual learners and/or study groups take advantage of quality theological instruction at an affordable price.

For your convenience, we have divided each *Foundations for Ministry Series* course into eight lessons so that two courses fit the educational "semester" system. We structured the *Foundations Series* courses so they can be taught in sixteen classroom hours, surpassing the well-accepted "CEU" (Continuing Education Unit) standards. (This allows for great flexibility in using the materials in your environment, over seminar, workshop, or multi-day teaching formats).

The *Foundations for Ministry Series* Packages
Our *Foundations for Ministry Series* course materials are available in one of two packages:

Training Resource Kit
This training kit may include the following (check the courses online to see what is included in a particular course package):

- Workbook: 6 - 8 lessons with appendices
- Audio files: MP3 files, each resource may have from 6 - 16 hours of audio.
- Course Syllabus: If you want to offer this resource to your students for credit, this will explain how to do that (TUMI Satellites may access this at *www.tumi.org/foundations*).
- Quizzes, Exams and Answer Key (TUMI Satellites may access this at *www.tumi.org* on the Satellite Gateway.)

Multimedia Training Resource Kit
This training kit may include the following (check the courses online to see what is included in a particular course package):

- Workbook: 6 - 8 lessons with appendices
- Audio files: MP3 files, each resource may have from 6 - 16 hours of audio .
- PowerPoint slides
- DVD/video
- Additional resources
- Course Syllabus: If you want to offer this resource to your students for credit, this will explain how to do that (TUMI Satellites may access this at *www.tumi.org/foundations*).
- Quizzes, Exams and Answer Key (TUMI Satellites may access this at *www.tumi.org* on the Satellite Gateway.)

As a satellite, your students may apply these courses toward a *Certificate in Urban Theological Studies* and/or a *Ministerial Studies Diploma* (see *Our Certificate and Diploma Programs* in this manual for more information).

Required Textbooks for *Foundations* Courses
Each *Foundations* course has assigned textbooks which are read and discussed throughout the course. We encourage students to read, reflect upon, and respond to these with their professors, mentors, and fellow learners. The OFFICIAL *Foundations for*

The Foundations for Ministry Series

Ministry Series required textbook list can be found at *www.tumi.org* on the Satellite Gateway.

Available Courses in the *Foundations* Series

Below is a sampling of some of the *Foundations* courses available. Please check *www.tumistore.org* for the most current listing.

- *A Biblical Vision: Mastering the New Testament Witness to Christ* (Biblical Studies)
- *A Biblical Vision: Mastering the Old Testament Witness to Christ* (Biblical Studies)
- *A Compelling Testimony* (Christian Ministry)
- *An Authentic Calling* (Urban Mission)
- *Church Matters: Retrieving the Great Tradition* (Theology and Ethics or Urban Mission)
- *Managing Projects for Ministry* (Christian Ministry)
- *Master the Bible: How to Get and Keep the Big Picture of the Bible's Story* (Biblical Studies, Theology and Ethics, or Christian Ministry)
- *Marking Time: Forming Spirituality through the Christian Year* (Theology and Ethics or Christian Ministry)
- *Ministry in a Multi-Cultural and Unchurched Society* (Christian Ministry or Urban Mission)
- *Sacred Roots Workshop: Retrieving the Great Tradition for the Contemporary Church* (Theology and Ethics)
- *The Gospel of John* (Biblical Studies)
- *Vision for Mission: Nurturing an Apostolic Heart* (Urban Mission)
- *Winning the World: Facilitating Urban Church Planting Movements* (Urban Mission)

It is highly recommended that groups of students work on the same *Foundations* course simultaneously and meet regularly to discuss their learning under the guidance of a mentor who can clarify the content, facilitate discussion about applications, and monitor the formal evaluations.

The Foundations for Ministry Series

Our Certificate and Diploma Programs

If you elect to grant a certificate or diploma through the auspices of *The Urban Ministry Institute* at your satellite, we provide you with several significant alternatives.

Certificate in Christian Leadership Studies: *Capstone**

*You may purchase each module individually and host your programming at your own scheduling convenience.

Our *Certificate in Christian Leadership Studies* is conferred upon all students who complete the 16 modules of our *Capstone Curriculum* (32 credits) at an approved satellite of *The Urban Ministry Institute* (*TUMI*). The modules must be taught by an approved mentor or professor. The students must read the texts and complete the required quizzes, final exam, exegetical and ministry projects for each module, attending 10 of the 12 classroom hours per module.

Certificate in Urban Theological Studies: Site Approved*

*Contact the Satellite Director of The Urban Ministry Institute for approval of your program.

Our *Certificate in Urban Theological Studies* is conferred upon all students who complete 32 credit hours of study at your satellite. You may utilize our curricula resources (*Capstone/Foundations* courses) and/or use a combination of your own courses taught by your qualified instructors (see Appendix 16.1 in the *Multiplying Laborers for the Urban Harvest* guidebook). While you have complete flexibility to select those courses which best meet the needs of your students, you must retain the balance of providing 8 credit hours in each department area: Biblical Studies, Theology and Ethics, Christian Ministry, and Urban Mission, and at least 50% of the course work for this certificate must be our *TUMI* courses. Be creative as you build a training experience that will suit your students' church and ministry needs. Please know that the *TUMI* staff are available to advise you in your program and courses of study.

Ministerial Studies Diploma: Site Approved*

*After you have designed your program, please be certain to send your draft to the Satellite Director of The Urban Ministry Institute for consultation and approval.

Your students may also pursue our advanced program, the *Ministerial Studies Diploma*, by completing an additional 32 credit hours of study (64 credit hours in total). The program begins with the completion of a required course: the Ministry Assessment Project. (Visit *www.tumi.org/mentor* for more details on this course.) This course helps a student assess their gifts, calling, and ongoing direction in ministry and brings their pastoral or denominational supervisor into the process of designing their diploma program and coordinating it with their ministry responsibilities. Again, in order to give you maximum flexibility in arranging your program, we encourage

**In order to qualify for the site-approved Certificate in Urban Theological Studies, your students must complete our Bible Interpretation course or Old Testament and New Testament Witness to Christ.

you to select the curriculum resources that best address the interests of your students. Your qualified instructors may teach courses in Biblical Studies**, Theology and Ethics, Christian Ministry and Urban Mission, as well as intersperse them with our curricula. Please retain the balance of 8 credit hours per department area and at least 50% of our *TUMI* courses for this diploma. What is of utmost importance is that you design a program that addresses and strengthens the vision, issues, and needs of your students.

We strongly encourage each satellite to recognize the students' faithful accomplishment of their certificate and diploma programs in the form of a graduation ceremony and service.

MAP Course and Process for Diploma Students

The MAP (Ministry Assessment Program) course and process helps students prepare for their next phase of ministry after their initial training and enables students to reflect on their gifts and calling in ministry, and determine the types of training they need to seek out in order to properly prepare for their future ministry directions. We desire to empower our TUMI students to minister effectively within their own church, with the leaders of their tradition and denomination. In our view, advanced ministry training should be integrated with the student's calling and service within their congregation's ministry vision. This course is required for admission into the TUMI Ministerial Studies Diploma program.

Please visit *www.tumi.org/mentor* and click on *MAP Process* for the following:

MAP Course Instruction Plan
This course instruction plan includes the course description and all of the assignments that the student will need to fulfill their coursework.

The MAP Process
This is an at-a-glance sheet that you can give to the Academic Advisor that will guide them through the MAP Process with a student. The resources below are all of the forms that they will utilize for this process and can be found on our website at *www.tumi.org/mentor* (see MAP Process).

- Sample Letter to the Student's Pastor/Letter to the Student's Pastor template
- Outline for First Interview
- Outline for Final Interview
- Agreement to Supervised Ministry Plan Paper

The Nicene Creed and Its Role in Leadership Development

The dangers of creed-making are obvious. Creeds can become formal, complex, and abstract. They can be almost illimitably expanded. They can be superimposed on Scripture. Properly handled, however, they facilitate public confession, form a succinct basis of teaching, safeguard pure doctrine, and constitute an appropriate focus for the church's fellowship in faith.

~ G. W. Bromiley

What is the relationship between Creedal Theology and Scripture? The Nicene Creed, while by no means can either be equated with or a substitute for the teaching of God's Word, is nonetheless a reliable plumb line of the essential claims that make plain the historic orthodox faith of the Church. Creeds are NOT equal to Scripture and in both the technical and spiritual sense, creeds in any form ought never to be placed on the same level of importance or place as Scripture. A creed is reasoned discourse, while the Scriptures are revealed truth.

~ Don L. Davis. *Sacred Roots Workshop: Retrieving the Great Tradition in the Contemporary Church.* Wichita, KS: The Urban Ministry Institute, 2011. p. 64.

A creed can, however, be an excellent summary of our historic orthodox faith, which the Nicene Creed, in fact does. Creeds are formally not present in the Bible (though councils and summaries of critical truth are everywhere found in both the Old and New Testaments), but creeds do mean to express essential biblical data and truth. In Christian history, three creeds have taken superior place: the Apostles' Creed, the Nicene Creed, and the Athanasian Creed.

Creedal Theology can shape our spiritual formation in the areas of baptism (incorporation), catechesis (discipleship), and ordination (laying on of hands), and the Creed has (and continues to) play a major role in our community life.

The Nicene Creed is a concise, elegant, and beautiful statement of what the earliest pastors, theologians, and leaders of the Church considered to be the elemental essentials of Christian orthodoxy.

What Is the Nicene Creed?
Rev. Terry G. Cornett, © 1997. The Urban Ministry Institute.

The original Nicene Creed came out of the first worldwide gathering of Christian leaders at Nicaea in Bithynia (what is now Isnik, Turkey) in the year 325. It was called to deal with a heresy called Arianism which denied that Jesus was God and taught that he was instead the greatest created being.

The council at Nicaea hammered out language that bishops could use to teach their churches who Jesus was. A little over fifty years later, new challenges were being faced. A modified form of the Arian heresy was making a comeback, and a new problem had also emerged. Some bishops and pastors had begun teaching that the Holy Spirit was not God (was not of the same substance as the Father) and was not really even a creature. He was thought of as a kind of power but not as a person of the Godhead.

To resolve this problem, a council of 150 bishops of the Eastern Church were gathered in 381 at Constantinople (modern day Istanbul, Turkey). This council reaffirmed the fact that Jesus was fully God and then turned their attention to the question of the Holy Spirit which the Nicene Council had left untouched. (The original Nicene Creed read simply, "We believe in the Holy Spirit.") The council turned this simple statement into a paragraph which explained more fully the person and work of the Holy Spirit.

The Nicene Creed

We believe in one God, the Father Almighty, maker of heaven and earth and of all things visible and invisible.

We believe in one Lord Jesus Christ, the only begotten Son of God, begotten of the Father before all ages, God from God, Light from Light, True God from True God, begotten not created, of the same essence as the Father, through whom all things were made.

Who for us men and for our salvation came down from heaven and was incarnate by the Holy Spirit and the Virgin Mary and became human. Who for us too, was crucified under Pontius Pilate, suffered and was buried. The third day he rose again according to the Scriptures, ascended into heaven and is seated at the right hand of the Father. He will come again in glory to judge the living and the dead, and his Kingdom will have no end.

The Nicene Creed and Its Role in Leadership Development

The term **catholic here refers to the Church's universality, through all ages and times, of all languages and peoples. It refers to no particular tradition or denominational expression (e.g., as in Roman Catholic).*

We believe in the Holy Spirit, the Lord and life-giver, who proceeds from the Father and the Son. Who together with the Father and Son is worshiped and glorified. Who spoke by the prophets.

We believe in one holy, catholic*, and apostolic church.

We acknowledge one baptism for the forgiveness of sin, and we look for the resurrection of the dead and the life of the age to come. Amen.

The Nicene Creed and Nicene Theology: Fidelity to Historic Orthodoxy

The Nicene Creed is our curricula's critical foundation. It serves as our understanding of historic orthodoxy, and provides us with the content to create various syllabi for catechetical teaching in Christian belief and doctrine. We are convinced that a vital, spiritual understanding of the Nicene Creed can ground new believers in the faith, serve as a basis for doctrinal and theological education for the Church, and can be effectively integrated as a key component in our services of worship (liturgy). Furthermore, we believe the Nicene Creed provides us with the essential outline for doctrinal formation of the church's leaders and undershepherds.

In the Early Church, credential for leadership training involved comprehending and defending the elements in the Nicene Creed. As a matter of fact, this document served as a basic "bottom line" for orthodoxy in preparing candidates for ordination in the Church. Not only can we appropriate the Creed in the same way for urban leaders, we can concentrate our theological training on the essentials of the faith itself.

Mastering this concise summary of the Story of God will empower leaders to better shepherd their churches and ministries. Memorize the Nicene Creed along with its biblical support to help you be able to defend its teachings biblically and theologically.

Do not hesitate to integrate the recitation and discussion of the Nicene Creed into the flow of every class session. As you will see in every *Capstone* module, time is set aside for the students to recite the Nicene Creed together before entering into the subject matter at hand. Resist the temptation to ignore this section in your class training. Form the habit of leading your classes in reciting the Nicene Creed together, referring to it throughout your discussions of theological issues, and reinforcing its centrality as you address and resolve doctrinal controversies. As a commentary of the ancient Church's rule of faith, as well as a coherent summary of Scripture and defense of historic orthodoxy, the Nicene Creed is a key pedagogical tool at the *Institute*. You will find, as we have, that employing it in this way can deepen your students' appreciation and understanding of orthodox teaching in their overall theological and leadership preparation.

Of course, many ways exist to review and memorize the Nicene Creed together with your students. One way to familiarize yourself with the Nicene Creed is through song. Dr. Don Davis has written the Nicene Creed in hymnic form, adapting it metrically in both common meter (8.6.8.6.) and 8.7.8.7. We've included a list of tune possibilities for use with these lyrics. (As you know, the hymn meter system allows any number of well-known hymn melodies to be assigned to various sets of hymn lyrics.) With the Nicene Creed in hymn form, you can select well-known hymn melodies and sing together the faith of the Creed as a class, with your whole heart!

- The Nicene Creed hymn – Common Meter (in the Appendix)
- The Nicene Creed hymn – 8.7.8.7 (in the Appendix)

Be creative as you help your students become familiar with this important, historic summary of our faith.

Additional Resources on the Nicene Creed

We offer the following documents (in the Appendix) to assist you in understanding the vitality and centrality of the Nicene Creed for both worship and leadership development.

- *The Nicene Creed with Biblical Support*

- *There Is a River: Identifying the Streams of a Revitalized, Authentic Christian Community in the City*
  This tabular document outlines what we believe to be the key tributaries of a renewed, authentic expression of the historic orthodox faith in the city. These elements together suggest the kind of spiritual formation and identity that can revitalize and regenerate urban Christian community. The theological foundation for this document is squarely built upon the elements of the Nicene Creed.

The Nicene Creed and Its Role in Leadership Development

- *Creedal Theology as a Blueprint For Discipleship and Leadership: A Time-tested Criterion for Equipping New Believers and Developing Indigenous Leaders*
  This document explores how we can employ the Creed as a primary tool in equipping and credentialing leaders for ministry in the urban church.

- *The Nicene Creed Bibliography*

Dealing with Theological Diversity: Holding Fast the Good

Note: we have included for your convenience a pdf printable version of this document on our website at www.tumi.org/mentor. We encourage you to print copies for your students, and discuss the principles in it. Without question, your students who learn the art of critical thinking can be used effectively in ministry to train others!

As an educational institution rooted in an interdenominational mission organization, *The Urban Ministry Institute* affirms the legitimacy of the various communions, organizations, and denominations which affirm the tenets of the historic orthodox faith. We are unashamedly evangelically orthodox, and seek to partner and collaborate with all those who affirm our Affirmation of Faith Statement, a document which is in sync with the classic Christian confession of Christ as Lord. God has greatly used our unabashed loyalty to the Great Tradition of the Faith, and we have formed numerous productive partnerships with other kindred churches and organizations that hold to the same confession.

A major role of your work as a Mentor will involve equipping your students to be clear regarding the historic orthodox confession and, at the same time, charitable and open to others who may differ on the non-essentials of the Christian confession. You will often find in many of your teaching sessions students from very different traditions, whose viewpoints diverge on numerous issues confronting the Church today. *The Urban Ministry Institute* is unashamedly evangelical but not sectarian. Your students may come from Baptistic, Reformed, Pentecostal, Methodist, Holiness, Independent or any other of the varied traditions that represent evangelical Christian belief.

Our theological framework is the Nicene Creed and our focus is on the essentials of the faith held in common by all orthodox Christian traditions. On non-essential issues of doctrine there is freedom to disagree. Your students will likely hold differing positions on such issues as the meaning of divine election, baptism in (with) the Holy Spirit, spiritual gifts, ordination of women, the Lord's Supper, modes of baptism, etc. We want to explain the boundaries of historic Christian orthodoxy and, to a lesser extent, help people see how and why it is that within those boundaries the traditions differ on more specific issues and how they scripturally support those positions.

Dealing with Theological Diversity

In addition to the focus on essentials, three principles should guide our classroom discussions when there is legitimate difference of opinion about theological truth.

- First, we respect the congregational traditions of our students and we are attempting to help them minister effectively within them. We want to encourage students to be loyal to their church or denomination and its vision, doctrines, leadership, and traditions.

- Second, we believe that theological discussion can highlight differences in a way that is irenic, that is, "leading toward peace." We are more interested in what we hold in common and in how differences in perspective can inform and sharpen each person's understanding of truth than we are in having one view "win out." During discussions that raise disagreements, Mentors and students should heed the words of James to be "quick to listen, slow to speak, and slow to become angry." Our experience is that classes which contain a diversity of views (within an evangelical and historic framework of orthodoxy) help students to become better thinkers and ministers.

- Third, this is leadership education. Students do not need to be protected from differing viewpoints but exposed to them. Critical thinking about issues, biblical defenses of positions, and understanding of the history of doctrinal development are a necessary part of all Christian leadership education.

As a Mentor, you will play a key role in creating a classroom atmosphere that is respectful and open toward the theological and ministry tradition of each Christian leader. Your job is not to undermine these but to help people sharpen their convictions, ground them in a firm biblical base, and integrate them within the context in which they are called to minister. We believe that the curriculums we provide will both model and build a framework in which you can accomplish this.

Holding Fast the Good:
Developing Critical Thinking Skills in Leadership Development

In order to be a responsible leader in the Church, a man or woman must have developed the ability to think critically, to weigh opinion without prejudice or bias, and possess a fairness in listening to diverse arguments and weigh evidence. Much of our effort as Mentors is enabling our students to engage widely divergent views on a controversial matter, discussing it fairly, in a respectful way, while listening to others in a way that encourages open dialogue. These kinds of skills undergird much of what ministry is, and we must learn ways to train our students to adopt these dispositions and employ these basic leadership tools in their Gospel work.

Theological Preparation:
The Historic Orthodox Faith and Teaching Critical Dialogue
TUMI is unashamedly committed to the historic orthodox faith, seeking to confess the same biblical truths proclaimed by the apostles, and defended through the ages by those faithful to Jesus Christ and to the Word of God. We firmly believe, too, that in order to rightly divide the Word and provide a clear and compelling witness to the lost in the city, we must be well versed in the Word of Christ enough to engage those who oppose our faith. For this reason, we expose students to ideas and notions with which we ourselves do not agree, and which may not be consistent with the truth as we know and confess it in Christ. The motive here is not to undercut our students' faith and convictions, but rather to strengthen them. Only if we are able to engage and refute the deceptively crafted falsehoods of much so-called biblical teaching can we protect those whom we are called to serve.

Do not be alarmed if in fact you come across materials or assertions in a textbook which seem off-center or out of sorts with what we consistently profess and teach in our modules. No leader can be effective today in our diverse, post-modern, and scientifically oriented culture without respectfully listening to positions that they do not agree with, and responding with the calmness and clarity which is due to all people, even those whose views are not consistent with historic orthodox teaching.

A Conflict of Visions: Sincere Christians Handling Disagreement
Battling wrong doctrine is not the only task of the Christian leader. He or she must also learn to converse and to agree to differ with believers whose views do not line up with their own. Our students represent many faith traditions holding to differing theological systems. It is easy to demonstrate historically that godly, sincere, and biblically grounded leaders and traditions have disagreed with one another. TUMI's emphasis on the Great Tradition captured in

Dealing with Theological Diversity

the Nicene Creed centers our common confession and anchors us in those essential truths held by Christians everywhere and by all.

In light of this, we strongly urge all our professors, mentors, and students to be willing to engage theological and ethical viewpoints which differ from their own. We believe that critically engaging such notions without endorsing them is essential to critical thinking. Our training must make us ready and willing to give an answer to those who ask us for our rationale for our ideas, or for reasons for our disagreement with theirs. Engaging different viewpoints can promote the kind of dialogue and discussion that shapes our thinking, and makes us better able to defend the truth.

Education Is Not Indoctrination: Critical Engagement and Respectful Demeanor

Education is not indoctrination; rather, we seek to help our leaders gain a critical mind-set, and to share with others with whom they disagree in a respectful and open manner. Truly, in things theological, we must be wise as serpents and harmless as doves. The ability to engage those with whom we sharply disagree, to offer counter-arguments to rebut their positions, and then to teach without shame the truth of the Scriptures in Christ as we understand them is an essential skill for all Christian leaders. This is especially so for those serving Christ in the city, those who encounter strange doctrines, alien viewpoints, and weird religious notions constantly, and in every form.

A major part of TUMI's training, then, is to equip our students to test everything, but to hold fast, to cling to that which is good (1 Thess. 5.21). Paul's exhortations to the Thessalonicans is the rule-of-thumb for all intellectual and academic dialogue in our TUMI modules and courses, and is itself our genuine desire for all our students. The aim of our TUMI studies is not to avoid knowing what others believe, as odd as some of those ideas may appear. Instead, our aim is to speak the truth in love, to engage others respectfully, grounded in the Scriptures, centered on Christ, with an aim to persuade those who find themselves believing in falsehoods and wrong doctrine. We desire both instructors and students to respect those who hold to views of Scripture that differ from their own, without giving up their own convictions regarding the essentials of the faith (Nicene theology). Throughout our modules you will find yourself, therefore, being exposed to views that contradict your views, or even call into question our cherished evangelical faith. We include these texts and viewpoints not to get you to endorse and embrace them, but in order to equip you to think critically, to engage others respectfully, and to grow intellectually, all with the intent to mature in Christ, and to disciple others in the truth.

Faith Seeking Understanding: Testing All Things, Holding Fast the Good
May God give all our entire network the grace and humility to test all things, to hold fast to that which rings true to Scripture and to Christ, and be ready and able to engage others who differ from your own viewpoints, especially those unwittingly caught in strange doctrines. The Holy Spirit, the very One who inspired the Scriptures, will enable us to confess the truth, defend it against falsehoods, to ground others in the true doctrine of our God and his Christ.

Let us, then, obey the admonition of Paul to the Christians in Thessalonica:

> But test everything; hold fast what is good.
>
> ~ 1 Thessalonians 5.21 (ESV)

May God give us grace to know and to defend the truth that sets us free!

Dealing with Theological Diversity

Section II

Understanding the Role of the Mentor

The Profile of a TUMI Mentor

Role Summary

In the TUMI pedagogical scheme, a Mentor plays a significant role in equipping students. With the context of their lives and ministries, and the actual engagement with the Scriptures and other training materials, the Mentor helps the student to both engage and contextualize their study data. The discussions they lead provide an opportunity for the students to reflect upon and critique the arguments and case studies that emerge throughout the course of study. Finally, and perhaps most importantly, the godly example and diligence of the Mentor himself/herself provides the students with a "living visual aid" to what it means to study the Word of God aggressively, with a passion to obey Christ and bear fruit, to God's glory.

In every way, then, Mentors serve as an anchor in the facilitation process, helping the students to develop a biblical framework for their own theological exploration and/or denominational commitments. As fellow students of Scripture, Mentors can give context and help students integrate their learning into the Story of God and their lives, aiding students as they grapple with the teachings of the faith while relating them to their own specific faith tradition. In many learning environments, it will often be the Mentor who makes all the difference in the training process for the students, as they strive to know, love, and live the story of God in their personal lives, their ministries, and in their lives in the church and community.

On the one hand, a Mentor's formal responsibility involves the specific tasks associated with facilitating a class of adult learners. You must implement courses by encouraging and recording student attendance, assisting the students in understanding and working together on the curriculum, overseeing video or audio content presentations to the Learning Group, teaching implications/applications of the core content, helping students select appropriate ministry projects, grading and evaluating student work, and reporting student needs and progress to the Site Coordinator.

On the other hand, your informal reality is that you will need to act as cheerleader and coach. You must learn to acknowledge their classroom and assignment performance, both encouraging and challenging them as they wrestle with difficult yet important

Mentor's Job Profile

subjects. Learning to properly evaluate student performance and grading is a critical part of serving as a Mentor. We are training many who have little or no background in traditional academic settings, and must be careful to edify our students in our training. We must challenge them to do their best, and to prepare themselves for the a particular task God has assigned them in their church or ministry. In everything, each faculty member and mentor must remind them of this call, work and the role God has for them to fulfill in the advancement of the Kingdom.

I. TUMI Mentor Character and Job Profile

A TUMI Mentor must first and foremost be a person of Christian character, one whose testimony is blameless in their own family, church, and community, and one who is available to the Holy Spirit to be used to facilitate training and growth in others. Two traits which are essential in this process are a passion for excellence and a deep abiding respect for what the Holy Spirit can accomplish through those whom he has both called and gifted.

A. A passion for and a demonstration of excellence in all things

> And whatever you do, in word or deed, do everything in the name of the Lord Jesus, giving thanks to God the Father through him.
>
> ~ Colossians 3.17

1. Maintain a compelling testimony as a mature disciple of Christ, honoring and glorifying God in your personal walk, your marriage and family, your work and employment, and in your neighborhood and community. Who we are is more important than and will determine what we do. We can never underestimate the power of a life lived well under God, and the impact this life can have before others. You are mentoring and facilitating for quality servant leadership, and you must let your light so shine before your students that who you are becomes a living epistle, known and read by them as a true model of Christian discipleship (1 Cor. 11.1; Matt. 5.14-16; 1 Pet. 3.15; 1 Tim. 4.7-16).

2. Be thorough and well prepared for your course. You are representing Christ. We have resources on our website to help you as you mentor TUMI courses.

Mentor's Job Profile

a. Visit *www.tumi.org/mentor* for resources and tools to help you as you equip leaders for the work of ministry.

b. Visit *www.tumi.org* and click on "help" at the bottom right of the screen to ask questions related to everything from administration, *Capstone* and specific module concerns, to reference texts, spiritual formation, and the like.

c. Visit *www.tumi.org/capstone* for the official required textbooks list for each *Capstone* module, along with the reading assignments for each module.

d. Visit the Satellite Gateway at *www.tumi.org* for our *Foundations for Ministry Series* courses with access to syllabi for those courses, along with course descriptions and the official required textbooks list for *Foundations* courses.

3. Manage your classroom in a professional, organized, and excellent fashion. All of your interactions with the students should be formal, warm, and respectful. Know your students, know what is important to them and pray for them. Be open to the Lord and to them to give a word of encouragement.

4. Nurture within them a spirit of bravado: David is TUMI's patron saint, and God the Holy Spirit selects and gifts whom he will to do what he desires.

5. Be professional, responsible, and diligent in all your duties as a mentor – preparation for class, counseling and assisting students, praying regularly for your class, and fairness and clarity in all grading and assessment. Your excellence will enable students to both trust and submit to your oversight and teaching, and will encourage them to mirror your fine work as they engage in their studies.

Mentor's Job Profile

B. A deep abiding respect for those whom the Holy Spirit has gifted and called

Whatever you do, work heartily, as for the Lord and not for men, knowing that from the Lord you will receive the inheritance as your reward. You are serving the Lord Christ.

~ Colossians 3.23-24

1. Recognize that the gifts and calling of God are irrevocable, given to individuals by the Holy Spirit himself, and that God almighty will lead them into the fullness of his power and ministry, for his glory's sake (1 Pet. 4.9-10; Rom. 11.34; Eph. 4.7-8). Know that God has a purpose and plan for each of your students, that they need not be like you or anyone else, and that the Lord will make known to them the specific ministries and opportunities that each one will fulfill for him. Acknowledging both the presence and power of the Holy Spirit in each student will enable you to be both patient and yet diligent in directing and assisting them as they learn.

2. Understanding the God-called nature of your students' lives and ministries, you need never then to patronize your students. God the Holy Spirit has called them, and he himself is outfitting them through this training for their own specific work of ministry. Expect the same thing from your students that you would from yourself. Challenge them to critically engage the materials as best as they can, and firmly and consistently push them to master the principles and ideas they encounter in the text. Your acknowledgment of them will make all the difference in their lives to either persevere in the midst of difficulty or balk at continuing on, especially as they encounter difficult, hard-to-understand materials.

3. Honor the readiness of your students and respect their decisions. If they do not want it, no amount of exhorting will change that. Timing is everything in the training of a leader. The contingencies of their lives will change, and you will have to change with them.

For our approved satellites, there is a syllabus along with quizzes and/or a final exam and their answer keys that can be found at www.tumi.org/ foundations for each **Foundations for Ministry Series course. The **Capstone Curriculum** does not require a separate Course Syllabus but we ask that you create a sheet for the students that shows the dates of class meetings, which lessons will be covered at each meeting, and due dates for assignments (see **Sample Class Schedule Chart** in the Appendix).*

**Contact and Connection sections are explained in "The Approach to Lessons: Contact, Content, Connection" found on pages 62-63 of this Mentor's Manual. Every Capstone Curriculum module comes with a "Mentor's Guide" that gives teaching helps for each lesson including: the lesson objectives, overview of student materials, and suggestions for planning and teaching the Mentor's portion of that lesson.

C. Providing efficient and professional oversight of your TUMI class (Job Responsibilities)

A Mentor should strive to provide efficient and professional oversight of his or her TUMI learning experience.

1. Plan and lead classes using TUMI's *Capstone Curriculum* or *Foundations for Ministry Series* courses.

   a. Before the course:

      (1) Thoroughly familiarize yourself with the Mentor's Guide, Student Workbooks, and audio or video presentation materials that make up the course you are teaching.

      (2) Work with your Site Coordinator to plan your Course Schedule Sheet*, and make sure that necessary student materials (workbooks, textbooks, etc.) will be available for your first class session.

   b. For each lesson:

      (1) Take attendance.

      (2) Administer quizzes and classwork/homework.

      (3) Play the audio or video teaching segment and answer student questions.

      (4) Plan and teach the "Contact" and "Connection" portion of lessons.**

2. Emphasize consistently the importance of faithful attendance, class participation, and completion of work.

3. Evaluate any materials, projects, or tests that are assigned as they are due. At the end of the course, calculate final grades and report them to the Site Coordinator.

Mentor's Job Profile

4. Be available to provide counsel and prayer for students as they engage in ministry.

5. Communicate with Site Coordinator about student needs, administrative questions, and course feedback.

Mentor's Job Profile

The Mentor and Cultural Contextualization

A key difficulty in all distance learning is the ability to take content that is designed for people in a wide variety of settings and make it practically relevant to specific people who face unique situations and challenges. This problem is particularly acute in regard to our curriculums at *The Urban Ministry Institute*. Our learners share in common a commitment to the Church and to the practice of urban ministry, especially among the poor, but due to the nature of our mission we have a particularly diverse audience to reach. Nationally, urban ministry involves outreach to a wide variety of people and people groups. Our material will often be taught in ethnic sub-cultures where attention to particular cultural issues and practices is vitally important. Our students come from a wide range of educational backgrounds. Some students will come with college educations already completed and yet many may also come without a high school diploma. Students will also be present from a variety of socio-economic levels and often represent a number of distinct urban neighborhoods and congregations.

This diversity, both within any given learning group, and between different learning groups across the nation, demands that Mentors play a key role in contextualizing the learning. In traditional education, contextualization describes the process of helping students to create meaning by connecting what is being taught in school to the everyday lives of the students. In theological and pastoral education, contextualization has as its goal:

> To enable, insofar as is humanly possible, an understanding of what it means that Jesus Christ, the Word, is authentically experienced in each and every human situation. . . . The gospel is Good News when it provides answers for a particular people living in a particular place at a particular time. This means the worldview of that people provides a framework for communication, the questions and needs of that people are a guide to the emphasis of the message, and the cultural gifts of that people become the medium of expression.
>
> ~ Dean Gilliland. "Contextualization."
> *Evangelical Dictionary of World Missions.* A. Scott Moreau, ed.
> Grand Rapids: Baker Books and Carlisle, Cumbria, U.K.
> Paternoster Press, 2000. p. 225.

The Mentor and Cultural Contextualization

The key to contextualization is understanding that while the gospel (Matt. 24.14; Rom. 1.16; 1 Cor. 15.1-2) and the "deposit of faith" (cf. 2 Tim. 1.14, Jude 1.3) are authoritative, timeless truth for all people, the implications and applications of that truth will be expressed differently from culture to culture and context to context.

We have deliberately designed our approach to distance education to include a person (the Mentor) who can guide students through the learning experience. As a Mentor, you are in face-to-face contact with a particular group of people that make up the class you are leading. You can, and should, discuss their ministry responsibilities and context, discern the ethnic and cultural make-up of their church and community, and understand what they hope to learn from the class. Your responsibility is to make sure that the lesson content is understood and applied in the context of those unique circumstances.

The burden to contextualize the truth to the situations in the life and ministry of our students is the Mentor's chief intellectual responsibility. By facilitating constant correlation of the truth to their situation the Mentor protects the student from merely listening to ideas without reflecting on the ramifications of those ideas for their lives. As Mentor, you must pay attention to the distance between the truths of Scripture and the life choices and environments of the students. Helping them integrate the truth into their lives is more of an art than a science, and you will get better at this fundamental teaching skill if you engage your students' contexts in the heart of your lesson discussions.

If you as a Mentor come from, or have some life experience in, the cultural context of the students you are teaching, this is a wonderful asset. It means that your own theological and ministry experience will be particularly helpful to your students. Even when this is not the case, however, you as a Mentor can contextualize by deliberately surfacing the questions that students bring to the material, by having students discuss their ministry situations and the challenges that they face, and by having students critically evaluate what the gospel means for the people, congregations, and the neighborhoods in which they minister.

The core content of each lesson will be delivered by the national TUMI faculty member who develops the course. In responding to this audio or video teaching, the Mentor must seek to draw out implications and applications relevant to these particular students and their cultural context. This means that you, the Mentor, must take seriously the questions and implications raised by the students. While you should freely share your own accumulated wisdom about ministry, there should also be a deliberate discussion of whether the implications and applications which you share will be applicable for all the cultures, sub-cultures and socio-economic classes represented by the students. Student-to-student interaction and peer learning can also be an important part of the contextualization process and should be encouraged.

While this emphasis on contextualization should guide everything you do in regard to your students, it is particularly important in the parts of the lesson that are prepared and taught directly by the Mentor, that is, in the *Contact* and *Connection* sections. The next pages of this manual are designed to introduce you to the structure of our lessons (including *Contact* and *Connection*) and to help you understand your role in teaching them.

The Mentor and Cultural Contextualization

Our Pedagogical Approach to Lessons: Contact, Content, Connection

Each lesson taught at *The Urban Ministry Institute* should be organized around the three basic stages of the teaching process: securing interest, communicating truth, and discovering applications. In order to do this we plan our lessons around the "Contact, Content, Connection" model of student engagement.

Contact

The *Contact* part of the lesson is designed to prime the students to engage the topic or theme of the day. It captures and focuses student attention on the subject matter by demonstrating its relevance for their lives and ministry, and/or seeks to stimulate the students' curiosity regarding the meaning of the themes under discussion.

> It helps the student answer the question: ***"Why is this important to me?"***

Content

Next, the *Content* part of the lesson seeks to engage the students in the discovery of, and interaction with, the important facts, stories, principles, experiences, ideas, and skills that comprise the subject being taught. It presents the truth claims of the lesson and facilitates critical reflection upon them in light of Scripture, reason, tradition, and experience.

> It helps the student answer the question: ***"What is the truth regarding this topic?"***

Connection

Finally, the *Connection* section of the lesson guides the students through a process of reflection on what the content means today, both for their lives and for their ministry situations. It is concerned with the ramifications of the truth, i.e., its implications for how they understand, evaluate, and act in light of the truths just discovered. It seeks to help them master and apply the learning in actual life. Furthermore, the *Connection* stage encourages the students to evaluate their current beliefs and practices in light of the new understanding they acquired in the content section, and to develop clear convictions about the topic.

It helps the student answer the question: *"What does this mean for me and what should I do about it?"*

Previously we spoke about the critical need to contextualize the curriculum to the students' situation, and your role as a Mentor in that process. You must understand your role as helping make the teaching relevant and meaningful in their own context. Therefore, the sections of the lesson most vital for your assistance in contextualization will be the *Contact* section (which helps students understand the relevance of the teaching to their own ministry situation), and the *Connection* section (which guides students in applying the truth learned to their ministry responsibilities). Devote a large amount of your preparation time (your study, prayer, and reflection) to helping make the curriculum relevant and on point with the life goals, situations, and opportunities of your students in the places where they live and work.

Since you engage your students in a face-to-face relationship, you, as Mentor, are in the best position to teach these sections of the lesson. You have the opportunity to learn the students' ministry contexts and to hear their questions on a weekly basis. This means that you must plan and teach these sections with the unique needs of your class in mind.

For instance, within the *Capstone Curriculum* you will be given guidance and suggestions for these sections from your Mentor Guide Notes for each lesson. However, you should feel free to adapt (or even replace) these suggested ideas with references, materials, and methods that take seriously the needs of the particular students you are teaching. Similarly, with the *Foundations for Ministry Series* courses, you should conclude each lesson by leading a discussion on the implications and applications to the local context. Creating the lesson objectives and core content taught in the *Capstone* and *Foundations for Ministry* curriculums is the responsibility of the national TUMI instructors. However, the responsibility to help your students understand the material and see its implications and applications for their particular lives and ministries is yours. Making the content come alive in their situations should be your express purpose and goal in each class session with your students.*

** For more specific information about how to plan the "Contact" and "Connection" parts of the lesson, see pages 96ff and 101ff in **Section Four: Understanding the Mechanics of Class Instruction**.*

The Approach to Lessons: Contact, Content, Connection

The Case for Case Studies: The Importance of Contacts and Case Studies in Capstone
Rev. Dr. Don L. Davis

If you have ever taught or sat in a Capstone class, you have noticed the presence of "Contact" stories or the "Case Studies" sections of the lesson. These are ubiquitous (everywhere present) in Capstone; more than 450 cases are offered at the beginning or end of the lessons, positioned to either introduce the lesson or to dig into the meaning of the lesson's content, at the end. They are numerous in number and thorny in character. Many suggest that they never seem to allow for a clear, simple resolvable answer to the problems they pose. Why include Contact stories and Case Studies in the lessons, in the first place?

While it may not be immediately obvious, the answer to this question is important. Case Studies are life application stories which highlight the importance of connecting truth that is researched with life that is lived. These stories, whether invented or actual, allow the learners to explore the relationship between the truths they discovered in their Bible study, and the tough, difficult decisions which emerge in the midst of our life circumstances. The method of engaging Contact stories and Case Studies in *Capstone* flows from the ancient rabbinic method of discerning wisdom through connecting the biblical truth to the facts of particular cases, in the light of the shared wisdom of tradition. It is a sound, helpful approach to discover truth together in a learning cohort.

What Exactly Is a Case Study? A Biblical Example
In the context of the *Capstone* lesson, what exactly is a case? A case is a life application story that is either posed or described in the Contact or Case Study section of the material. It is based on biblical examples which reveal the ancient practice of careful observation of situations, and the corresponding act of making generalizations and discovering principles after you have observed and analyzed a particular situation.

A clear biblical example of this practice is given in Proverbs 24.30-34 (ESV):

I passed by the field of a sluggard, by the vineyard of a man lacking sense, [31] and behold, it was all overgrown with thorns; the ground was covered with nettles, and its stone wall was broken down. [32] Then I saw and considered it; I looked and received instruction. [33] A little sleep, a little slumber, a little folding of the hands to rest, [34] and poverty will come upon you like a robber, and want like an armed man.

Note the order of this investigation: first, careful, critical consideration is made of a particular situation (i.e., a case). This situation is noted carefully, looking at the various facts and conditions associated with it. (This is important: cases are built on a careful knowledge of the facts of the situation). Next, the observer reflects on the *meaning* of what he sees; he considers it, looks at it, and then "*receives instruction.*" Finally, the observer, after gathering the facts of the situation and reflecting on their meaning, generalizes a principle, a truth, that can be used not only to understand the case under investigation, but other cases of similar kind that may arise. "A little sleep, a little slumber, a little folding of the hands to rest, and poverty will come upon you like a robber, and want like an armed man."

Notice how this process of case study dovetails into the discovery of a biblical insight or principle that is listed in the form of a "proverb," a short, pithy, memorizable statement that summarizes the insight received from the observation and reflection. Of course, to test the generalization, other cases can be consulted, and the principle applied to them, to see if similar results are discovered. Still, the process is clear: observation, interpretation, generalization, decision.

Of special interest here is the connection of cases to rabbinic methods of truth seeking and truth telling. Case study is an ancient, rabbinic way to discern God's truth and will in a difficult and/or controversial situation.

Case Studies and Rabbinic Methods of Wisdom

A clear biblical example arises from the case of Gamaliel in his comment on the Sanhedrin's thoughts regarding the apostles. He demonstrated this ancient rabbinic practice in his response to the Sanhedrin Council's determination to kill Peter and the apostles (Acts 5.33-39). After hearing Peter and the apostles' courageous defense against the Council's threat for them to be quiet and to cease speaking of Jesus of Nazareth, they wanted to kill them, presumably for blasphemy and false teaching among the people.

The Case for Case Studies

The Case for Case Studies

On hearing this, Gamaliel warned the Council not to act on such a decision, and made an argument to them based on his working knowledge of relevant cases dealing with the futility of rebellious movements to succeed or sustain in the face of God's judgments.

Gamaliel then referred to two cases which illumined the situation they were facing with the apostles. The first dealt with Theudas with his 400 insurrectionists, whose rebellious cause produced his own death, the dispersal of his followers, and the total elimination of his movement (Acts 5.36). The second involved Judas the Galilean whose rebellion rose up during the days of the census, and drew some folk after him. (Josephus the historian actually gives a comprehensive account of his actions.) Like Theudas, Gamaliel says, Judas perished, and everyone who followed him was scattered as well (Acts 5.37).

After considering the lessons associated with these cases, Gamaliel makes his argument based on the principle gleaned from his observation of the cases of Theudas and Judas.

> So in the present case I tell you, keep away from these men and let them alone, for if this plan or this undertaking is of man, it will fail; but if it is of God, you will not be able to overthrow them. You might even be found opposing God!" So they took his advice.
>
> ~ Acts 5.38-39

Although the Council decided to not kill the apostles, they did unfortunately foolishly and unjustifiably beat the apostles and charged them not to speak any more in the name of the Lord Jesus (vv. 40-41).

Gamaliel's approach in this situation should be seen as a rabbinic tested method of dealing with difficult and controversial problems and issues. He related the particular situation of Peter and the apostles to a bigger picture of the futility of rebellious movements. When confronted with a problem that called for a conclusive, biblical answer, Gamaliel immediately referred to two relevant cases judged to be of the same subject. He recited the cases, summarized his findings from his reflections on them, and then generalized a principle that related directly to what they ought to consider with the apostles in their situation, right then and there. This method of Gamaliel was a standard rabbinic approach to applying Scripture to life – observation of the facts of a case, reflection on other related, relevant cases, the generalization of a principle, and connecting that principle to life.

Historically speaking, a rabbi was a "keeper of the cases and their interpretations" for the community, in sync with the traditions of the elders. As a student-pastor-counselor of the tradition, he could draw from his internal storehouse the various cases and their relevant biblical principles to the different issues of life that were brought to him. As he encountered situations, he would reflect on the facts, and relate those to the law and to tradition's understanding of it. His duty was to be as aware as possible of the body of cases and their corollary biblical principles which related to various questions or concerns as they would come up. The rabbi was trained in assessing relevant and appropriate cases and relating them to the Law and to tradition. In any given question, what were the relevant cases, or the "seminal" (precedent setting) cases connected to it? What were the "opposite" or "contrary" cases that reveal a breaking of the principle under consideration? What might be considered either borderline or hybrid cases, those stories containing elements that were hard to categorize, both puzzling and difficult to ascertain?

In the same way the rabbis were equipped to relate the truth of the Scripture to actual cases and historical instances, so we hope our students, through the use of the Contacts and Case Studies, will be better outfitted to relate their learning to real life happenings.

Case Studies and Communities of Learning

In a similar vein, Case Studies also offer a community of learning (like a module cohort) a solid, testable approach to discovering and applying truth together, as a group.

Case approaches assume the priority of the community's reflection and interaction with life over time. Through its own told and lived history, a community builds up shared knowledge which it trusts, has tested, and shares with its members. This knowledge is codified in principles, and passed down generation to generation through tradition and shared insight. These "insights" gleaned over time must still be tested and proven by experience, but the method and process is solid. Cases are considered, observed, interpreted. Principles are discovered and tested in experience. These principles are then cherished, learned, and used to make decisions in difficult situations, and to set direction in carrying out what we believe God's will to be in a given circumstance.

As we think about this, we ought not be too abstract. The easiest way to think together is to tell stories and interpret them together.

The Case for Case Studies

The Case for Case Studies

Case Studies should be seen as stories (whether invented or historical) that enable a community to wrestle with its commitments in the context of a real experience. Stories are the heart of our lives together as communities. We live in actual situations which, when we speak of them, take the shape of specific stories we share.

A story makes the truth come alive; it forces us to think about the meaning of what we have learned in a way that actually impacts our lives and our circumstances. Cases become living pictures, the kind that are worth a thousand words, and help us draw out the wisdom that it invites us to see and apply. More than this, Case Studies invite a community to connect its research, its problems, its opportunities to real truths.

In a nutshell, Case Study dialogue in a group forces all participants to share their observations and findings, and allows the group to engage in its members' thoughts and reflections. Because of this shared nature of case study, it forces those in a group to be convinced but less dogmatic in asserting the finality of their individual opinions and judgments with others. Case Study is therefore difficult; it can be hard to see the facts the same way, or even weigh the same facts in the same manner. To explore cases sometimes requires much time and open dialogue among those engaging the stories with the truth.

Even in light of these challenges, though, Case Studies are highly effective in training members to both listen and reflect together. Other members will emphasize things we do not, and they will offer different interpretations on the meaning of the facts we discover. We must learn to learn together, and not abstractly. Case Studies call the learners to connect their knowledge with actual life situations, and forces the researchers to become problem-solvers, counselors, and deliberators together. The insights gleaned are gleaned by us together. The Case Study becomes the lens by which we together discover truth and relate it to life. Cases provide data, but also emotion, insight, and wisdom. There's no better method of biblical counseling than using case studies to explore God's will.

Case Studies: Tell the Stories and Learn Together

In conclusion, Case Studies are demanding, but properly understood and engaged, they provide an open-ended, communal approach and strategy toward effective life application of truth. Allocate your lesson engagement time blocks to generously give as much time as you can to both the Contact and Case Study sections of the Capstone lesson. Carefully review the facts and issues introduced in the various cases, and prayerfully discern which ones you will concentrate on, what principles you will explore, and what other relevant cases you might discuss.

Also, realize that the Contacts and Case Studies are offered to give you a ready-made platform to test your students' abilities to relate the truth to life, to connect principles with practice. This is "on-the-job training" for Christian leadership, without the horrible consequences of their poor or unjustified decisions! Allow the Case Studies to be the testing zone of how your students relate the insights of the Scripture to the challenges of real life situations.

Do not forget that Case Studies do not lend themselves to "right/wrong" kinds of dualistic approaches. Their observation of the facts, reflection on their meaning, and generalizing of principles will neither be easy nor clean. However, the lessons they learn in how to approach the tough issues of life will be invaluable. Even if the answers do not always resolve into "the one right answer," it will be heartening to see that there may be more than one "right answer!" (God tells husbands to love their wives as Christ does the church, but he does not tell them to all buy flowers and have a date night on the third Sunday of each month! The command is clear, but we have freedom in how we apply the command to a particular situation [2 Cor. 3.17].)

Continuing in the word of Christ as his disciples demands that we relate his word to our lives (John 8.31-32). Let us never neglect the cases of our own lives, and the ways in which the Scripture can make us wise to salvation in Christ, in the very center of our days as we live them (2 Tim. 3.15-17).

The Case for Case Studies

Literacy and Language Issues: Helping Students Succeed

The key distinctive of our student application and acceptance process is that a pastoral recommendation is the primary criteria for acceptance. This implies a number of things about the students you will mentor.

- Your students are not just potential leaders. They are already leaders. It has been established that they are already functioning in some type of lay or pastoral ministry in their church. They are called by God and gifted by the Holy Spirit. Our job is not to confirm their fitness for ministry but rather to invest in them so that they become even better at what their church has already entrusted them with.

- Your students are involved in the life of a church and represent a congregational or denominational tradition that creates the framework for the practice of ministry.

- The church's entrustment of leadership, not prior academic training, qualifies them for investment. As a result, your students may have a wide range of academic backgrounds. Some students may not have completed high school while others may have college degrees. Because our focus is on training leaders "especially among the poor," it is not uncommon for some to have had less academic opportunity than middle-class church leaders. Although oral skills are usually strong among any group of leaders, some of your students may struggle with low literacy or writing skills.

- Because of the multi-cultural nature of city populations and the high number of immigrants, some students may be very gifted inside their cultural context but lack some skills, training, or behaviors that people expect from leaders in the dominant culture. When possible we want to offer training in the primary language of the leaders. However, because of the large number of language groups in the city you will sometimes have students who are being trained in English even though it is not their first language.

These dynamics affect our classes and teaching in several ways:

Grading

Traditional seminary education has a difficult time helping people who do not come with existing academic credentials and skills. A certain level of proficiency in the dominant culture's language, education, and values is required before the investment can be attempted by them. This is especially significant because in many cases the seminary is being used as a way to see if the student qualifies for leadership. They must, in essence, "weed out" the unqualified, and this is generally done, not on the basis of calling or spiritual gifting or evaluation of the student's ministry in the congregation, but on the basis of academic achievement. Grades are used as a way to evaluate a person's fitness for ministry. If a person earns a Master of Divinity degree, they become part of the potential leadership pool that churches in the dominant culture can draw from for pastoral leaders.

In our context, leadership education is not used to evaluate a person's leadership potential but to enhance their existing ministry skills. We are not trying to determine whether they are fit leaders because their church has already determined that they are. This means that we are only interested in helping people succeed.

The primary use of grades in our system is to help a student assess their own progress. Students should fail courses only if they did not complete the assignments. Students who complete all the course requirements to the best of their ability should receive a passing grade although the nature of the grade will obviously vary according to the degree of competence achieved. This does not mean that challenging content should not be offered or that high standards should not be maintained. It does mean that investment in motivated Christian leaders is the primary goal and evaluation is a subordinate goal.

NOTE: *It should be stressed to students that they are not ever being graded on their ministry calling or competence but only on their current mastery of the particular subject matter in the course.*

Assigned Reading

Students are required to read, reflect upon, and be ready to discuss selected assigned textbooks for every TUMI course. These textbooks are selected to enhance the student's mastery of the subject,

Literacy and Language Issues

Literacy and Language Issues

to be exposed to the views of various authors on the subject, and provide additional, supplemental data that is relevant to the issues covered in class. Please encourage your students to be diligent in their reading and response to these texts, and challenge them to discuss their meanings with you and their classmates.

While we have required texts, we do incorporate them differently than normal academic classrooms. For instance, our courses require that every student purchase, read, and reflect upon the textbook(s) for the course. They must complete the reading assignment for each class session, which involves reading a section in each required textbook and writing a precis (concise summary) of its main point, as they see it.

In the student precis, we ask them to summarize the major theme and argument of the section, and then give a careful response to it. Our desire is that our students learn how to critically analyze a text, that is, to read it, understand its thesis (main point), articulate its argument in a respectful way (whether they agree with the author or not), and then respond as to why they agree or disagree with the thesis. This practice will help them dialogue with others, engage different opinions in a respectful way, and learn to listen to dialogue with others whose beliefs are different than their own.

Because some of our students may be challenged by the reading involved in academic study, we think carefully about both the level of reading and the amount of reading that is required. This does not mean that we never assign difficult books, but it does mean that we take exceptional care to find the best books possible and limit the number of books that students are required to read compared to a traditional seminary setting. Instructors take seriously that the books chosen are meant to equip a wide range of urban church leaders. We want to challenge and stretch our leaders but not discourage them.

Four other safeguards help us with those students who find the reading exceptionally challenging. First, very few graded assignments are based on the outside reading for the course. The outside readings will be extremely helpful for any student's understanding of ministry but the majority of the course can be completed successfully by class participation and working with materials that have been presented orally as well as in written form. Second, we encourage Mentors and/or students to form reading groups in those courses where the reading may be more challenging or student literacy is exceptionally low. Having students discuss the readings together during the week or immediately prior to a class can make a genuine difference in overall comprehension. Third, as Mentor, you may assist your students greatly by offering a brief summary of the reading assignments for that week. Such summaries will focus their attention on key principles emerging from the readings, and help them know what you believe is most relevant for your current week's lesson. Fourth, if a student has a particularly acute problem with literacy, we encourage you to speak to your site coordinator about literacy programs in your area that can serve as a further resource to these students.

Because even poor churches function in a highly literate society and because their leaders often are called to negotiate the gap between the dominant society and their members, we encourage our students to work on their reading skills.

Written Work

Students should always be given the option of completing any written assignment (Scripture memorization, quizzes, ministry project reflection papers, etc.) orally. This may be done in person or in recorded form, whichever is more conducive to the joint needs of Mentors and students. If poor writing skills seem to be affecting the ability of the student to communicate their knowledge on a particular assignment, Mentors should feel free to request a follow-up with the student to have them orally fill in what is missing.

Summary

Mentors should do whatever possible to keep differences in class, culture, or language from hindering a student's ability to learn or to communicate their learning. We are concerned with maintaining academic integrity and high standards but we believe that the cultural forms in which those standards are evaluated should remain flexible and adaptable. In all cases, we should offer students an atmosphere of respect befitting their status as Christian leaders and also a clear sense of our belief in their calling and abilities. Balancing respect, high expectations, and cultural flexibility is fundamental to the Mentor's role, and should be part of the relationship that you build between yourself and your students.

Literacy and Language Issues

Reading Standards

Question

How do you deal with the different levels of literacy of students taking classes? According to the reading requirements that Don Davis lays out, many of the courses have three books to read with hundreds of pages of reading . . . and most are theologically deep and not easy to digest. How do you keep the bar high, yet at the same time not overwhelm students who, many of which, don't even have a high school diploma?

Answer

In dealing with literacy, it is very important to understand the way in which the reading assignments are designed in TUMI courses. As a rule, unless otherwise noted, the reading assignments are given as exposure and supplementary material to the actual classroom lectures, dialogues, and discussions. Albeit various readings and articles are used to provide conceptual outlines for some materials, as well as referred to selectively within teaching segments, the readings themselves are not the substance of the teaching. Our philosophy is to use texts to support the basic conceptual and intellectual skeletons which are constructed in the actual outlines of the course; professors profess, students learn, and texts support. As such, we do not directly quiz nor test from the books. This is not to say that the texts are either unnecessary or irrelevant; as mentioned above, often we selected the texts on the basis of their ability to cover the central concepts while, at the same time, be somewhat manageable and readable. For students who cannot read well or who find the assignments burdensome, we ask that they do as best as they can with the reading assignment, allow the mentor to highlight the key concepts associated with the book, and integrate as much of the concepts into the actual discussion of the lesson topic, where applicable.

Question

As a satellite, do we have any freedom to substitute some of the required reading books for certain courses with other books of our choosing?

Answer

Capstone is an integrated curriculum; the books were selected not because there were not more difficult or different books on the subjects, but because they were the books best suited to supplement the concepts we want to cover. By definition, texts are geared both to professorial discretion and subject matter. We have history with the texts included, and have tested them in real world settings with real leaders. They supplement the concepts we seek to cover. In an integrated curriculum, you must be careful to teach in sync with the objectives of the lesson and module, and frankly, we cannot guarantee where mentors will go if we were to grant blanket authority to sites to change every and anything. The concepts of the texts are integrated in the outline, supplemented within them for emphasis and focus. (Remember certain issues of interdenominational status, historic orthodoxy, and nonsectarianism were hammered out in selecting these books. We selected them on their ability to enhance our lessons while avoiding idiosyncratic and tangential directions).

As theological educators, we had a dramatically broad reservoir of potential texts on every subject, and selected these on the basis of our learning objectives and mandate to be interdenominationally open and historically orthodox. So, as a rule, texts should not be substituted. Of course, denominations and worshiping communities will want to articulate their own distinctive doctrines and practices, and you should feel free to add (but not substitute) texts to further reflect those distinctions. You should always be extraordinarily careful to reiterate the lesson and module objectives lest you wind up teaching idiosyncratically and not integrally.

Knowing that this curriculum is being employed in various theological communions by diverse Mentors and students can help you understand the priority of preserving our unity and diversity as we serve very distinctive communities of the King. We love them all, and serve them all.

Reading Standards

TUMI Course Credit and Accreditation

TUMI Course Credit and Accreditation

As a training center dedicated to honoring and glorifying God in all we do, TUMI is unashamedly committed to academic excellence and quality leadership education. Every resource and program represents our commitment to excellence and God-honoring leadership education that rivals the most rigorous and prestigious programs today. Nevertheless, we have deliberately chosen to forego seeking academic accreditation, remaining for the indefinite future as a non-accredited educational school. Why?

To be sure, accreditation in most cases and venues is commendable and beneficial for any leadership training center, affording its students the credibility of accredited studies and the ability to transfer credit to other sister institutions. However, exorbitant prices and academic standards preclude the involvement of most urban leaders from attending traditional schools. Accreditation standards inadvertently may severely shrink the pool of prospective students for ministry education, and effectively shut out the vast majority of urban applicants in our traditional seminaries and Christian liberal arts schools. Moreover, the pursuit of accreditation, if won, would dramatically limit the number and kinds of leaders that we currently serve, especially those who would not qualify for traditional theological education because of lack of funds, academic background, or cultural distance.

In light of these unfortunate circumstances, TUMI has elected to remain unaccredited, not as a cover for supposed mediocrity, but as our way of ensuring that all of our premiere programs and resources can be accessed by any urban leaders who are serving their churches and advancing the Kingdom of Christ in the city, and who also may not have either the large sums of funds or the academic background to qualify for that training.

The Case For and Against Accreditation

In a real sense, the process of academic accreditation was designed to protect students from fraudulent and unethical diploma mills that were suspect academically and criminal ethically. Who among us has not heard of a get-certified-quick kind of enterprise promising a Ph.D. through a phone call and a money deposit? *The Urban Ministry Institute* affirms and embraces the legitimacy of the various credentialing associations, and believes them in the main to be helpful, responsible, and credible enterprises that move forward responsible scholarship and higher education.

Nevertheless, TUMI maintains proudly our non-accredited status. This decision in no way speaks of any desire to ignore traditional academic and ministry standards for its educational programming. On the contrary, we deeply respect and partner with accredited institutions who are equipping leaders for the Kingdom. Rather, we have chosen not to participate in formal accreditation processes in order to remain available to as many urban leaders as possible. While accreditation establishes strong criteria to ensure educational and professional excellence, the process can both unknowingly and unfortunately eliminate or exclude many deserving potential students. Without realizing its power to exclude, accredtation may block many students who, because of lack of funds or poor educational background, may be disqualified from leadership education opportunities.

From the beginning, TUMI has asserted that the call of God and the gifting by his Holy Spirit are the ground of all authentic leadership service. In conjunction with this, practical ministry experience becomes one of the most essential prerequisites for those desiring and deserving ministry training. We believe it is our responsibility as a missions-based training center to remain available to students who are called of God regardless of financial status or academic background. Therefore, we unashamedly make our training available to students who, under traditional circumstances, would never be able to participate in seminary-level instruction. Truly, it is not by power, nor by might, but by the Spirit of the Lord that men and women are called into the ministry of the Gospel (Zech. 4.6).

Again, our decision to remain non-accredited does not, in any way, reflect a lack of commitment to academic excellence. On the contrary, we believe that those preparing to do God's work deserve a faculty who has been well prepared academically and programs that present an intellectual challenge. At *The Urban Ministry Institute*, students will find courses that are both stimulating and demanding, along with a faculty of experienced ministers and missionaries who have earned degrees from outstanding colleges and universities.

For specific information on the actual hours and training for *Capstone*, refer to *Capstone Student Educational Learning Hours* in the Appendix.

TUMI Course Credit and Accreditation

Accredited Partnership Training

Although TUMI has chosen to be and remain non-accredited in order to keep our resources available to deserving urban leaders who seek our training, we also are unashamedly committed to academic excellence and quality leadership education. We demonstrate this commitment not only in the quality of our educational programming, but also in how we partner with accredited liberal arts schools and seminaries where our faculty teach and offer courses.

We affiliate with the Association of Higher Biblical Education (ABHE), a fine accrediting association of schools and seminaries, and we also enjoy ongoing, positive relationships with academic partners of TUMI. We have established both formal and informal training partnerships with these accredited liberal arts schools and seminaries, and these partners offer our students credit for the successful completion of the *Capstone Curriculum*. This credit can be transferred to these schools which recognizes them for graduate-level credit. Please check online (*www.tumi.org*) for the latest information on current TUMI partnerships.

TUMI Course Credit and Accreditation

Section III

Understanding the Essentials
of Class Administration

Facilitating for Excellence:
Organize Your Classroom for Success

All the remaining items in this Section of the manual refer to specific dimensions of mentoring that make the difference in whether your classroom experience is truly excellent or not. To be a solid facilitator and mentor of adults in training demands that you be well organized, clear in your communication regarding assignments and duties, and careful in your record keeping. In many cases, the difference between a good and unsound mentor is their attention to detail, especially in managing their schedule, processing grades, communicating assignments, and offering specific counsel at the appropriate times throughout the course. Pay attention to the insights below, and incorporate them into your own mentoring regimen. Doing so will ensure a more pleasant learning experience for your students, and less headaches and fretting from you!

Managing the Class Schedule

Coordinate with the Site Coordinator the timing and overall schedule of the course you will be teaching, selecting the timetable that is best for you and your students.

Class Format

TUMI courses may be taught in a variety of formats (e.g. weekend, four-week, eight- or nine-week, etc.) depending upon your circumstance. (See *Ways to Schedule Your Training Programs* in the Appendix for a variety of options.) You should feel the freedom to select the format that is best for you.

While you are free to employ any teaching format that works for your students, we are convinced that the eight- or nine-week teaching format is best, with a clear rationale and solid advantages.

Rationale for an Eight- to Nine-Week Class Format

1. *It enables students to better process the great amount of material contained in each module.* Because each content segment contains a large amount of material that will be new and/or challenging to the students, there is value in allowing them to process smaller pieces of it in a given week. The danger, of course, is that the material becomes fragmented. Avoiding this requires effort on the part of the teacher to review and make connections. However, with this danger managed, the eight-week format allows students to focus on comprehending a single lecture, and then building on that comprehension with another single lecture. This yields greater total comprehension at the end of the course.

2. *It tends to be more in sync with the volatile schedules of many bi-vocational urban leaders.* The assignments, especially the readings, present a time problem for many bi-vocational students. The lengthening of the course from four to eight weeks provides much-needed additional time for completion. Between work and ministry, many students have precious few free hours in the week. Shortening class from 3/3.5 hours down to 2/2.5 hours eases some schedule difficulty.

Managing the Class Schedule

3. *It allows the students time to better gain perspective in the context of their family and ministry lives.* A longer period for meditation and consideration of the truth allows students to think about the correlation of their learning within the specific contexts of their personal lives and ministries in the church. Such time can make all the difference between rushing through material and making the principles their own.

Advantages of an Eight- to Nine-Week Class Format

1. It allows students the *time needed to process* the large amount content given in each segment.

2. It encourages students to develop learning and helping relationships among themselves as they process the data over time. (The entire "cohort" theory of adult learning reinforces the importance of shared dialogue and interaction for urban learners.) The repeated gatherings and additional time together reinforces and strengthens this kind of communal learning environment.

Studying and Planning: Your Personal Preparation

Excellent teaching demands that you comprehend the material in its broadest scope, getting the big-picture perspective of all the key issues and concepts, and drafting a plan to hit each point squarely, deeply, and appropriately.

In preparing for the course, you should make it a priority to look over the Mentor's Guide and review the overall scope of the course or module. This would include all its key elements, including:

- Course title and overview
- Objectives
- Devotional material
- Contact questions
- Response to the video segment questions
- Mentor notes
- Case studies
- Key concepts
- Assignments

Review the video/audio several times to grasp the themes and concepts of the course.

Each course also has specific assigned readings to enhance student discussion and understanding. These readings were selected to emphasize the course's central concepts, oftentimes covering various positions or angles related to the themes. Make it your priority to study these texts, correlated with the workbook outlines. This kind of careful, critical review will enable you to help your students grasp the key truths and principles covered under the course's core themes. Of course, it will also be important for you to provide any additional clarification you desire, consulting Bible dictionaries, theological dictionaries, and commentaries to clarify any major topics you wish to explore.

Finally, regularly check the help button on our website (*www.tumi.org*) for questions or comments related to this particular module or course.

Studying and Planning:
Your Personal Preparation

Preparing Class Paperwork

Managing your classroom records is an essential task of effective classroom administration. Below you will find a listing of the key elements of this management along with explanations and instructions for each. All of the forms listed here can be accessed at *www.tumi.org/mentor*.

Create Documents Related to Student Information

The Site Coordinator will give you a list of students registered for your class. Create an *Attendance Sheet* (to track student attendance), a *Student Info Sheet* (so you can get in touch with the students outside of class), and a *Grade Recording Sheet* (in order to record quiz totals and final assignment grades for each student). See samples of each form in the Appendix.

Access Online Listings of Required Textbooks and Reading Assignments

Each *Capstone* module or *Foundations for Ministry Series* course has assigned textbook readings which are to be read and discussed throughout the course. While students are not tested on these readings, they nevertheless represent a key addition to the overall learning and dialogue of the course. Encourage your students to read and engage these readings, and dialogue about them in the classroom, their assignments, and their ministry situations.

Required Textbooks

The textbooks that we select are often subject to varying degrees of issues with availability, pricing, and access. Because of the fluidity of access (e.g., books going out of print, getting permission for reprinting), the required textbook list will change, and will most likely differ from the listing in your *Capstone Curriculum* or *Foundations for Ministry Series* workbook. Please visit our website to see the latest, official required textbook list for your course. The website posting will always represent our most up-to-date listing of all TUMI required texts.

A. Visit *www.tumi.org/books* for our OFFICIAL *Capstone* required textbook listing (English).
B. Visit *www.tumi.org/libros* for our OFFICIAL *Capstone* required textbook listing (Spanish).
C. Visit *www.tumi.org/foundationsbooks* for our OFFICIAL *Foundations for Ministry Series* required textbook listing.

Preparing Class Paperwork

Print Handouts of All Key Materials for Students

A key part of your class preparation involves creating and distributing handouts for your students to keep them abreast of the course schedule, the weekly reading assignments, and the importance and nature of critical thinking.

Course Schedule and with Notes

Create a course schedule for your students which includes the days and dates for your class, the key subjects covered in each class session, as well as dates for quizzes and due dates for class assignments. This information will help your students anticipate assignments, know what to read and prepare for each class session, and meet all due dates on time. See *Sample Course Schedule* in the Appendix, create a course schedule for your class, and print copies for your students.

Reading Assignments

The *Capstone Curriculum* reading assignments posted on our website are keyed specifically to the lesson format of their modules. Please visit *www.tumi.org/capstone* and click on the reading assignments link for your module. There you will find the reading assignments list for your course. Printable (pdf) Reading Assignement Forms are located at *www.tumi.org/mentor* (listed by module).

Important note: Depending on how you structure your course's sessions, you have complete flexibility to break up the reading assignments into units that best match your actual class sessions. In other words, if you are running an eight-week course, simply break up the reading assignments to match your sessions. What is critical is that you focus on the lesson as the basic unit of teaching in your *Capstone* and *Foundations* courses.

Finally, know that your students will most likely have different levels of reading ability. Regardless of their level of reading proficiency, you should emphasize that your students, as leaders, must strive to read and think critically, reading as much of the assignments as possible, and critically engaging the portions they do read. Of course, you should inform your students that they will be tested only on notes from the Workbook and classroom, and not on the data of their reading assignments. Nevertheless, your role as mentor is to demonstrate the richness of discovering insights from the reading, and integrate those insights in your summaries, questions, comments, and teaching.

Preparing Class Paperwork

Preparing Class Paperwork

Holding Fast the Good:
Developing Critical Thinking Skills in Leadership Development

A major goal of our ministry training is helping our students not to over-react or respond unthinkingly to ideas and viewpoints different from their own, especially those they encounter in their textbooks, or in heated class discussions. In order to help us understand how to train our students in the skills of dialogue and critical thinking, Dr. Davis has written a short but fine essay that every student should read. This essay deals with how we have to handle diversity of thought and opinion in our training. Again, this file is located at *www.tumi.org/mentor*. Please print a copy for each of your students.

Scripture Memory Grading Form

In order to fulfill their credit requirements for their courses, the students will need to memorize and self-grade select Scripture passages connected to the course. Students are allowed the rough equivalent of *one mistake per verse* for *full* credit. Additionally, they are also allowed the equivalent of *two mistakes per verse* for *one-half* credit. More errors than these per verse results in the student receiving no credit for their assignment. (Punctuation and misspellings do NOT count as a mistake.) Your students should grade their own verses, and note on their form their credit amount in order to receive credit for this assignment. There is a sample *Scripture Memory Grading Form* in the Appendix, and printable forms can be found at *www.tumi.org/mentor*.

Assignment Submission Envelope

Students tend to take their work more seriously if we provide opportunity for them to be as responsible for their work as possible. In light of this, we strongly suggest that you purchase 10x14 clasp envelopes and print labels to put on these envelopes that list the assignments they will need to submit for class.

The envelope method is an easy way for your students to organize their work and to ensure that they store and turn in every assignment at the end of class. Furthermore, this method can help you force the students to manage their own documents, helping you keep in proper order the many papers you will receive to grade at the end of your course. This simple method of students archiving their own assignments throughout the course has proven to be an excellent tool, for student responsibility as well as classroom management.

An editable label form is available for you on our website at *www.tumi.org/mentor* detailing the assignments due at the end of a *Capstone* module. (Please note, quizzes are not listed on the label as students will take the quizzes during the course. Plan on grading the quizzes yourself, recording the scores, and returning the graded quizzes to the students in order that they can review these for their final exam. Students do not need to submit quizzes with their final paperwork.)

Make Copies of Course Quizzes and Take-Home Final Exam
Every *Capstone* module contains prepared Quizzes based on each Lesson's content, excluding Lesson Four, whose content is covered in the Final Exam. (The Final Exam reviews the material from the entire course.) These Quizzes and Final Exams for all the courses in our *Capstone Curriculum* as well as our *Foundations for Ministry Series* can be found on our website or the Satellite Gateway at *www.tumi.org.*

Our *Final Exams* are designed to be take-home, closed-book exams that the students complete, and at a later date hand in for grading. (Of course, if you have the time and prefer to set aside time for them to take the exam at your site, you may do so.) For your convenience, we have created an editable cover page to attach to your *Final Exam* that provides a line for the student's name, gives instructions on the test, and its due date for the exam's return. In preparation for your class, we suggest that you print the appropriate number of quizzes for the class, as well as the final exam with the cover page you edited. Again, you can find the editable cover page template at *www.tumi.org/mentor.*

Preparing Class Paperwork

Readying Your Facilities and Classroom

A comfortable, clean, and well-lit learning space adds dramatically to your students' ability to participate in a meaningful learning experience. Excellence should be the standard for every dimension of your learning and teaching venue, and your preparation, even in the smallest details of classroom management, will enhance the overall enrichment of your course and sessions. As in everything we do, we serve the Lord Christ, and he is worthy of our very best, to God's glory (Eccles. 9.10; Col. 3.17, 24; 1 Cor. 10.31).

Facilities

Give proper time to setting up your physical space in order to ensure maximum learning and dialogue. Prepare your room excellently, ensuring that your room is neat, clean, and well organized. Seek to make your classroom as presentable and inviting as possible. Remember, something as small as your room will speak volumes regarding what you believe about your training of these leaders for Christ and his Kingdom. Ensure that the carpet is clean and the floor swept, the tables are wiped off, and the chairs neatly arranged. Clean or touch up your classroom walls. (Truly, a simple can of paint is inexpensive yet does wonders to the look of a classroom.) A sloppy, ill-kept learning environment can sabotage your training experience and negate all your good teaching and preparation. Always make it a priority to make and keep your classroom space tidy and presentable.

Classroom

Make sure you take the time to prepare your classroom prior to the start of your class. Set up and wipe off tables and chairs, and ensure the room is properly arranged well before students arrive. Additionally, size your room for your students. For instance, if you have twenty students registered for class, do not set up the classroom for thirty-five. Take down extra tables and chairs so the room does not feel empty or the class appear to be poorly attended. Use dividers if you have a large room and few students. Finally, check the room temperature. Set heat/air conditioning at a comfortable level for you and your students. (It's better to err a little on the cool side to help the students stay alert.)

Equipment

Without question, effective technology can be used to dramatically enhance our teaching and training, and should be counted as a great blessing in the furtherance of the Gospel and training disciples and leaders. While this is true, technology can also be the bane of your classroom if you fail to set it up well in advance, and make certain that it works. Wherever technology exists, things usually can and will often go wrong in any setting, but you are less likely to have issues if you set up and test it ahead of time. *Do not wait until class time to set up your technologies for class!* Instead, always set up laptop/DVD with projector and screen for video projection, and test all connections, making certain all is functioning properly.

Supplies

Set up whiteboard, markers, and eraser for class discussion. Put out hand cleaner, Kleenex, extra pens/pencils, a quiz basket for students to turn in their completed quizzes, and anything else the students or you may need as you host the class. While detail to items such as these may seem minor, these little touches of thoughtfulness in preparation show your students the excellence that you want them to reflect in all they do.

Snacks: To Eat or Not to Eat

We encourage satellites to arrange for snacks during class breaks. It is welcoming and hospitable to the students and provides for a refreshing break in the midst of their concentration. Snacks do not need to be costly or tax you in terms of preparation. Popcorn is a tasty, inexpensive, and healthy snack that can provide physical refreshment. You can invite your students to bring snacks to share with everyone, which will help in both cost and variety. Whatever you decide to do – have snacks or not, it is important to allow for a break in the midst of the class to give students a chance to shift their thinking for a few minutes. Strategically arranged and well-ordered breaks enable students to catch their breath, intellectually speaking, and gain some refreshment through drinks, in restroom use, or simply standing up and engaging each other for a few moments.

Even if you do not provide snacks, it is good to have coffee and water available for students during their class breaks. Of course, you will need to be sure that you start the coffee early enough for students to receive a cup before class starts.

Readying Your Facilities and Classroom

Assigning, Recording, and Processing Student Grades

In some cases, these guidelines may not address specific situations in your context. It may be necessary to consult your ministry's leaders for specific direction. While we want all TUMI sites to stay consistent with TUMI standards, you may be more specific in the guidance from your leadership. For example, in a jail or prison it may not be wise to allow fellow students to grade each other, and take-home finals may be impossible.

Your satellite and its training experiences exist to facilitate and equip leaders for the urban church. A formative and central element of that training is accurate and regular record keeping of student information and grading. Careful record keeping helps you know the status of each student, keeping current in their contact information, and following their progress academically and ministerially. You will need a solid, efficient system designed to track the student courses and grades. Keep your system simple, and design a structure easy enough for you to maintain and follow. These records must be confidential, not accessible to the public or left where others can see them. Establish a clear, doable process, and then follow it consistently. You are representing the Lord and your students in this, and excellence shows your respect for both.

Again, a key part of the Mentor's role is to record individual student assignment grades, calculate their overall grades, and inform the Site Coordinator of the students' grades so transcripts can be created and students formally notified of their final grades. Although TUMI classes are not driven primarily by academic aims, we do take student performance seriously. And, of course, your students will anxiously await their **transcripts at the end of each course**. The following steps (and sample appendices) will help you process your students' work and submit their records to your Site Coordinator promptly, appropriately, and accurately.

Receive Completed Assignments

Throughout or at the end of each course, you will receive assignments from your students. Ensure that these are put away and kept out of view of other students. Create a system that you can follow in which to receive the assignments and keep them confidential. (Recall our suggestion of the envelope method, which emphasizes student organization of their own materials, to be turned in at the end of class).

Grade Paperwork

The course requirements and weights are already assigned for each *Capstone* or *Foundations* course. (Each *Capstone* module has a syllabus in the front of the student workbook, and each *Foundations for Ministry Series* course or workshop syllabus may be accessed by our site coordinators on our website, *www.tumi.org* on the Satellite

Gateway.) Below is a sample of a *Capstone* module's course requirements and grading system:

Requirement	Percentage	Points
Attendance and Class Participation	30%	90
Quizzes	10%	30
Memory Verses	15%	45
Ministry Project	10%	30
Exegetical Project	15%	45
Readings and Homework Assignments	10%	30
Final Exam	10%	30
Total	100%	300

Assigning, Recording, and Processing Student Grades

The students' submitted assignments will include Scripture Memorization (self-graded passages turned in to you on a date you designate); Ministry Project, Exegetical Project, Reading Assignments, Final Exam (with essay question answers attached). The total points for each assignment are listed in the course syllabus in *Capstone* and *Foundations*.

Attendance

Attendance at each class session is a course requirement and, as you can see above, is a key part of the student's grade. Be sure you take attendance throughout the course, and then note their point totals as part of your grading process.

Quizzes

The quizzes for both *Capstone* and *Foundations* are located on the Satellite Gateway at *www.tumi.org*. Grade the quizzes, marking the correct answers on the questions they got wrong, record their point totals on the *Grade Recording Sheet* (see Appendix) and return the quizzes to the students (so they can use them to study for the Final Exam).

Memory Verses

The students' submitted assignments will include Scripture Memory. (These will be self-graded by the students before they give them to you.) Record their point total for each assignment (according to the points assigned for this assignment in the course syllabus) on the *Grade Recording Sheet.*

Ministry Project

The goal of the ministry project is not only to apply the learning but also to reflect on what happened as your students shared their insights with others. In their reporting students should both describe what they did and what they learned through the experience. In evaluating the reports look for evidence that the students thought about what happened during the application and gained insight that will help them in the future. Refer to the course syllabus for the point total for this assignment.

Exegetical Project

Your students should be evaluated on all aspects of the criteria listed in the assignment. (Please note that we evaluate based on the concepts of which they are writing, not the grammar or spelling in their writing. You will find that students are at various skill levels in those areas. The key is the student's ability to understand the Scripture and explain/interpret it in such a way as to help relate it to their lives and ministry. Refer to the course syllabus for the point total for this assignment.

Reading Assignment

Your students will most likely have different levels of reading ability. No matter what level, it is important that as leaders, your students read as much as they can and engage what they read. The students are required to do this assignment for each required textbook for the course. Refer to the course syllabus for the point total for the required reading assignments.

Final Exam

The final exam for most of our courses is a closed-book, closed-notes take-home final. Students are not allowed to refer to anything other than their memory to take this exam (except in some cases where it is specifically written on the final exam that a Bible is allowed). The answer key for this is on the web at *www.tumi.org* on the Satellite Gateway.

Calculate and Record Final Grades

A central element in your satellite's effectiveness involves doing the work of a *Registrar* of a college or university. Simply put, the record of our students' performance (i.e., their grades) and the ability to retrieve those grade reports over time actually begins with your conscientious work as Mentor. In order to help you do this, we have created a *Microsoft Excel Grade Recording Sheet*. (See *Sample Grade Recording Sheet* in the Appendix, and download the *Excel Grade Recording Sheet* from our website at *www.tumi.org/mentor*.) You can enter student names, and points for each of the above course requirements, as the course progresses. The column on the right will automatically calculate the points as you add the totals for each student.

List each student's points for every assignment they turn in on the *Grade Recording Sheet* created for this course. (See sample in the Appendix). Depending on the system you set up, you will receive the students' assignments either throughout the course, or all at the end of the course together (as in the envelope method). Once the course is over, the assignments graded, and points totaled, you should use the *TUMI Grade Scale* (see this document in the Appendix) to determine the appropriate grade for each student. List that grade on the *Grade Recording Sheet* for each student and save your final edits on the *Grade Recording Sheet*.

Submit Final Grades to Site Coordinator
Always double-check your grade point calculations according to the Grade Scale, and when confident your records are correct, submit the final *Grade Recording Sheet* to your Site Coordinator along with the *Course Attendance Sheet*. The Site Coordinator will send out grades to the students and save the *Grade Recording Sheet* with their records for backup.

Assigning, Recording, and Processing Student Grades

Wrapping Up Final Details

Closing out a course is as important as preparing for its start. Once all the students' and Mentor's duties are completed and you have submitted final grades to your Site Coordinator, turn in all extra workbooks, textbooks, supplies, building keys, Mentor Guide and DVD to your Site Coordinator. Celebrate your students' accomplishments and your facilitation of a meaningful experience. Of course, continue to maintain regular contact with your Site Coordinator in anticipation of your next opportunity to mentor a course for your site.

Section IV

Understanding the Mechanics of Class Instruction

Leading a Capstone Module or Foundations for Ministry Series Class Session

Flexible structures that can be adapted for your site's needs are a staple in TUMI's educational philosophy. With so many dozens of contexts employing our training regimens and materials, it would be impossible to insist on a single, "perfect" means of teaching, hosting, and facilitating meaningful training experiences in all our partner sites. You and your colleagues will need to use your wisdom and follow the Spirit's leading as to how you will structure your training. Feel free to experiment as you strive to find the most appropriate and edifying structure that best suits the needs of your students and serves the availability of you and the other Mentors.

Below you will find our suggestion of what kind of format best suits an effective facilitation of our *Capstone* modules and *Foundations for Ministry Series* courses. These resources are specially formatted to be similar in structure, which enhances both student and mentor familiarity with the course outline and approach. They do differ, however, with several notable exceptions: first, our *Capstone Curriculum* utilizes video in teaching format whereas our *Foundations for Ministry Series* uses audio. Second, our *Capstone Curriculum* video teaching is approximately four hours in total length, whereas our *Foundations* courses' audio teaching runs anywhere from eight to sixteen hours in length. Also, some of our *Foundations* courses have PowerPoint resources accessible to review while listening to the audio teaching. Some of our Mentors have chosen to listen to the audio of the *Foundations* courses, and then teach the course materials themselves.

These materials have been designed for flexible use. However you choose to structure your learning format, and whatever you choose to do, the following outline of managing a class session can help you facilitate a classroom meeting thoroughly and excellently.

Curriculum	Video	Audio	PowerPoint	Mentor Guide
Capstone Curriculum	4-6 hrs	No	---	Yes
Foundations for Ministry Series	No	8-16 hrs.	Some courses	No

Leading a Capstone or Foundations Class Session

I. Before the Course Begins

A. Look over the Mentor's Guide notes along with the lesson outlines in order to gain an understanding of the content that will be covered in the course (*Capstone*) OR the Course Syllabus which outlines the course objectives and requirements for students (*Foundations*).

B. Read and review the course's resources carefully, familiarizing yourself with the content of the course's materials, and how they are designed to work together in a particular classroom session (e.g. video, audio, PowerPoint, handouts, etc.).

C. Read any assigned readings associated with the curriculum, whether textbooks or handouts.

D. Review the key theological themes associated with the course by using Bible dictionaries, theological dictionaries, and commentaries to refresh your familiarity with major topics covered in the curriculum.

E. Think about key questions and areas of ministry training that you would like to explore with students in light of the content that is being covered.

II. Before Each Lesson

A. Watch the video segment(s) for that class session that is found on the DVD (or listen to the audio for the course).

B. Create a *Contact* and *Connection* section for this lesson.

C. Review and summarize the required text reading assignments due for this lesson segment. (Highlight the central principles and key points you intend to emphasize as you engage the materials in class.)

III. Preparing and Teaching the *Contact* Section

A. Review the Mentor's Guide to understand the lesson objectives and gather ideas for possible *Contact* activities.

B. Create a *Contact* section that introduces the students to the lesson content and captures their interest. As a rule, *Contact* methods fall into three general categories.

1. *Attention focusers* capture student attention and introduce them to the lesson topic. Attention focusers can be used by themselves with motivated learners or combined with one of the other methods described below:

   a. Singing an opening song related to the lesson theme

   b. Showing a cartoon or telling a joke that relates to an issue addressed by the lesson

   c. Asking students to go stand on the left side of the room if they believe that it is easier to teach people how to be saved from the Gospels, and to stand on the right side if they believe it is easier to teach people from the Epistles

2. *Story-telling methods.* The instructor may tell a story that illustrates the importance of the lesson content or ask students to share their experiences (stories) about the topic that will be discussed.

   a. In a lesson on the role of the pastor a Mentor may tell the story of conducting a funeral and share the questions and challenges that were part of the experience.

   b. In a lesson about evangelism the Mentor may ask students to describe an experience they have had of sharing the Gospel.

3. *Problem-posing activities* raise challenging questions for students to answer and lead them toward the lesson content as a source for answering those questions, or they may ask students to list the unanswered questions that they have about the topic that will be discussed.

   a. Presenting case studies from ministry situations that call for a leadership decision and having students discuss what the best response would be.

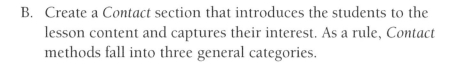

Leading a Capstone or Foundations Class Session

    b. Problems framed as questions such as "When preaching at a funeral, is it more important for a minister to be truthful or compassionate? Why?"

C. Understanding *Contact* as *point of contact* between the student's life and interest and the biblical material

    1. Regardless of what method is chosen, the key to a successful *Contact* section is making a transition from the *Contact* to the *Content* of the lesson. When planning the *Contact* section, Mentors should write out a transition statement that builds a bridge from the *Contact* to the lesson content.

    2. For example, if the lesson content was on the truth that the Holy Spirit is a divine Person who is a full member of the Godhead, the *Contact* activity might be to have students quickly draw a symbol that best represents the Holy Spirit to them. After having them share their drawings and discuss why they chose what they did, the Mentor might make a transition statement along the following lines:

Because the Holy Spirit is often represented by symbols like fire or oil in Scripture rather than with a human image like the Father or the Son, it is sometimes difficult to help people understand that the Spirit is a full person within the Godhead who thinks, acts, and speaks as personally as God the Father or Jesus Christ. In this lesson, we want to establish the scriptural basis for understanding that the Spirit is more than just a symbol for "God's power" and think about ways that we can make this plain to people in our congregations.

This is a helpful transition statement because it directs the students to what they can expect from the lesson content and also prepares them for some of the things that might be discussed in the *Connection* section that comes later. Although you may adapt your transition statement based on student responses during the *Contact* section, it is important, during the planning time, to think about what will be said. *How will you bridge the discussion from the introductory concepts to the actual content of the lesson?*

D. Things to remember as you teach the *Contact* section you have created

1. Employ the stories, comments, and questions in the *Contact* section to "prime the pump" of your students' curiosities as you prepare to engage the biblical content of your module's lesson.

2. Be careful to manage your time well while teaching the *Contact* section. Designed to provoke response and challenge students to engage each other on topics of contemporary importance, the *Contact* section can quickly consume a large portion of your teaching time! Be wise in how you allocate your time as you discuss the stories, and make the transition to playing the first video lesson segment for the students.

E. Three useful questions for evaluating the *Contact* section you have created are:

1. Is it creative and interesting?

2. Does it take into account the needs and interests of this particular group?

3. Does it focus people toward the lesson content and arouse their interest in it?

IV. Preparing and Facilitating the *Content* Section

A. Orient your students to the material they will engage in the Content session.

1. Prepare the students to review the content of your module's lesson by viewing the video teaching together.

2. After teaching the *Contact* section (including the transition statement), play the video segment for the students, or listen to your designated audio segment. (For *Capstone*, each lesson has two video teaching segments of approximately 25 minutes in length; for *Foundations* courses, audio segments tend to be 50

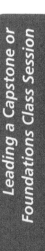

Leading a Capstone or Foundations Class Session

Leading a Capstone or Foundations Class Session

minutes in length, but can be divided up as you see fit for student comprehension.)

3. Remind the students that they can follow along with the video presentation using their Student Workbook which contains a general outline of the material presented and Scripture references as well as other supplementary materials referenced by the speaker. For *Foundations* courses, the workbooks coincide with the audio teaching, with some adjustment for student interaction.

B. Adapt the flow of the *Content* sections of your courses with the capability and comprehension of your students.

1. Do not hesitate to stop the video and review the material with the students if it is plain that they are having difficulty with the concepts being presented. Additionally, you may wish to view or listen to a portion of the teaching a second (or twenty-second time!) in order for the issues, concepts, or questions to be fully understood.

2. Once you have viewed the *Capstone* video segment, answer the *Segue One* questions to review the ideas covered on video. Focus on questions they may have about the content, and confirm that they grasp both the data and implications of the presented content.

3. After this discussion, you may need to take a break or change the pace of your presentation. Exploring the content of your lessons will be both exhilarating and exhausting! Monitor how your students are wrestling with the data, and do all you can to make their learning as hassle-free as possible.

4. The rule of thumb is simple: *organize the Content section in order to ensure that the students understand the critical objectives being covered by the content in any classroom session.* The goal is not to cover ground but to master concepts and principles which help us grapple with the overall objectives of the course, whether a *Capstone* or *Foundations* course.

C. Master the *Content* section in stages and phases; be careful not to cover too much ground per classroom session.

    1. After you have completed your discussion together on the first video segment, play the second video segment for the students. *Depending on how you structure your class, this second segment may be viewed an entire week later!* Pace is paramount when covering new concepts with adult learners; be like the bee (gather honey) not the butterfly (covering ground).

    2. Use the same discernment and oversight to ensure through the viewing and the discussion of the *Segue Two* questions that your students grasp the scope and meaning of the content presented. Having covered carefully the main ideas of the lesson, you will now be ready to teach the *Connection* section of the lesson.

    3. Highlight the central principles, insights, and concepts covered in the *Content* section. Typically, students will be exposed to a considerable amount of material, and it will be easy for them to get lost in the volume. Remember the lesson, module, and course *objectives*, and correlate *the material covered* with *the actual educational objectives* you have in the class itself.

V. Preparing and Facilitating the *Connection* Section

A. Review the Mentor's Guide to understand the lesson objectives and gather ideas for possible *Connection* activities.

B. Create a *Connection* section that helps students form new associations between truth and their lives (implications) and discuss specific changes in their beliefs, attitudes, or actions that should occur as a result (applications).

    1. *As you plan, be a little wary of making the Connection section overly specific. Generally this lesson section should come to students as an invitation to discover, rather than as a finished product with all the specific outcomes predetermined.*

2. At the heart of every good *Connection* section is a question (or series of questions) that asks students how knowing the truth will change their thinking, attitudes, and behaviors. Because this is theological and ministry training, the changes we are most concerned with are those associated with the way in which the students train and lead others in their ministry context. Try and focus in on helping students think about this area of application in the questions you develop.

3. Utilize any one of a number of different formats for the *Connection* section. Students can discuss the implications and applications together in a large Mentor-led group or in small groups with other students (either open discussion or following a pre-written set of questions). Case studies, also, are often good discussion starters.

4. Regardless of the method, in this section both the Mentor and the learning group itself should be seen as a source of wisdom. Since your students are themselves already Christian leaders, there is often a wealth of experience and knowledge that can be drawn on from the students themselves. Students should be encouraged to learn from each other as well as from the Mentor.

C. Several principles should guide the *Connection* discussions that you lead:

1. The primary goal in this section is to *bring to the surface the questions* that students have. In other words, the questions that occur to students during the lesson take priority over any questions that the Mentor prepares in advance – although the questions raised by an experienced Mentor will still be a useful learning tool. A corollary to this is to assume that the question raised by one student is very often the unspoken question present among the entire group.

2. Try and focus the discussion on *the concrete and the specific* rather than the *purely theoretical or hypothetical*. This part of the lesson is meant to focus on the actual situations that are being faced by the specific students in your classroom.

3. Do not be afraid to share the wisdom that you have gained through your own ministry experience. You are a key resource to students and they should expect that you will make lessons you have learned available to them. However, always keep in mind that variables of culture, context, and personality may mean that what has worked for you may not always work for everyone. Make suggestions but dialogue with students about whether your experience seems workable in their context and, if not, what adaptations might be made to make it so.

D. Principles to remember in facilitating an effective *Connection* section:

1. *Focus in on the central questions raised in both the Contact and Content sections, and dialogue with them.* Use your Mentor's Guide to review any relevant questions or data, and to check for additional help as you cover the *Summary of Key Concepts* section. This section is designed to provide you with a handy and ready review of the key principles and concepts covered in both of the video segments and segue questions. Use the summary to clarify any incomplete understandings that students may demonstrate in their answers.

2. *Think through the principles using actual case studies.* Review the *Case Studies* found in the student material and/or Mentor's Guide. Be careful to allow for proper time with each case study you choose to cover. While it is not necessary to cover all of the *Contacts* and *Case Studies* in a lesson, the more you challenge your students to relate their understanding to actual lived experiences, the better they will comprehend the truths you are teaching.

3. *Concentrate on their life situations as you correlate the biblical truth.* Make certain that you allow time to discuss with your students the relevance of the key lesson principles for discipleship and ministry. These questions can be derived either from those they initiate with you, or select ones you raise during this section.

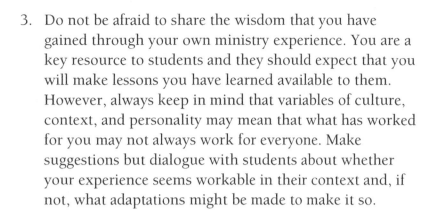

Leading a Capstone or Foundations Class Session

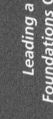

Leading a Capstone or Foundations Class Session

4. *Don't be afraid to repeat the obvious.* Always make sure that you "pile-drive" the thesis and central theme of the lesson at the end of your study, restating the thesis of the lesson, and reviewing its main points.

5. *Suggest further exploration.* Draw your students' attention to the resources and bibliographies listed for those wanting to inquire more deeply into the subject, or to consult for further study.

6. *Facilitate new ways of thinking about applying the material in their lives.* Take time each lesson to reinforce the importance of planning and following through on their Ministry Projects. Spend time discussing possible directions for this as needed, and remind them of its importance in their overall learning and training program. Because the Ministry Project is the *structured application project* for the entire course, it will be helpful to set aside part of the *Connection* section to have students discuss what they might choose for their project and to evaluate progress and/or report to the class following completion of the assignment.

E. Three useful questions for evaluating the *Connection* section you have created are:

1. Have I anticipated in advance what the general areas of implication and application are likely to be for the teaching that is given in the lesson?

2. Have I created a way to bring student questions to the surface and give them priority?

3. Will this help a student leave the classroom knowing what to do with the truth they have learned?

F. Remind the students of all upcoming assignments.

1. It is imperative that students stay on top of the various assignments they are responsible for in their study of this module. Remind them, therefore, of deadlines they will soon be facing, including their Scripture memorization duties, assigned required text readings, their Exegetical

and Ministry Projects, as well as any other tasks you have assigned them.

2. Emphasize good planning and discipline as the keys to efficient study and preparation.

G. Close your lesson with prayer and challenge.

1. End your time of study, reflection, and discussion with prayer for your students, thankfulness to God for his truth and his Word, and petition the Lord that the truths that the Holy Spirit has given them will become an intimate part of their hearts, lives, and ministries.

2. Make yourself available to your students after class (as possible) to explore any additional questions or comments they may have concerning the lesson, class, assignments, or anything else that may arise from your time together.

Leading a Capstone or
Foundations Class Session

Handling Projects and Student Assignments

In some cases, these guidelines may not address specific situations in your context. It may be necessary to consult your ministry's leaders for specific direction. While we want all TUMI sites to stay consistent with TUMI standards, you may be more specific in the guidance from your leadership. For example, in a jail or prison it may not be wise to allow fellow students to grade each other, and take-home finals may be impossible.

The Exegetical Project

The Scriptures are God's potent instrument to equip the man or woman of God for every work of ministry he calls them to (2 Tim. 3.16-17). In order to complete the requirements for each course, each student must select a passage and do an inductive Bible study (i.e., an exegetical study) upon it. The paper highlights a class topic, and challenges the student to relate their exegesis of the biblical text to that topic. Through this process our hope is to equip our students to engage openly and fairly a biblical text in such a way that they come to understand its meaning in its original context, discern its principles of truth, and be able to relate those truths to their lives and ministries in a powerful way.

1. *General Description:* The purpose of this project is to give the student an opportunity to do a detailed study of a major passage of Scripture. The hope is that, as they study the passage, they will be able to relate its meaning to their own walk as well as to those God has given them to lead. It is important that they learn how to exegete (explain, interpret) Scripture for themselves and for others. This is a Bible study project, and, in order to do exegesis, the student must be committed to understand the meaning of the passage in its own setting. Once they know what it meant, they can then draw out principles that apply to all of us, and then relate those principles to life. A simple three-step process is given in the assignment that can guide them in their personal study of the Bible passage:

   a. What was God saying to the people in the text's original situation?

   b. What principle(s) does the text teach that is true for all people everywhere, including today?

   c. What is the Holy Spirit asking me to do with this principle here, today, in my life and ministry?

2. Exegesis and hermeneutical method: *approaching the Bible critically and openly.* Once they have answered these questions in their personal study, they are then ready to write out their insights for their paper assignment. We are seeking to help students approach the Scripture in a structured, disciplined, and

stage-oriented way that leads from observing the text in its original context, discerning timeless principles in that context that apply to all life, and then identifying specific and particular applications of those principles in their lives and ministries. This is the essence of *The Three-Step Model* which underlies TUMI's biblical hermeneutic (cf. *The Three-Step Model* in our Appendix). Assisting our students in thinking with these steps in mind is essential for their effective completion of the Exegetical Projects.

3. *Guidelines for the Mentor*

   a. Your students should be evaluated on all aspects of the criteria listed in the assignment. (Please note that we evaluate based on the concepts of which they are writing, not the grammar or spelling in their writing. You will find that students are at various skill levels in those areas. The key is the student's ability to understand the Scripture and explain/interpret it in such a way as to help relate it to their lives and ministry.

   b. Concentrate on enabling your students to understand and apply the principles of the *The Three-Step Model* hermeneutic. Don't get bogged down in the voluminous side paths and roads associated with traditional biblical exegesis. If your students comprehend and become well practiced at the activities, mindsets, and procedures connected to the three major steps of biblical exegesis, eventually they will become skilled workmen and workwomen who need not be ashamed, readily able to rightly handle the Word of truth (2 Tim. 2.15).

   c. Print out copies of the appendices *The Three-Step Model* and *The Exegetical Project: Using the Three-Step Model to Exegete Scripture* for your students. Both of these appendices can be found at *www.tumi.org/mentor*.

Handling Projects and Student Assignments

The Ministry Project

Learning that is not experienced and shared often times is lost, and that, very quickly. All TUMI course offerings require our students to connect their learning to life in practical ways, and to discover ways in which to communicate that learning creatively, concisely, and effectively in the various contexts of life where they live, work, and minister. We refer to this opportunity to share and communicate the truth as the student's Ministry Project.

1. *General Description:* A Ministry Project is an assignment that requires students to integrate some key element of the course learning by:

   a. Determining a personal ministry situation in which they can use the course knowledge.

   b. Preparing to use that knowledge and submitting that preparation to the Mentor for evaluation and suggestions.

   c. Using their learning in ministry and reporting on the learning that results from the experience to their class and/or instructor.

2. *Predefined, or not?* In some cases, the nature of the ministry project is predefined in the curriculum. In other cases there is wide latitude given for the student to shape and define the application. *Do not feel limited or bound to the Ministry Project designated in any given module or course.* As Mentor, you may allow your students great freedom in discerning how and in what context they will share with others the insights gained in their learning this session.

   Generally speaking, the project should involve an activity that is a normal part of the student's ministry responsibility but should seek to increase their competency by using knowledge, techniques, or principles learned in the course. In every case, the focus is on students consciously using what they have learned to affect the way in which they minister. Some examples are:

   a. Preaching a sermon or teaching a lesson which is informed by course learning.

Handling Projects and Student Assignments

b. Using a principle from the course in an evangelistic or community service outreach.

c. Creating artwork, songs, or poetry which can be used in their ministry and which communicate truth learned in the course.

d. Discussing with others what they learned from their exegetical project for this course.

Any ministry activity which incorporates course learning is potentially acceptable as long as it allows the student to make a *concrete application* and provides *an opportunity to reflect* on the results.

3. *Guidelines for the Mentor*

a. Give firm due dates for the completion of the project and the reporting on it.

b. Whenever the schedule allows, have students orally report on their learning to others in the class.

c. The goal of the ministry project is not only to apply the learning but also to reflect on what happened.

d. In their reporting students should both describe what they did and what they learned through the experience. In evaluating the reports look for evidence that the students thought about what happened during the application and gained insight that will help them in the future.

e. Students who prefer to do so should be allowed to report on the project to the Mentor orally (in person or in recorded form). Students who choose this option should be reminded to think through their oral presentation in advance (just as they would a written assignment) and make a clear presentation of what they did and learned.

f. Students who are taking more than one course at a time through TUMI should be allowed to combine/adapt ministry projects from the other classes and have them serve "double-duty" for both courses. In these cases they should turn in a report to both Mentors. Although the description of what

Handling Projects and Student Assignments

they did for their project should be the same in each case, the reflection and learning section should be different since it is specifically applied to the learning of each course.

The Book Reading and Précis Assignment

A critical element in the preparation of urban Christian leaders is their ability to engage the ideas and claims of others in a rigorous and respectful manner, that is, to read what others have written, and restate their position clearly and fairly, whether or not they believe it. Only when the student understands and restates the author's argument fairly can they then be in a position to evaluate its truth value. The student must strive to understand before they seek to judge.

1. *General Description:* We require students to purchase, read, and reflect upon the textbook(s) for each course. Students must read each required textbook and write a precis (concise summary) of its main point, as they see it. They will need to summarize its major theme and argument, and then give their concise evaluation of it. It is of utmost importance to equip your students to analyze a text, that is, to read it, understand its thesis (main point), articulate its argument in a charitable way (whether they agree with the author or not), and then respond as to why they agree or disagree with the thesis. The criteria for this assignment are given in the course itself.

2. *Texts on point.* The reading assignments for the *Capstone Curriculum* found on our website are keyed specifically to the lesson format of their module. Please note that, depending on how you are structuring your course sessions, you have complete flexibility to break up the reading assignments to match your actual class sessions. In other words, if you are running an eight-week course, simply break up the reading assignments to match your sessions. What is critical is that you focus on the lesson as the basic unit of teaching in your *Capstone* courses.

3. *Guidelines for the Mentor*

   a. Your students will most likely have different levels of reading ability. No matter what level, it is important that as leaders, your students read as much as they can and engage what they read.

b. This practice helps students to engage different opinions in a respectful way, and to learn to listen to others and respond with clarity and respect. In this way, they can learn to dialogue with and discuss with others whose beliefs are different than their own.

c. The students are required to do this assignment for each assigned textbook for the course.

d. Students are tested only on what is covered in class, not on their reading assignments.

Scripture Memory

The canonical Scriptures provide the authoritative testimony of God's saving work in Jesus Christ, and as such, must be mastered by every urban Christian leader for life, teaching, preaching, and counseling. Memorizing the Word of God, therefore, should be a central priority for those who intend to represent Christ Jesus as an ambassador of the Kingdom. Scripture Memorization provides us with 100% knowledge of the Scriptures in our hearts, allowing for easy retrieval and multiple, constant use in all aspects of our lives and ministries.

1. *General Description:* We require students to memorize several passages of Scripture related to the theme of the content of the course. Scripture memory helps prepare us for ministry, giving us the tongue of a disciple that we may know how to sustain those who are weary with a healing, encouraging word (Isa. 50.4). Furthermore, having the Scriptures readily available in our minds and hearts enables us to give an answer to everyone who asks us for a reason of the hope that is within us (1 Pet. 3.15). Truly, those who know the Word can therefore through the Holy Spirit "preach the word; be ready in season and out of season; reprove, rebuke, and exhort, with complete patience and teaching" (2 Tim. 4.2).

   Remind the students that God's Word is a treasure, and his Word hidden in the heart renews the mind, enriches the soul, and outfits for ministry. Let us honor him and his Word by hiding it in our hearts, meditating on it with a mind to obey, and looking for opportunities to teach his truths concerning Jesus Christ to others. God will be glorified as we allow the Spirit to transform our lives through the hidden treasures of God's Word.

Handling Projects and Student Assignments

2. The fundamental requirement for Christian leadership: *mastery of the Bible, in your own language.* Our conviction at TUMI is that while mastery of the original languages of the Bible can provide unique insight and refreshment into its meaning, our modern translations represent accurate, comprehensive, and well-researched translations of the Holy Scriptures. Because of this conviction, we have deliberately chosen to highlight the primacy of Scripture in the theological arguments undergirding the Nicene creedal theology of our *Capstone Curriculum.* While we refer to and encourage familiarity with the biblical languages, we believe that one can be spiritually mature and ministerially competent without a mastery of the biblical languages. The Scriptures in one's native tongue has been the foundation of missions and church development, and is arguably the most significant element in ongoing spiritual formation in the Church, seeing how the Scriptures play the formative role and serve as a key foundation in virtually all spiritual disciplines.

   This elevates the need for TUMI students and graduates to demonstrate a comprehensive, accessible knowledge of the Bible, and Scripture memorization contributes to this mastery. (For more on the importance of Scripture memorization, please review our *Master the Bible* resources, training tools specifically designed to help urban learners and leaders master Scripture's story and content. Visit our website *www.tumistore.org* for more information. Also, see *Comparing the Scripture Memorization Lists in the Capstone Curriculum and Master the Bible System* in the Appendix).

3. *Guidelines for the Mentor*

   a. While it is normal for adult learners to bemoan their inability to memorize and recall Scripture, we must not relax what God commands for his leaders and his people (Josh. 1.8; Ps. 119.9-11; Jer. 20.7; 2 Tim. 2.15; 3.15-17). Students should be challenged to do their very best to ingest and digest the Word of God, and strive to remember and retain as much of the Bible as possible. Again, Scripture memorization represents 100% Bible knowledge; the prophets, Jesus, and the apostles all reveal in their lives and ministries a deep knowledge through the memorized Word, and doing so provided them (and will empower us) to possess and wield a ready and effective weapon against the lies and machinations of the enemy (2 Cor. 10.3-5; Eph. 6.10-18).

b. Strongly resist the temptation to give in to arguments regarding the "impossibility" of some students' ability to memorize the Word. Gently encourage them to continue, to ask the Spirit for help, to develop ongoing, disciplined habits of review and recitation. Remember, leaders in the Church of God know his Word. Challenge them not to give up or give in to the struggle. Encourage them to try different memorization methods, to pray for God's grace and help in this, and to keep at it. The Lord will reward them.

c. The *Scripture Memory Grading Form* should be provided to your students at the beginning of class. (See the sample in the Appendix, and find a printable version at *www.tumi.org/ mentor.*)

d. In order to fulfill their credit requirements for their courses, the students will need to memorize and self-grade select Scripture passages that relate to the theme of the course. They are allowed the equivalent of one mistake per verse for full credit. Additionally, they are allowed the equivalent of two mistakes per verse for one-half credit. If they make more errors than those allowed, they receive no credit for their assignment. (Punctuation and misspellings do NOT count as mistakes.)

e. The students must grade their own verses and record their credit amount in order to receive credit for this assignment.

Handling Projects and Student Assignments

Dealing with Difficulties in the Classroom

Doctrinal Controversies

To operate a TUMI site is to experience a fair amount of controversy, conflict, and debate. This kind of interaction in the classroom is both inevitable and invaluable, given that your students may have been spiritually formed in diverse theological persuasions in their respective Christian denominations. A significant role of your intellectual responsibility in the classroom will be serving as referee and facilitator as you maneuver through difficult and thorny issues with your students. As you negotiate various kinds of interactions between and among them, you will need to constantly be aware of the dangers of extremism and dogmatism. Ignoring the reality of conflict won't eliminate it; we must face it, charitably and directly, and trust the Holy Spirit to make us clear, loving, and helpful as we deal with these issues.

Of course, you will need to be sensitive to the genuine differences in doctrine and practice among your students. Differences are neither cosmetic nor unimportant; rather, as the adage goes, differences make all the difference in the world! In doctrinal and theological discussion, you should strive to recognize and affirm the real, substantive differences among your students and the traditions they represent. You will need to emphasize our common commitment to the ancient consensus of faith, as well as the interdenominational status of TUMI. We seek neither to alter nor dictate what our students represent in their various communions, but only to show all legitimate traditions of the Christian faith derive their identity and substance from the orthodox Christian core of belief and practice, settled since the apostolic age.

You may need from time to time to silence the controversialist among you, i.e., that student whose singular desire is to argue over every obtuse point of theology and doctrine. While we ought to encourage dialogue and interaction, seek to emphasize the importance of etiquette and courtesy as we engage one another, and realize that how we resolve our differences is as important as *the subject matter* of them. Let us strive to allow for freedom in the non-essentials, for fidelity to the essentials of the faith, and for charity, love, and grace in all matters of theology and doctrine that gets discussed in our classrooms.

Dealing with Difficulties in the Classroom

Academic Challenges

Unavoidably, you will encounter TUMI students who are challenged with less-than-satisfactory academic background, those who have no real solid academic training or accomplishment, and who, by normal standards, would be disqualified from typical seminary inclusion. These individuals, from our vantage point, are precisely why TUMI was created. God's standard of his own called, gifted warriors is a call to godliness and holiness, not a call to academic prowess and mastery. Eloquence is not required to be a Christian leader; being filled with the Holy Spirit certainly is.

As you grade your students and engage their academic deficiencies, you must remember that you are training ministers of the Gospel, not scholars. While we employ traditional models of assessment in our classes (e.g., giving quizzes, exams, and grade reports), these are not the final indicators of success in a TUMI classroom. Grades are important, and we use this system unapologetically, but grades matter for reasons not obvious in its traditional educational settings. We are not seeking to fake out our students by creating detractors, questions, and exams that swoop down with the normal "Gotcha!" of traditional leadership assessment. It matters that our students are called of God *and* tend to be from less-than-stellar academic backgrounds.

Arguably, this is one of your most challenging tasks as a TUMI mentor: to use traditional models of assessment without being enslaved by them. You must learn to acknowledge the effort and engagement of your students as well as their performance on quizzes and projects. Concentrate on character and excellence in all things, not merely in tokens of intelligence or their ability to recite back a particular point. Be fair, always being careful to challenge your students to learn, but refusing to penalize them for simply not having the background of your typical seminary candidate.

Enough room is given to you as a mentor to grade the students fairly and in sync with their efforts and engagement. Do not assume that neglect in one's academic background is to be equated with an inability to think or engage in solid dialogue about difficult, important matters. (Unfortunately, we have had mentors who falsely assumed that being poor was to be equated with being less than bright; poverty and stupidity have nothing in common, and we should avoid all crass stereotypes that would seek to connect them together!) Seek the Lord's guidance as you work with your

Dealing with Difficulties in the Classroom

students, and be careful of the tendencies to make a TUMI class an academic environment and not a leadership development environment.

Absenteeism or Student Dropout

As much as we seek to enthusiastically encourage students to achieve in our classes, we must be careful not to make the corollary mistake of gross sentimentalism. As one of the most common practices among instructors toward those who have been susceptible to underachievement, sentimentalism is that patronizing position where we deliberately or unthinkingly behave toward our students in a condescending manner, as if they are not able to perform. The worst thing a mentor can do is to manifest this condescension by constantly excusing the absence of students from class, or their premature exit from a class. As a mentor, you must neither, on the one hand, treat them harshly and unfairly, or, on the other hand, behave as if they cannot accomplish excellence in their work. Simply put – not all students will complete their training, and some may even exit our class offerings altogether.

Our TUMI pedagogy sees the classroom component as an essential element of an overall development strategy of a student, a strategy which also includes the domain of their personal Christian walk among their family, associates, and peers, as well as their life and ministry through their local assembly. You should be aware that students will face a vast array of contingencies during a class which may alter or change their ability to stay in the class. No student will enter our classrooms with the leisure and ease enjoyed by many students who summarily skip classes on their college campuses. Pressures of time, money, family, children, ministry will unavoidably encroach on the lives of your students, and, in some cases, impact their absenteeism.

You must therefore be encouraging, but also open to the Lord's leading with your students and their classroom environment. Let students leave, if they must or if they wish. The Spirit endows our students with challenges, gifts, opportunities and resources, all of which are integrated into the tapestry of their lives and ministries. Our classes are an essential thread in that tapestry, but will never be the entire tapestry. We can contribute to their development, but we cannot nursemaid them into maturity. To change the metaphor, we are spiritual midwives to their spiritual birthing and

Dealing with Difficulties in the Classroom

development. Feel no sense of defeat if students ebb and flow in and out of your classroom, and do not be alarmed even if, during certain seasons, you wind up offering no classes at all. Know the volatility of the urban environment and your students' lives, and always be ready to offer a class when and where you have students who are also ready to learn.

Student Discouragement

Any endeavor worth striving for in the spiritual realm is bound to be laden with challenges, tribulations, and defeats. Every Christian leader must learn to navigate through the bogs of discouragement and exhaustion, of boredom and temptation, of weakness and doubt. You must equip your students to persevere in the midst of trial, and oftentimes our training can be the very tool the enemy uses to create discouragement and despondency in our students, for several reasons.

Many students in taking your class will clearly expose themselves to their lack of academic training, making them vulnerable to the enemy's attack once they experience less-than-satisfactory academic performance. Students who considered themselves adequate if not excellent in their understanding of a subject may, after engaging the material in a course, come to see they were not trained at all. Comparing their performance with their peers can be used by the devil to suggest their own inadequacy as to fitness for leadership, and the enemy may further propose that they drop out altogether – that they were wrong in even starting up studies in the first place. These and countless other flaming arrows will be flung by the enemy upon your students as they matriculate through your class.

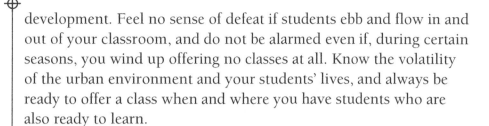

You must see, therefore, that your teaching is a spiritual enterprise, and your classroom a battlefield with the confidence and conviction of your students being assailed every class session. The devil is a liar, and your students are not immune to his attacks (John 8.44). If your students are spent, tired, and exhausted, remind them that they *ought to be* tired: they are facing, as all Christians and especially Christian leaders, the devastating and potent mix of engaging life and ministry in perpetual battle with the world, the flesh, and the devil. Fighting doubt and fear is the Christian's duty, and the battle will certainly rage in the life of a developing leader.

Do not overreact to their fatigue, fear, or discouragement: the Bible's who's who of discouraged leaders is pretty impressive

(Moses, Jonah, David, Paul, Elijah). All these and more in Scripture faced challenges and were all victims of chronic, difficult discouragement. As the saying goes, "What's good for the goose is good for the gander." The leaders of God's Church worldwide are facing challenges, and so will they. You will need to help them manage their studies in order to assist them to combat stress and discouragement. This is not easy, but will prove terribly rewarding; your role as mentor is to help them to organize their efforts in such a way as to stay ahead of the deadlines, in tune with the assignments, and always open to the Lord's leading, even in the midst of their studies. For the discouraged and stressed-out student, there is always hope, because it is truly not by power nor by might but always by the Spirit of the Lord (Zech. 4.6).

Don't hesitate to monitor the hearts and spirits of your students, and constantly offer words of encouragement and support for those who, for whatever reason, seem to be discouraged or overwhelmed by their studies. A clear word of counsel and acknowledgment, given at the right time and in the right way, can make all the difference with a student who finds himself deflated and overcome by the rigors of tough-minded intellectual work.

Appendix

Our Distinctives

Appendix 1
Our Distinctives:
Advancing the Kingdom among the Urban Poor

God Has Chosen the Poor

One does not have to read many pages into the New Testament to discover where the early Church got the idea that the poor were specially chosen by God to receive the Gospel and spread it throughout the earth. Jesus, himself, had announced publicly that he was intentionally preaching the Gospel to the poor (Luke 4.18, 6.20) and even suggested that this action helped demonstrate that he was, indeed, the Messiah (Matt. 11.2-6).

Building on Jesus' teaching, it is not unusual to find very explicit statements in the Epistles about God's choice of, and expectations for, those who are without power, resources, or money. For example, James teaches:

> Listen, my dear brothers: Has not God chosen those who are poor in the eyes of the world to be rich in faith and to inherit the kingdom he promised those who love him?
>
> ~ James 2.5

*The words "chose" and "chosen" in James 2 and 1 Corinthians 1 come from the Greek word **eklégomai** which means "giving favor to the chosen subject. . . . It involves preference and selection from among many choices." In other contexts, it is used to describe God's choice of the "elect" (Mark 13.20) and Jesus' choosing of his disciples (Luke 6.13).*

In a similar manner, Paul writes:

> But God chose the foolish things of the world to shame the wise; God chose the weak things of the world to shame the strong. He chose the lowly things of this world and the despised things-and the things that are not-to nullify the things that are, so that no one may boast before him.
>
> ~ 1 Corinthians 1.27-29

These ideas are not a new theme introduced by the New Testament writers. Instead, they faithfully reflect the Old Testament teachings about how God relates to the poor. One scholar summarizes the Old Testament teaching about the poor in three principles.*

** Douglas J. Moo, **James**, Tyndale Old Testament Commentary Series, Gen. Ed. Leon Morris, (Leicester, England-Grand Rapids, MI: IVP-Eerdmans, 1985), pp. 53-54.*

1. God has a particular concern for the poor.
2. God's people must manifest a similar concern [for the poor].
3. The poor are frequently identified with the pious and the righteous.

"In the teaching of Jesus, material possessions are not regarded as evil, but as dangerous. The poor are often shown to be happier than the rich, because it is easier for them to have an attitude of dependence upon God" (R.E. Nixon, "Poverty," The Illustrated Bible Dictionary, eds. J.D. Douglas, et al., [Leicester, England: IVP, 1980], p. 1255).

Who Are the Poor?

To understand God's choice of the poor it is necessary to understand who the "poor" are. The way that Scripture uses the term "poor" is both alike and different from the way we often use the term.

1. The Greek word used in the New Testament means essentially the same thing as our English word "poor." It describes someone who is economically deprived, someone who doesn't have enough money or resources. However, when this word is used by the New Testament writers, they seem to also rely on the Old Testament understandings of the word "poor." Thus, in the New Testament, the poor are both "those who don't have enough money" (Greek understanding) *plus* "something else" (the Hebrew understanding).

2. This "something else" was an understanding developed over time in the Hebrew Scriptures. In the Old Testament, "the poor" are those who are so powerless and dependent that they are vulnerable to being misused by those who have influence in the society. The emphasis is *on being on the wrong end of a relationship* with those in power. Therefore, in the Old Testament, the poor came to mean those people who were characterized by three things:

   a. They lack the money and resources they need,
   b. They are taken advantage of by those who do have money and resources, and
   c. The result is that they must humbly turn to God as their only source of protection.

3. Therefore, from a theological point of view, we could say that Scripture defines "the poor" as:

   Those whose need makes them desperate enough to rely on God alone.

Biblical scholar Robert A. Guelich makes exactly these points when he writes about the development of the term "poor" in the Old Testament.

Our Distinctives

The most common of these words [for the poor], *'ny* and its later relative, *'nw*, have a much broader scope than simply to denote a socioeconomic status . . . The *'ny* refers to one so powerless and dependent as to be vulnerable to exploitation by those who have the power base. Thus the accent falls on a socioeconomic *relationship* rather than on material possessions as such. Yet this powerless and dependent relationship caused one to rely upon God for one's needs and vindication. This humble posture of *the poor* devoid of pretension before God reflects the religious dimension and comes out frequently in the Psalms . . . But the religious dimension is never exclusive of the socioeconomic. Both elements are integral to *'ny* . . . . In summary, the poor in Judaism referred to those in desperate need (socioeconomic element) whose helplessness drove them to a dependent relationship with God (religious element) for the supplying of their needs and their vindication.

~ Robert A. Guelich. *The Sermon on the Mount*.
Waco: Word Books, 1982. pp. 68-69.

This understanding helps us perceive how Luke can record Jesus' teaching as "Blessed are *the poor* for yours is the Kingdom of God" (Luke 6.20); while Matthew records "Blessed are the poor in spirit for theirs is the Kingdom of heaven" (Matt. 5.3). In both accounts the point is the same: blessed are those who have become desperate enough to rely on God alone. Only people who are willing to acknowledge their helplessness can receive this help from God. As Clarence Jordan points out:

When one says 'I don't need to be poor in things; I'm poor in spirit,' and another says, 'I don't need to be poor in spirit; I'm poor in things,' both are justifying themselves as they are, and are saying in unison, 'I don't need.' With that cry on his lips, no man can repent.

~ Clarence Jordan. *Sermon on the Mount*, Rev. ed.
Valley Forge: Koinonia-Judson Press, 1980. p. 20.

What are some life experiences besides poverty that often help people realize their desperate need for God?

Obviously, people who are not poor can come to this point of being desperate enough to rely on God alone. (The Bible records many examples, such as Zaccheus or Joseph of Arimathea, to make this apparent.) *It is also clear that many poor people may refuse to acknowledge their need before God.* However, Jesus and the apostles consistently teach that it is even more difficult for the affluent to acknowledge their need for God (Matt. 19.24; Mark 10.23; James 2.6-7) and that the poor should be expected to respond with faith. This confidence in God's choice of the poor is so profound that one scholar can say: "In the New Testament the poor replace Israel as the focus of the gospel" (C.M.N. Sugden, "Poverty and Wealth,"

New Dictionary of Theology, eds. Sinclair B. Ferguson, et al., [Downers Grove: InterVarsity Press, 1988], p. 524).

Four Fundamental Responses

When we recognize that the Scriptures treat the poor as a group with theological significance, it forces us to consider what our response will be. Both as Christians, and as missionaries, there are at least four responses that we should make.

1. Respect

God's choice of the poor fundamentally challenges the normal way that people respond to the poor. Within society, people avoid the poor, disdain their ways, and expect little from them in any area. Certainly they are not seen as the natural place to search for leaders.

God, however, identifies himself with the poor. The Scriptures say that to oppress the poor is to show contempt to God himself (Prov. 14.31). God's identification with the poor and God's choice of the poor (James 2.5) should make a profound difference to anyone who acknowledges Christ as Lord. Simply put:

- If we respect God, we will respect the poor.
- If we obey God, we will identify with the poor.
- If we believe God, we will see the poor as the potential leaders of his Church.

Sadly, many people look at those who are poor and see them primarily as objects of benevolence. Such people view the poor only as those who need their help. While it is certainly right to help the poor (see point two below), such help will create dependence and a loss of dignity if it is not firmly coupled with deep respect for the poor as those that God has chosen. We believe it is not a sacrifice, but rather, a privilege and delight to be called to make disciples among the unreached urban poor.

2. Love, Compassion, and Justice

Christians are called to respond to others with love, compassion, and justice. This response to the poor is the same response that Christians give to all people everywhere. What makes it unique is that the world system mitigates against applying this concern to the poor. Theologian Thomas C. Oden says:

Our Distinctives

"To live in radical obedience to Jesus Christ means to be identified with the poor and oppressed. If that is not clear in the New Testament, then nothing is" (Jim Wallis. *Agenda for Biblical People*. [New York: Harper & Row, 1976], p. 94).

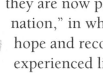

Our Distinctives

"One of the ways that St. Francis described his relationship with the poor (and others) was through the word 'cortesia.' We use the word 'courtesy' to mean manners. Originally, it meant the behavior and etiquette expected of one who served at a noble court . . . . For St. Francis . . . cortesia was a way of seeing and acting towards others" (Lawrence Cunningham, **St. Francis of Assisi**, [San Francisco: Harper & Row, 1981].

Although Christian charity is due everyone, the poor are Christ's particular concern, precisely because they are the neediest.

~ Thomas C. Oden. *Pastoral Theology: Essentials of Ministry.*
San Francisco: Harper & Row, 1983. p. 268.

God emphasizes our response to the poor, not to play favorites, but because otherwise they would be overlooked.

The Scriptures constantly underscore the responsibility of God's people to share with the poor and help them escape from the grinding effects of poverty. God's Word places responsibility on us to work for justice for the poor. Working for *shalom* (peace, fullness, abundance, wholeness) means that we will never be content to leave the poor to their poverty while any of us have the means to affect change.

3. Preach the Gospel

Out of all our responses to the poor, none is more important than preaching the Gospel. It is exactly what Jesus himself did. Nothing is more revolutionary in liberating the poor than bringing them into relationship with God through Christ.

No project or program can ever achieve what salvation does for the poor. In coming to acknowledge Jesus as Lord and Savior, the poor experience radical liberation through the acquisition of an entirely new identity.

- They move from being at the bottom of the social structure to being an adopted child of the King of kings.
- God's favor, protection, and resources are made available through Christ.
- They are given authority over sin, hell, and death, and every evil thing that would seek to destroy them.
- They are incorporated into a new community (the Church) which offers equality, respect, love, sharing, fellowship, and the opportunity to exercise their gifts and calling from God.

Salvation means that the presence of the living God is active among the poor bringing freedom, wholeness, and justice. It means that they are now part of a "royal priesthood," "members of a holy nation," in which they serve as "Christ's ambassadors" announcing hope and reconciliation to those around them who have not yet experienced liberation.

*"The intercession of a poor man is acceptable and influential with God" (The Pastor of Hermas, Bk. 3, **Ante-Nicene Fathers**, Vol. 2, eds. A. Roberts and J. Donaldson, [Peabody, Hendrickson, 1995], p. 32).*

4. Expect Great Things

There is, perhaps, no more surprising statement that comes from Jesus' lips than the word he gives to his disciples in John 14.12-14.

> I tell you the truth, *anyone who has faith in me will do what I have been doing. He will do even greater things than these*, because I am going to the Father. And I will do whatever you ask in my name, so that the Son may bring glory to the Father. You may ask for anything in my name, and I will do it.

On the surface, the idea of accomplishing greater things than Jesus seems absurd. And yet, in just a few short years the Book of Acts records more conversions than ever happened within the life and ministry of Jesus.

Two principles underlie this amazing statement. First, Jesus said discipleship reproduces students who are like him (Luke 6.40). Second, when Jesus returned to the Father and sent the Holy Spirit (John 14.16; Acts 2.38), he made his power universally available to all who believe (John 14.14).

It would be easy to expect little from the poor because of their lack of resources. However, when Scripture disciplines our thinking, a new dynamic emerges. We expect congregations of the urban poor to do greater works than Jesus did on earth because they enter into a discipling relationship with Jesus who freely gives them his Holy Spirit.

As we plant churches we must:

- *Encourage the poor to believe in the calling, gifts, and abilities that God has given them* (both individually and corporately). We must have faith in what God will do through them even before they believe it themselves.
- *Set high standards*. The only acceptable goal for any Christian is to become like Jesus. Being poor is never an excuse for ignoring God's commands or shirking the responsibilities he gives every believer.
- *Teach people to rely on Jesus, not on us*. Missionary resources are limited. God's resources are unlimited.
- *Instill a passion for reproduction* (evangelism, follow-up, discipleship, and church planting). "You did not choose me, but I chose you to go and bear fruit – fruit that will last.

Then the Father will give you whatever you ask in my name" (John 15.16).

One veteran missionary, who has served in both U.S. and Brazilian cities, describes successful churches among the urban poor in this manner:

> Churches . . . that used a "we-help-you-in-your-need" methodology were not winning the lower, working class. People were helped but the spiritual direction of their lives did not change . . . . [whereas] churches that lacked financial and earthly resources were filled with poor people, were led by barely literate lay preachers, and made hard demands on people. New members were expected to be faithful tithers, to wear clothes that conformed to a rigid dress code, to carry their Bibles to church, and to dedicate a large amount of time to worship services, healing services, home prayer meetings, street meetings, and outreach visitation. The churches that gave the most and expected the least were not growing, but those that gave the least material benefit and demanded the most were growing fastest. They demanded conversion from sin and preached that Christ had the power to make it happen, and that this power could be received though faith and prayer.
>
> ~ Charles D. Uken. "Discipling White, Blue-Collar Workers and Their Families." Discipling the City: A Comprehensive Approach to Urban Mission, 2nd ed., ed. Roger S. Greenway, Grand Rapids: Baker Book House, 1992. p. 180.

We honor both God and the poor when we respect them enough to believe that they will function as full-fledged disciples of Jesus Christ.

Appendix 2
The Key Components of "In Context" Theological Education

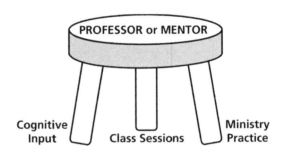

** The stool graphic and model is adapted from Stewart G. Snook, **Developing Leaders through Theological Education by Extension: Case Studies from Africa.** (Wheaton, IL: Billy Graham Center, Wheaton College, 1992.) p. 107.*

The three legs of the stool* shown above represent three of the four key components in our learning model. These first three are:

Cognitive Input
The learner must be exposed to content (the facts, data, ideas, stories, analysis, and concepts). Biblical and theological truth is presented to the learner at home through books and self-study materials and in class through video teaching and the mentor's input.

Ministry Practice
The learner must be engaged in lay or pastoral ministry through the local church. The learner generates questions that emerge from these "Field Experiences" and applies their learning in the ministry situation. Each class requires students to undertake a ministry project that uses their course learning in their ministry situation.

Class Sessions**
The classes serve three primary purposes: First, to introduce new content and allow learners to interact with a mentor who can help clarify that content. Second, to allow learners to raise questions and dialogue about the implications and applications of the content in their ministry situation. Mentors should consider the peer learning that takes place through dialogue among the learning group to be a key part of the educational process. Third, to monitor the learner's progress and evaluate their understanding of the material.

** Although weekly classes are the norm, student needs may require more flexible scheduling (either a more compact or a more extended meeting schedule). The key is that you host regularly scheduled classes at times when your students may conveniently attend.

The fourth component is the Mentor [teacher]:

> These three [*components*] connect to the most important, the seat, which represents the teacher. The legs are inserted into the seat and completed by it. When you have the seat into which the legs fit, you have a useful stool. . . .If teachers are not faithful in all their duties, students will get discouraged and quit. If they lecture and are boring, students will get discouraged and quit. Teachers not only have to provide an interesting class – above all else they must model the truths being taught. The program will only be as strong as those who teach.
>
> ~ Snook, pp. 106-107.

A Mentor

The mentor [teacher] must not only present and clarify content but also facilitate discussion so that the group raises and grapples with actual questions from the local context. It is essential that the mentor strive to develop a learning environment where students interact with each other (as well as with the mentor) to find answers. Whether an academic theologian or a pastor, the mentor must have a *praxis** orientation toward theology which considers the actual implementation of the learning through the church and its ministries to be the real goal of theological education.

Conclusion

These components allow for considerable freedom, innovation, and adaptation in the practice of theological education, but they are each vital elements which must be present in some form for maximum effectiveness.

* Praxis is the intentionally willed action by which a theory becomes a practical social activity.

The Key Components of "In Context" Theological Ed.

Appendix 3
Overview of the Capstone Curriculum and Summary Objectives

Overview of the *Capstone Curriculum*

A project of over eight years, the *Capstone Curriculum* was released in the spring of 2006. Containing 10,000+ pages of text, this curriculum includes 16 modules; 72 Lessons, 128 thirty-minute video segments; 166 memory verses; 41 required textbooks; 217 recommended supplemental textbooks; 380 case studies; 8,080 Scripture passages.

The *Capstone Curriculum* is a sixteen-module training program, designed to be engaged at a seminary level, to serve as the most essential knowledge and skill learning necessary for effective urban ministry and church leadership. Based on an expanded and detailed discussion of the critical sections of the Nicene Creed, the *Capstone Curriculum* seeks to equip learners in the foundational truths of the Great Tradition of the Church. It was constructed to offer solid, historically orthodox, Christ-centered, biblical training to urban leaders that is both culturally sensitive and entirely affordable to those who normally would be excluded from training because of academic background or cultural distance.

The curriculum is organized around four departments or categories, Biblical Studies, Theology and Ethics, Christian Ministry, and Urban Mission. Each department contains four modules or courses, each with four lessons which contain the content of the material in a structured, systemic manner. Each module consists of a *Mentor's Guide*, a *Student Workbook*, and *DVDs* (two video discs containing four hours of video). Additionally, each module includes a full complement of training tools (case studies, quizzes and exams, exegetical and ministry projects, Scripture memorization assignments, and required and suggested textbooks).

The *Capstone Curriculum* is specifically structured to be used in a variety of formats, time frames, and teaching venues. As a complete training curriculum, it may be accessed through *The Urban Ministry Institute's* Satellite Certificate Program. This curriculum provides a Christian leader all they need to be effective servant leaders in their family, church, and ministry contexts.

Summary Objectives of the *Capstone Curriculum*

While each individual module in the *Capstone Curriculum* possesses its own unique set of learning objectives based on the theme and goals of the course, the following objectives are our "across-the-curriculum" objectives for the entire set. These objectives represent the pedagogical constellation of aims that every module and all modules seek to represent. In that sense they comprise the key, fundamental goals of the entire resource, and ought to be remembered and referred to regardless of the individual module under consideration.

1. To ground emerging urban leaders in the Gospel of Christ, enabling them to know the basics of conversion and their own calling to salvation and leadership

2. To root our students in the indispensability of the Church to serve as both agent and locus of the Kingdom, and for them to serve the church practically and specifically in the local assembly

3. To equip urban leaders with the necessary skills to study, apply, teach, preach, and minister the Word of God in the urban context, employing their learning in the context of their own personal lives and church ministries

4. To challenge urban leaders to regularly memorize select portions of Scripture, and develop the discipline of review to retain and utilize texts both devotionally and in ministry

5. To establish urban leaders in a Christ-centered vision of Scripture, and equip them in a Nicene-based, biblical theology that is congruent with the historic orthodox faith of the Great Tradition

6. To provide a biblical foundation for both understanding and practicing Christian leadership in the context of the Church, with a special emphasis and appreciation for spiritual formation in urban communities, especially among the poor

7. To train urban leaders to evangelize, disciple, plant, pastor, and minister within evangelical urban churches which will be spiritually vital, culturally conducive, and aggressively

Overview of Capstone and Summary Objectives

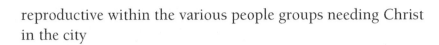

reproductive within the various people groups needing Christ in the city

8. To encourage urban leaders to find practical, meaningful ways to promote justice and demonstrate mercy with the broken and needy in urban communities, and discover ways to display hospitality, generosity, and compassion in the places where they live and minister

Overview of Capstone and Summary Objectives

Appendix 4

Teaching Objectives for the
Capstone Curriculum, by Module

Module Description

Capstone Module 1 – Conversion and Calling

As disciples of Jesus Christ, we affirm our deep belief in the creative, convicting, converting, and calling power of the Word of God. To understand the wonderful blessing of conversion and calling, we will need to critically evaluate the place of the Word of God in the Church.

Our first lesson, *The Word That Creates*, explores the nature of the Holy Scriptures as the Word of God. We'll see that God's own perfect integrity guarantees the absolute trustworthiness of the Scriptures. Furthermore, we'll discover how God created the universe through his Word, and how he identifies himself completely with the Word in Jesus Christ. Being the means by which the Holy Spirit creates new life in those who believe, we prove to be disciples by abiding in Jesus' Word. As members of the Church we receive the Word together in community, the same which provides us with the ultimate purpose of the created universe, which is the glorification of Almighty God.

In the next lesson, *The Word That Convicts*, we'll look at how God's Word convicts of sin, righteousness, and judgment. The Word teaches that sin is universal in scope and corrupting in its character. The Word of God also convicts regarding righteousness, revealing God's perfect righteousness and our moral inadequacy. And, it convicts regarding judgment, instructing that God will judge Israel and the nations, the Church, Satan and his angels, and all the wicked dead by his just determination. God's Word also convicts us of the truth--of Jesus Christ, the Kingdom of God, and the integrity of his Word through his messengers, the prophets and the Apostles.

Lesson three, *The Word That Converts*, concentrates on the power of the Word of God to produce new life in the believer. This Word that converts is synonymous with the Gospel of Jesus; it is the good news of salvation which causes us to be "born again," to experience the washing of regeneration, and renewal of the Holy Spirit. The Word produces in we who believe concrete signs of God's renewing power. This same Word that creates new life, sustains us, provides spiritual nourishment, causes our growth, and enables us to defend ourselves against the devil's lies.

Finally, lesson four, *The Word That Calls*, explores the concept of (*metanoia*), that is, repentance towards God, and to faith (*pistis*). Faith in Jesus Christ is the way that God saves, delivers, and rescues the believer from the penalty, power, and presence of sin. As we turn from sin to God in Christ, the Word leads us to receive God's new nature (regeneration) and become incorporated (adopted) into the people of God (to the *laos* of God) by grace through faith alone. The Word that calls us to salvation also calls us to discipleship (as bondslaves of Jesus), to freedom (as redeemed children) and to mission (to make disciples through our witness and good works).

Truly, the Holy Scriptures are a Word that are profitable for teaching, correction, instruction, and training so that God's person might be completely equipped for any task (2 Tim. 3.16-17). May God bless you as you explore the richness of his God-breathed Word that creates, convicts, converts and calls!

Objectives for *Capstone* Module 1, Conversion and Calling
After your reading, study, discussion, and application of the materials in this lesson, you will be able to:

Objectives for Lesson 1 The Word That Creates

1. Defend the idea that the Holy Scriptures are the Word of God, a written record of the Lord's own living and eternal Word.
2. Show from Scripture that the God of the Bible, the Triune God, guarantees the truthfulness of the Word of God, which makes it absolutely trustworthy. All things in the universe were made through God's creative and life-giving Word.
3. Describe how the Lord God identifies himself completely with the Word of God, especially in Jesus Christ, the Second person of the Trinity, through whom God reveals himself, redeems the world, and will restore the universe under his righteous rule.
4. Prove from Scripture that the Word of God, infused as it is with God's very life, is the means by which the Holy Spirit creates new life in those who believe.
5. Discuss how continuing in and receiving this implanted Word of God is the true sign of discipleship and authentic adoption into the family of God. As saints of God, we receive the Word of God together in his covenant community.

6. Demonstrate how the Word reveals the ultimate purpose of the created universe, which is the glorification of Almighty God.
7. Recite from memory a passage relating to the creative power of the Word of God.

After your reading, study, discussion, and application of the materials in this lesson, you will be able to articulate and defend with Scripture the truth that:

1. The Word of God is that Word that convicts of sin, righteousness, and judgment.
2. Of all the ways we can understand the person and works of God, it is the Word of God in Scripture that enables us to understand sin – that it is universal in scope and corrupting in its character.
3. God's Law convicts us of our sin, revealing the distance between our actions and intentions and God's holy demands.
4. The Word of God convicts regarding righteousness, revealing our inadequacy in keeping God's Law, and revealing God's righteousness by faith through the death and resurrection of Jesus Christ.
5. The Word of God convicts regarding judgment, revealing God's intent to bring to account all creatures everywhere, and his upcoming judgment on Israel and the nations, the Church, on Satan and his angels, and all the wicked dead.
6. The Word of God produces conviction regarding the nature of truth, i.e., what is true concerning God, his work in the world, and the destiny and purpose of humankind.
7. The Word of God also produces conviction about the primary subject of the Scriptures: the revelation of the person and work of Jesus Christ.
8. God's Word also produces conviction regarding the overarching backdrop of all of God's revelation: the revelation of his kingdom plan.
9. God's Word produces conviction through the integrity of God's chosen messengers, the prophets and the Apostles, who were given the task to represent and to speak of God's person and plan.

*Objectives for Lesson 3
The Word That Converts*

When you have completed your work in this module, we trust that you will be able to understand, articulate, and defend the truth that:

1. The Word that converts is synonymous with the good news of salvation by faith in Jesus Christ. The Gospel of Jesus Christ is the Word that converts.
2. This potent Word effectively leads us to *metanoia*, that is, repentance from sin and a turning towards God in Jesus Christ.
3. This Word which works so effectively repentance (*metanoia*) to salvation, works with the same power to produce faith (*pistis*) in the believer. This faith saves, delivers, and rescues the believer from the penalty, power, and presence of sin.
4. The Word of God, once activated by repentance and faith, produces confirming signs of God's forgiveness and the Holy Spirit's power in the life of the believer.
5. Inwardly, the believer displays signs of new life in Jesus Christ including a knowledge of God as heavenly Father, a new experience of prayer, an openness to the Word of God, and a willingness to follow the inner leading of Jesus' voice.
6. Outwardly, and in a corresponding way, the Word that converts produces outward signs including such things as an identification with the people of God, the display of a new Christlike character and lifestyle, a love for other believers, and a desire to see the lost won to Christ.

*Objectives for Lesson 4
The Word That Calls*

After your reading, study, discussion, and application of the materials in this lesson, you will be able to understand, articulate, and defend the truth that:

1. The Word that effectively leads us to salvation and conversion also calls us to live as disciples of Jesus, obedient to his will.
2. This Word that calls us to discipleship demands that we make ourselves available to Jesus that we might love him supremely, above all other loves, including marriage and family, in such a way that we may serve him as Lord above all.
3. The call also asks us to embrace our new identity in Christ as aliens and sojourners in this world, those men and women who act and work as citizens of the Kingdom of God in the midst of the world, as representatives of Jesus.
4. The lifestyle of discipleship is demonstrated when we respond favorably to the call to live as sacrificial servants

to his glory. As slaves of Christ, we commit all we are and have to glorifying him and accomplishing his will in the world, as he directs.

5. We are also called to live and work in community, as members of God's glorious family in the people of God (*laos*).

6. The disciple of Jesus is called to live in the freedom of Jesus Christ, to use their freedom as an opportunity to fulfill the Great Commandment, and to give clear witness for the purpose of saving others for the cause of Christ.

7. The word that calls to discipleship, community, and freedom also calls us to mission. As agents of the Kingdom of God, we are called to fulfill the Great Commission, to do battle with our spiritual enemy the devil, and to demonstrate the life of the Kingdom through our love and good works.

Teaching Objectives for Capstone, by Module

Teaching Objectives for Capstone, by Module

Module Description

Capstone Module 2 – The Kingdom of God

Of all the subjects preached and taught by Jesus of Nazareth, none are as significant and controversial as the subject of the Kingdom of God. Both conservative and liberal scholars agree that Jesus' favorite subject, the one he preached and taught upon most often, is the Kingdom of God. It was his salvation message, master plan, and heart theology. Sadly, the modern Church seems to pay little attention to what Jesus considered to be most important in his prophetic and Messianic ministry. Our hope is that your heart will be gripped by the kingdom story – the King and his Kingdom – and see its importance in the life of personal discipleship and ministry.

The first lesson, *God's Reign Challenged*, focuses upon God as the sovereign majesty. It discusses how the absolute sovereignty and lordship of God was defied, both by the devil and his angels, and the first human pair, Adam and Eve, through their willful disobedience in the garden. This rebellion produced tragic results in the world, in human nature, and the release of the demonic into the world. In spite of our rebellion, however, God intends to restore all heaven and earth back under his reign, and constitute again a universe where his name is glorified, and his justice and peace rule forever.

In our second lesson, *God's Reign Inaugurated*, we will explore God's intent to eradicate all disobedience and rebellion as a result of the Fall – God becomes a Warrior in this fallen realm. God made a covenant with Abraham as his solemn promise to bring a Seed through whom the shalom and justice kingdom reign would be brought back to earth. This covenant promise was renewed with Isaac and Jacob, to the Israelite nation, to the tribe of Judah, and finally to the family of David. Here we trace in bold line the origins of the Messiah, so the reign of God would be brought back into this fallen and sin-cursed world. Jesus of Nazareth is the Kingdom's presence realized, with God's reign demonstrated in his incarnation, death, resurrection, and ascension.

Lessons three and four deal with *God's Reign Invading* and *God's Reign Consummated*, respectively. Now that our Lord Jesus has died, risen, and ascended into heaven, the Kingdom of God is being proclaimed throughout the world by his Church. The Church of Jesus Christ is the locus – the place or context – of God's salvation, of the empowering presence of the Holy Spirit, and of authentic kingdom shalom, the place where God's presence and power are freely being displayed. The Kingdom of God will be consummated at the Second Coming of Jesus, where death, disease, and all evil will be put down, all heaven and earth shall be renewed, and God will become All-in-all.

The Story of the Kingdom is the story of Jesus, and God's intent is to bring the world back under his rule in him. Our prayer is that your love and service to him will abound as you study the Word of God on the forever rule of God!

Objectives for *Capstone* Module 2, The Kingdom of God

After your reading, study, discussion, and application of the materials in this lesson, you will be able to:

Objectives for Lesson 1 God's Reign Challenged

1. Describe how God as Lord, reigns over all, but that his reign was challenged through satanic rebellion in the heavenlies, and through the voluntary rebellion and disobedience of the first human pair on earth.
2. Demonstrate how this challenge resulted in the curse upon creation, leading to death, and the greatest of all human tragedies, called by the Church, "the Fall."
3. How this disobedience by Satan and the first human pair has produced tragic and corrupting results in three spheres of personage and existence: *kosmos* (the world), *sarx* (fleshliness of human nature), and *kakos* (ongoing influence and chaos of the evil one).
4. Recite from memory a passage relating to the challenge of God's reign.

Objectives for Lesson 2 God's Reign Inaugurated

After your reading, study, discussion, and application of the materials in this lesson, you will be able to:

1. Show from Scripture that since the Fall, the reign of God has been inaugurated in this present world.
2. Describe how God is bringing his reign concretely into the world in an intentional way, firstly, in his own predisposition as a Warrior over his enemies.
3. Show how through the covenant promise of deliverance given to Abraham God worked out his Kingdom's inauguration, and through the history of God's dealings and workings with Israel, his covenant people.
4. Articulate how Jesus of Nazareth in the world represents the Kingdom's presence realized in his incarnation, death, resurrection, and ascension.

Teaching Objectives for Capstone, by Module

5. Recite from memory a passage relating to the inauguration of God's reign.

*Objectives for Lesson 3
God's Reign Invading*

After your reading, study, discussion, and application of the materials in this lesson, you will be able to:

1. Show that the Church of Jesus Christ, as his body and agent, is itself the locus (the place and/or context) of God's salvation, of the empowering presence of the Holy Spirit, and of the authentic expression of the Kingdom's life and witness.
2. See that the Church of Jesus Christ is not only a context, but an agent, a willing and available servant to God in order to advance kingdom purposes in the world.
3. Recite from memory a passage relating to the invasion of God's reign.

*Objectives for Lesson 4
God's Reign
Consummated*

After your reading, study, discussion, and application of the materials in this lesson, you will be able to:

1. Define eschatology and its significance for Christian discipleship.
2. Outline briefly the biblical conception of death, and then discuss together the Bible's teachings on the intermediate state.
3. Focus on the Second Coming of Jesus Christ, the resurrection from the dead and the final judgment, and the Kingdom consummated with God as All-in-all.
4. Recite from memory a passage related to the consummation of God's reign.

Module Description

Capstone Module 3 – Theology of the Church

The Church of God in Jesus Christ is one of the most refreshing and important themes of all the Scriptures. Jesus of Nazareth, through his death, burial, and resurrection, has been exalted as head over his new people, those called to represent him in the earth and bear witness of his already/not yet Kingdom. To understand the Church's role in God's kingdom program is critical to every facet of personal and corporate discipleship; there is no discipleship or salvation apart from God's saving action in the Church. Grasping what God is doing in and through his people empowers God's leader to represent him with wisdom and honor. We invite you with enthusiasm to study the Church in order to fully appreciate the nature of ministry in the world today.

The first lesson, *The Church Foreshadowed in God's Plan*, focuses upon how the Church is foreshadowed in God's exalted purpose to bring glory to himself by saving a new humanity through his covenant with Abraham. You will see how the Church is foreshadowed in the unfolding of his gracious plan of salvation to include the Gentiles in his work in Christ Jesus, and learn of God's intent to create for himself a unique and peculiar people, the laos of God. You will also discover the richness and meaning of salvation, what it means to be rescued from the lostness and separation from God caused by sin. Through our union with Christ we become joined to "the people of God" who inherit the Kingdom he promised. United to Christ is to be united to his people, those people whose hope is in God creating a new heaven and a new earth with a new humanity under the rule of God which will completely reverse the effects of sin and death on the world.

In our second lesson, *The Church at Worship*, we'll consider salvation as the foundation of the Church's worship. We'll see that salvation comes by God's grace alone and that human beings can in no way earn or deserve it. Worship, therefore, is the proper response to the grace of God. We will also explore some of the insights from Christian reflection about the Church's worship, including a brief study of the terms "sacrament" and "ordinance" as well as varying views of Baptism and the Lord's Supper applied to the Church's worship. Furthermore, we'll discover the theological purpose of the Church's worship, which is to glorify God because of his solitary holiness, his infinite beauty, his incomparable glory and his match-less works. Approaching the triune God through Jesus Christ, the Church worships through praise and thanksgiving, and through

Teaching Objectives for Capstone, by Module

Liturgy, which emphasizes the Word and the Sacraments. The Church also worships God through its obedience and lifestyle as a covenant community.

Lesson three is entitled *The Church as Witness*, and focuses on the mission of the Church. In this lesson we'll cover the most significant aspects of the doctrine of election as it applies to Jesus Christ as the elect of God, to his chosen people Israel, to the Church, and to individual believers. We'll discover Jesus Christ as the Elect of God, the One through whom God saves out of the world a people for himself, and briefly explore the dimensions and definition of the concept of God's chosen people as it is defined both in Israel as the people of God and the Church of Jesus Christ. As God's instrument of his Great Commission, we'll take notice of three critical elements within it: the Church gives witness as she evangelizes the lost, as she baptizes new believers in Christ (that is, to incorporate them as members into the Church), and as she teaches her members to observe all the things Christ commanded.

Finally, in lesson four, *The Church at Work*, we will discover the various dimensions and elements of the Church. Special attention will be given to how we may detect authentic Christian community by concentrating on certain marks which have been proven to be true signs of the Church's actions and lifestyle. We'll consider the marks of the Church according to the Nicene Creed, as well as according to the teaching of the Reformation. We will also look at the Church through the lens of the Vincentian Rule, a helpful guide to understand and evaluate traditions and teachings claiming to be binding upon Christians. We'll end this study by concentrating on the ministry of the Church through various images of the Church mentioned in the New Testament, the image of the household of God (God's family), through the image of the body of Christ and Temple of the Holy Spirit (God's agent of the Kingdom of God). We will also look through the lens of God's army, as the Church does battle in the Lamb's war. These images offer great insight into how we are to understand the Church's identity and work in the world today.

Without question, the Church of Jesus Christ is God's agent for his Kingdom, and the people of his presence. May your study of this material and the Word of God produce in you a deep love and devotion to live for and build up the holy people of God, the Church!

Objectives for *Capstone* Module 3, Theology of the Church

*Objectives for Lesson 1
The Church
Foreshadowed
in God's Plan*

After your reading, study, discussion, and application of the materials in this lesson, you will be able to:

1. Explain how the Church is foreshadowed in God's exalted purpose, that is, God's determination to bring glory to himself through a new humanity through the covenant he would make with Abraham.
2. Recite relevant Scripture and concepts connected to the Church foreshadowed in the unfolding of his gracious plan of salvation, his goal to unveil the grand mystery of his inclusion of the Gentiles in Christ Jesus.
3. Detail and tell how the Church is foreshadowed in God's revealed plan of Scripture, that from the beginning, God's intent was to create for himself a unique and peculiar People, the *laos* of God.
4. Give a biblical definition of salvation and understand how it relates to participation in the Church.
5. Recite from memory a Bible passage that describes the Church in light of its relationship to the Old Testament people of God.

*Objectives for Lesson 2
The Church at Worship*

After your reading, study, discussion, and application of the materials in this lesson, you will be able to:

1. Defend the idea that salvation comes by God's grace alone and that human beings can in no way earn or deserve it.
2. Recognize that worship is the proper response to the grace of God.
3. Explain the difference between the terms "sacrament" and "ordinance" and describe the theological perspective that lies behind each term.
4. Understand the meaning of baptism and the Lord's Supper and discuss the key differences in the way Christians think about their meaning.
5. Recite the primary purpose of the Church's worship of God, to glorify God because of his solitary holiness, his infinite beauty, his incomparable glory, and his matchless works.
6. Articulate that the Church worships the Triune God through Jesus Christ. We worship Yahweh God alone, through Jesus Christ, in the power of the Holy Spirit.

Teaching Objectives for Capstone, by Module

Teaching Objectives for Capstone, by Module

7. Know and apply how the Church worships through praise and thanksgiving, through liturgy, which emphasizes the Word and the sacraments, and through our obedience and lifestyle as a covenant community.

Objectives for Lesson 3
The Church as Witness

After your reading, study, discussion, and application of the materials in this lesson, you will be able to:

1. Outline the most significant aspects of the doctrine of election as it applies to Jesus Christ as the Elect Servant of God.
2. Describe how God's election relates both to his chosen people Israel as well as to the Church.
3. Explain the relationship of God's election of individual believers "in Christ," that is, in connection to Christ as they cling to him by faith.
4. Articulate how the Great Commission provides an overall outline for the Church's threefold witness in the world to make disciples.
5. Recite how the Church fulfills Christ's commission by obeying Jesus' call to evangelize the lost, by baptizing new believers in Christ (incorporating them as members into the Church), and by teaching true converts to observe all the things Christ commanded.

Objectives for Lesson 4
The Church at Work

After your reading, study, discussion, and application of the materials in this lesson, you will be able to:

1. Articulate the various dimensions and elements of the Church, and be able to say how we may detect authentic Christian community through the Church's actions and lifestyle.
2. Discern the marks of the Church according to the Nicene Creed.
3. Recognize the dimensions and definition of Church according to the teaching of the Reformation.
4. Recite the standard of doctrinal unity through the lens of the Vincentian Rule, a helpful guide to understand and evaluate traditions and teachings claiming to be binding upon Christians.
5. Describe the character of the Church's works in the world by exploring various images of the Church mentioned in the New Testament.

6. Provide insights into the Church's nature and function through the lens of the household of God, the body of Christ, and temple of the Holy Spirit, through the ambassadorship of the Church as the agent of the Kingdom of God, as well as God's army, the Church's work as doing battle in the Lamb's war.

Teaching Objectives for Capstone, by Module

Module Description

Capstone Module 4 – Foundations for Christian Mission

The theme of mission has not received the kind of focus and attention in our urban churches that it should. Having been seen largely as a work across the ocean in far flung corners of the world, we have failed to give it the kind of critical analysis that it deserves. From one vantage point, the entirety of the Christian faith could be seen as a response of mission, the call to go to the nations and proclaim Jesus of Nazareth as Lord and King of the reign of God. The NT is a collection of missionary documents given to churches that were founded by the apostles, the original missionaries of the Christian faith. God himself is the original missionary, coming to the world in Christ and reconciling it to himself (2 Cor. 5.18-21). Indeed, Christianity is mission.

This module, therefore, deals with this key subject with the intent to help you, God's emerging leader in the city, to understand both the theology and ramifications of mission from a biblical point of view. In a real sense, we cannot understand what God is doing in the world through mission without an overview of the vision of God's purpose and working. So, in our first two lessons we will look at mission through four distinctive lenses: mission as drama and promise, and mission as romance and warfare respectively.

In our first lesson, *The Vision and Biblical Foundation for Christian Mission (1)*, we deal with the perspective of Mission as the Drama of All Time. Out intent here is to provide a framework for understanding the work of mission from the Scriptures themselves. We will begin by giving a general definition of mission, and then outline a quick summary of the critical elements of a biblical understanding of mission. We will look at mission through the lens of story and drama, showing from Scripture that mission is God's sovereign working through history through the various epochs or sections of time to bring about redemption in Christ. We also explore Mission as the Fulfillment of the Divine Promise, envisioning mission as God fulfilling his promise as the covenant God of faithfulness. We will describe the role of biblical covenants in the Scriptures, and trace God's action as response to his covenant promise to Abraham, confirmed in his sons and the patriarchs, identified with the tribe of Judah and clarified in the promise to David to have a perpetual heir on his throne. In the person of Jesus of Nazareth, the promise of Abraham and David has been fulfilled, and now, through mission proclamation of the Gospel, the promise of new life is offered to the nations through the preaching of the cross.

In lesson two, *The Vision and Biblical Foundation for Christian Mission (2)*, we will explore Mission as the Romance of the Ages and as the War of the Spheres. These images in Scripture allow us to see just how critical mission is to our theological framework as believers. As the romance of God, we see God's determination to draw out of the world a people for his own possession. We will review this grand theme, beginning with the history of Israel as the wife of God, and her unfaithfulness through idolatry and disobedience. We will trace this theme in the person of Jesus, and see how the new covenant expanded the people of God to include the Gentiles. As the warfare of the ages, we see the proclamation of God's kingdom rule in the person of Jesus of Nazareth. Beginning with the clear affirmation of God's sovereignty, we see God has determined to reestablish his rule over his creation, which fell from his grace through the rebellion of the devil and humankind at the Fall. Since this time, God has taken the position of warrior to bring the universe back under his rulership. In the person of Jesus of Nazareth, God is reasserting his right to rule over the universe, and mission is the proclamation of that Kingdom come in Christ.

In lesson three, *Christian Mission and the City*, we turn our attention to the object of mission and God's intent for the city and the poor. We begin by looking at the ancient city, its organization and characteristics, especially its symbolic feature as a sign of rebellion against the Lord. We will consider the spiritual significance of the city, looking at God's interaction with a number of cities in Scripture, and exploring their meanings. We will see how God has adopted the city concept for his own purposes, overruling its association with rebellion and idolatry, and redeeming its meaning for mission, and for the future glory of the Kingdom. In this lesson, then, we will also provide a rationale for our involvement in urban mission. As the seat of influence, power, and spiritual activity as well as the magnet for the oppressed, the broken, and the poor, we as 21st century disciples must strive to speak and live prophetically to the city. As the picture and symbol of our spiritual destiny and inheritance, we must do all we can to evangelize, disciple, and plant churches in our cities, both at home and abroad.

Finally, in lesson four we explore another critical component of Christian mission. In *Christian Mission and the Poor*, we will examine the concept of the poor and mission through the lens of the rich biblical concept of shalom, or wholeness. As the covenant community of Yahweh, the people of Israel were called to live in such

Teaching Objectives for Capstone, by Module

faithfulness to the Lord's covenant that poverty would be replaced with justice and righteousness. Building on the fact of God's deliverance of his people from Egypt at the Exodus, God gave his people in his covenant a blueprint for justice that would address the issue of poverty and oppression. Armed with this biblical vision, we will then consider how Jesus as Messiah and Head of the Church fulfills the Messianic prophecy regarding the One who would bring justice and peace to the poor. Jesus as Lord and Head of the Church continues to express God's mandate for shalom among the people of God, and through his people, to the world. The Church, God's new covenant community by faith in Jesus, is called to live in shalom and demonstrate both to its own members and to the world the justice of God for the broken. This is possible now because of the Holy Spirit who empowers and strengthens the people of God today.

As believers in Jesus Christ, each of us, every congregation has been redeemed in order that we might be redemptive, proclaiming and living out the truth of God where he has placed us. Truly, to be Christian is to be mission-oriented and mission-formed; we were born from above to become co-laborers with God in his mission to win the world for his Son (Acts 9.15).

Objectives for Lesson 1 The Vision and Biblical Foundation for Christian Mission, I

Objectives for *Capstone* Module 4, Foundations for Christian Mission
After your reading, study, discussion, and application of the materials in this lesson, you will be able to:

1. Outline a "prolegomena" ("first word") or "big picture" overview to mission.
2. Define mission as "the proclamation of God's offer of salvation and redemption in the person and work of Jesus Christ in the power of the Holy Spirit to all people groups."
3. Reproduce the elements of a biblical understanding of mission, including its need for a clear understanding of God and his purposes for the universe, to relate all the details of history to a single unified whole, to be rooted in the Scriptures themselves, to be anchored in the person and work of Jesus Christ, and to take seriously the biblical way of discussing mission through image, pictures, and stories.
4. Lay out the four theological frameworks/pictures of mission in Scripture, i.e., Mission as the Drama of all time (God as the major character in the greatest plot motif of all time), as the Fulfillment of the Divine Promise (God fulfilling his

covenant promise in Jesus Christ), as the Romance of the Ages (God as the bridegroom of his redeemed humanity), and as the War of the Spheres (God as the warrior reestablishing his rule over the universe).

5. Give an overview of the major elements in the *Drama of All Time* in terms of the major phases of God's unfolding purpose, including *Before Time* (which highlights God's pre-existence and purpose, the mystery of iniquity and the rebellion of the powers), *Beginning of Time* (which includes the creation of the universe and humankind, the fall and the curse, the *protoevangelium*, the end of Eden, the reign of death, and the first signs of grace), and the *Unfolding of Time* (which includes the Abrahamic promise, the Exodus, the Conquest of the Land, the City-Temple-Throne, the Captivity and Exile, and the Return of the Remnant).

6. Complete the phases of God's unfolding purpose with the *Fullness of Time* (which includes the incarnation, the Kingdom revealed in Jesus, the passion, death, resurrection, and ascension of Christ), the *Last Times* (including the descent of the Holy Spirit, the formation of the Church, the inclusion of the Gentiles, and age of world mission), the *Fulfillment of Time* (which includes the end of world evangelization, the apostasy of the Church, the Great Tribulation, the *Parousia*, the reign of Christ on earth, the Great White Throne, the Lake of Fire, and turning the Kingdom over to God the Father), and finally *Beyond Time* (which includes the new heavens and new earth, the descent of the New Jerusalem, the times of refreshing, and the ushering in of the Age to Come).

7. Summarize the implications of Mission as the *Drama of All Time*: how God's sovereign purpose underwrites all human history, God as the central character in the unfolding phases of the divine drama, mission as the recovery of that which was lost at the *beginning of time*, and the making of disciples among all nations as our part in *fulfilling our role in the script of Almighty God*.

8. Give an overview of the major elements of Mission as the *Fulfillment of the Divine Promise* beginning with a definition of covenant as a contract between two parties, whether individuals, tribes, or nations, with both having obligations to fulfill, and benefits and advantages as a result of the fulfillment of those conditions.

Teaching Objectives for Capstone, by Module

9. Outline key characteristics of covenant making in Scripture including how they were invoked by a witness, were sober (i.e., breaking them was seen as a great moral evil), were given witness by giving gifts, eating meals, and setting up stones of remembrance, confirmed with an oath and with sacrifice.

10. Provide several examples of covenants in the Bible, including marriage, the covenant with Noah, the covenant of Sinai with the children of Israel, all of which speak to the solemn contract between individuals, or God and individuals.

11. Trace the framework as Mission as *Fulfillment of the Divine Promise* from covenant made with Abraham, with its condition that he leave his country and kindred to go to a land of God's own choosing, with the corresponding blessing that God would make him a great nation, bless him and make his name great, bless and curse those who did the same to him, and bless all the families of the earth in him.

12. Highlight how this Abrahamic covenant was renewed, confirmed in both Isaac and Jacob, and related to Judah as the tribe out of which the divine Messiah would come, and show how the royal Seed of Abraham's blessing would come through God's covenant with David and his house, whose heir would reign forever over the house of Israel and be a blessing to the nations.

13. Show how this promise was fulfilled in the person of Jesus of Nazareth, who represents the embodiment both of the Abrahamic and Davidic promises. Through his life, death, resurrection, and ascension, the covenant promise of God is fulfilled.

14. Explain how mission is the proclamation of the Good News regarding God's covenant faithfulness, with the Great Commission as a responsibility to proclaim the promise fulfilled for the salvation of all humanity, beginning at Jerusalem, to the very ends of the earth.

15. Show the linkage between the role of mission in this age and the declaration that in the person of Jesus of Nazareth, the promise of Abraham and David has been fulfilled, and now, through mission's proclamation of the Gospel, the promise of new life is offered to the nations through the preaching of the cross.

After your reading, study, discussion, and application of the materials in this lesson, you will be able to:

1. Lay out the divine romance between God and his people as one of the major motifs of mission in Scripture, that is, God's determination to draw out of the world a people for his own possession, a possession fulfilled and completed in Jesus' love for his Church.

2. Outline the notion of the bride and bridegroom in the OT, including its connection to the idea of mirth and gladness in Scripture, its use as a basic image of God's relationship to his people (as seen in the book of Song of Solomon), and the way in which God's relationship with his people matured, from the pitiful origins of Israel to its judgment and exile by God due to her unfaithfulness.

3. Detail the remnant's return to the land, from Cyrus' decree for the remnant to return, its actual reentry into the land through Ezra, Zerubbabel, and Nehemiah, and God's promise for a new covenant, not based on their obedience and faithfulness but rather his writing his law on their hearts and giving them a new spirit. Ultimately, his people would be restored to God, who would dance and rejoice over his people like a bridegroom over a bride.

4. Trace some of the major hints of the promise of a new covenant given in the OT, including the Abrahamic covenant and its prospect of Gentile inclusion, and show how with Jesus, the bride metaphor is extended and completed. Jesus becomes the source and life of the Church, his new bride, with John the Baptist being the friend of the bridegroom.

5. Show how the idea of God's people was revealed through the disclosure of the mystery revealed through the apostles and prophets, that Gentiles are fellow heirs with the Jews in the new covenant promise of God, and through it, are welcomed as members of God's new humanity and Christ's bride.

6. List the major doctrinal points associated with Gentile inclusion in the bride of Christ, including their welcome through faith, the resolution of the issue at the Jerusalem Council, the power of the blood of Christ to include them in the covenant, how the heart of apostolic ministry is preparing God's people as a bride, whom Christ will receive at his coming blameless in his sight.

7. Detail how the divine romance will be consummated with the coming of the New Jerusalem from heaven, the dwelling place of God and his people, who will totally identify with Christ, the bridegroom, in being made like him, becoming joint-heirs with him, being in his presence forever as his co-regent.

8. Draw out the main implications of the divine romance, including God's desire to draw from all nations a people for his own, a drawing that includes both Jews and Gentiles, and therefore mission is the testimony that God is drawing members of his kingdom community from both the Jews and Gentiles who will live with him forever.

9. Outline the motif of *Mission as the War of the Spheres*, which is perhaps the most dynamic image of mission in Scripture, the proclamation of God's kingdom rule in the person of Jesus of Nazareth.

10. Give an overview of the reign of God in Scripture, beginning with the Lord as creator and sustainer of all, and the mystery of iniquity (the satanic rebellion in the heavenlies), which resulted in the temptation and fall of humankind, and the curse, yet ended with God's promise to crush the head of the serpent through the Seed of the woman. As a result of the Fall, the universe is at war and God is a warrior.

11. Lay out the major points of God as the divine warrior in the OT, including God as warrior defeating evil in its symbolism as a river and sea, defeating Pharaoh and his armies, who led his people into victory as the great Lord of armies, and who fought against his own people because of their disobedience and rebellion. Also, Israel's prophets pictured God as a divine warrior who through his Messiah would finally destroy all evil once and for all time.

12. Show how the promise of the Messiah in David's heir represented God's intent to provide a king who would restore the reign to his people, rule the nations with justice and righteousness, and bring a knowledge of God to the entire earth as Lord and King.

13. Argue from Scripture how God's promised rule has been inaugurated through the person and work of Jesus Christ, who is the one from the Davidic line who will restore the reign of God. In him and the various aspects of his birth, teaching, miracles, exorcisms, deeds, death, and resurrection, the Kingdom of God is now here, already present in the life of the Church.

14. Explain the "already/not yet dimension" of the Kingdom of God; although the Kingdom of God has come in the fulfillment of the Messianic promise in the person of Jesus, the Kingdom will only be consummated at his Second Coming, when the full and final manifestation will occur. The Church is both sign and foretaste of the Kingdom present today, who is authorized to proclaim and demonstrate the victory of Christ over Satan and the curse as his agent and deputy.

15. Draw out the main implications of the *Mission as the War of the Spheres* motif, including the reassertion of God's rule today over his universe in Jesus Christ, God as the warrior who through his anointed One has defeated the power of the devil and the effects of the curse, and how mission through this lens becomes the display and proclamation of the rule of God here and now. Making disciples among all nations is advancing the reign of God by testifying to its coming in the person of Jesus of Nazareth.

*Objectives for Lesson 3
Christian Mission
and the City*

After your reading, study, discussion, and application of the materials in this lesson, you will be able to:

1. Define the concept of the city from the Bible, including the fact that cities were a collection of houses and buildings surrounded by walls, were significant and impressive for their time, and that some were dependent for protection and supply upon others. Cities, common in the ancient world, were relatively small, typically unpaved, strengthened by thick walls and high towers, and seats of government and power.

2. Lay out the spiritual meaning of the city, that is, the ways in which cities were associated with human rebellion and idolatry (*Enoch*, the city of Cain), with independence and arrogance (as in the case of the Tower of Babel), and with evil and godlessness (as with Babylon). Cities were judged by God for their sinfulness (e.g., Sodom and Gomorrah, Jericho, Nineveh), and denounced for their false sense of security and power (specifically, Jerusalem).

3. Show how God adopted the city as symbol of his dwelling place and blessing, i.e., his selection of Jerusalem for himself, and his determination to make her a praise in the earth. Show further the divine irony of God transforming the image of rebellion into an image of refuge (i.e., the cities of Refuge), as well as the image of a place which can know and

experience his forgiveness and blessing (i.e., Jonah and the experience of Nineveh).

4. Detail how, because of God's own mercy and graciousness, there can be hope for any city which repents in the face of his judgment, yields in the face of his demands, and seeks his mercy in the face of his punishment.

5. Give evidence of the three critical reasons why urban mission must be a priority for all mission activity today. These include the following: the city as the seat of influence, power, and spiritual activity in the world, is becoming a magnet for the oppressed, the broken, and the poor, and is seen as the picture of our spiritual destiny and inheritance.

6. Show how Jesus' own ministry was rooted in city work, and his proclamation mandate included the preaching of the Kingdom in Jerusalem; also, how Christianity was birthed in a city, and spread through the Roman empire in the first century via the great urban centers of the time (in places such as Damascus, Antioch, Corinth, Philippi, Thessalonica, Athens, and Rome itself). The apostolic ministry (including the Pauline journeys) were urban in character, centers which proved to be the gateways to the larger Roman empire.

7. Give an overview of the size, scope, and population of some of the major urban centers today. Further, show how these cities serve as centers of government, education, health-care, information, entertainment, trade, commerce, business, industry, jurisprudence, the military, and religion. Outline the cities in regard to their significance in terms of cultural cities (which lead the world in fashion, trends, and ideas), *political and administrative cities* (centers of worldwide decision making bodies, or those containing governments and their bureaucracies), *industrial cities* (noisy, blue-collar, factory centers host to central manufacturing industries) *commercial cities* (giant marketplaces or bazaars where goods and services are exchanged on worldwide basis), *symbolic cities* (cities where great historical struggles are fought, settled, and symbolized), and *primary cities* (those which combine all of the characteristics together).

8. Lay out the ways in which cities today serve as magnets for the oppressed, the broken, and the poor, including the biblical focus on God's heart for the poor, the trend of urbanization (and its concentration on the poor) as the most powerful characteristic of modern times, and the logical argument that if God is concerned for the poor, he likewise

is concerned about the American inner city because of its staggering number of underclass and poor families.

9. Summarize the key biblical data on how the city is the picture and symbol of our spiritual destiny and inheritance, in the sense of the hope of the New Jerusalem; this will be the city not where God is absent and where arrogance rules, but where God is present, and Jesus is adored as Lord of all. Show how the explicit goal of mission is to rob the cities of the world in order to *fill up and populate* the New Jerusalem, the true mother of all believers (*God's final urban renewal project*).

10. Restate the key implications for understanding the centrality of the city for urban mission, i.e., how in all our mission praying, giving and sending we must focus on the cities, we must recruit more spiritual laborers to serve in the city, strategize how to affect unreached cities with the Gospel, and pray for the city and seek its safety, finding our safety in its preservation.

Teaching Objectives for Capstone, by Module

Objectives for Lesson 4 Christian Mission and the Poor

After your reading, study, discussion, and application of the materials in this lesson, you will be able to:

1. Define the concept of the poor in light of the biblical vision of *shalom*, or wholeness: *shalom* is the Hebrew term for "fullness of human community in fellowship with God and with one another."

2. Outline the elements of *shalom* including its experience of health and wellness, safety and protection, harmony between neighbors, prosperity and material sufficiency, and the absence of malice and conflict – genuine peace. This also includes the idea of *shalom* as God's gracious provision, as connected with the coming of the Messiah who is the Prince of *shalom*, as well as shalom as the standard for the people of God.

3. Explain how poverty is the denial of God's *shalom*, how his blessing was to prevent the occurrence of poverty, and the commands to the covenant community were designed to ensure justice and righteousness among Yahweh's people, and that faithfulness to the covenant was designed for the continuation of *shalom* among the Israelites as they obeyed his voice and met its conditions.

4. Show how God is identified with the poor, i.e., it is his design to lift and bless them from their state, to punish those who oppress them, and to demand that his people demonstrate the same concern that he has on behalf of the broken, poor, and the oppressed. The Exodus is a key event which embodies God's identification with the poor and the oppressed, revealing his heart of justice, the creation of his covenant community which was called to be a reflection of his holiness, a model of justice and mercy, and a beacon for the nations.

5. Lay out the biblical causes of poverty, including natural disaster and calamity (e.g., famine, drought, storm, etc.), personal laziness and slothfulness (e.g., bad decisions, immoral character, idleness, hard-heartedness, etc.), and oppression and injustice from the hands of the powerful (e.g., mistreatment, exploitation, defrauding wages, etc.). The term "the poor" in the Scriptures is linked to a number of different concepts which serve as synonyms, including "the widow," "the fatherless," and the "stranger."

6. List the standards God gave to his covenant people in regard to the generous and just treatment of the poor as a witness. These include special provisions for the care of the poor which were factored into the harvest and gleaning stipulations of the Law, justice in the courts where all matters, measures, and transactions were to be done honestly and rightly, regardless of person, and resources were to be shared in the Sabbatical year, with the poor provided a share of the produce of the fields and vineyards.

7. Further list out the standards, including how the people of God were forbidden to charge interest to the poor, fair timely payment for a day's work (i.e., wages to be paid the same day with no oppression or defrauding allowed), with radical hospitality to be practiced to the poor (an "open hand policy"), and resources to be set aside for them (i.e., certain portions of the tithe and bounty to be given to the most needy and vulnerable in the midst of the community). The poor were to be included in all celebrations, and in the year of Jubilee, the poor were to recover their property, with provision made for those whose funds were short or absent.

8. Note the implications of these standards for God's covenant community: God's people were in all their dealings to reflect God's identification with the poor, informed by God's deliverance of them at the Exodus, and were to demonstrate

the Lord's shalom in all their relationships and dealings with others.

9. Give evidence how Jesus' founding of the Church is God's new covenant kingdom community, called to demonstrate the same shalom in the midst of the people of God.

10. Explain how Jesus' Messiahship was inaugurated in acts of healing the oppressed and preaching Good News to the poor, who were the object of his attention, calling, ministry, and purpose, and authenticated his Messiahship to John the Baptist through works of justice and preaching to the poor. Further show how he verified and confirmed the salvation of others by their treatment of the poor, and how he identified without reservation to the "least of these" (i.e., the hungry, thirsty, the stranger, the naked, the sick, and the prisoner).

11. Show the connection between Christ's kingdom community, the Church, and its responsibility to demonstrate mercy and justice in the kingdom community, i.e., it is called to proclaim the Good News to the poor as the body of Christ in the world, and how it is called to give evidence of the life of the Age to Come in its display of justice on behalf of the poor. Also demonstrate that in the life and mission of the Church, empowered by the Holy Spirit, the *shalom* of God's OT covenant community is enjoyed and displayed.

12. Demonstrate how the new community displays radical generosity and hospitality to the needy within the community, especially to the widows, fatherless, and poor in our midst, as well as makes provision for other churches during times of calamity and distress.

13. Lay out how the new community is called to be an advocate for the poor, which is a hallmark of authentic Christian mission. This advocacy includes not being partial or bigoted on account of class or difference among the members of the body, possessing a commitment to be a community of good works on behalf of the poor and vulnerable, and working to help meet the practical needs of the hurting, especially those in the household of God.

14. Discern the implications of the Church as the new community of the Kingdom for urban mission, including the demand to proclaim the Good News to the poor (i.e., respecting the poor as those who have been chosen by God, with whom Jesus identified, who are never to be patronized but dealt with justly and compassionately with full expectation of their transformation and contribution).

15. Summarize further implications of this vision, including that the Church must act in accordance with God's choice of the poor (i.e., defending their cause, maintaining their rights, providing advocacy for them, and showing no partiality in our affairs in the Church); we are to be generous and hospitable in meeting the needs of the poor, sharing our own goods, being hospitable to strangers and to the imprisoned, and showing love as we have been shown.

16. Lay out the final (and perhaps the most important) implication which is that the Church must seek justice and equity in dealing with the poor in our midst and in the world; we are not merely to meet necessities but strive to impact structures and relationships that will lead to a more just situation. As the Lord in the OT demanded that the covenant community give the poor resources, so the Church is to "live the true prosperity Gospel," by seeking justice and equity on behalf of the poor in all dealings and issues.

Teaching Objectives for Capstone, by Module

Capstone **Module 5 – Bible Interpretation**

Module Description

According to the clear testimony of the Scriptures themselves, God equips his representatives through the Spirit-breathed Word of God, the Scriptures. Everyone God calls into the ministry must determine to discipline themselves so as to master its contents, submit to its injunctions, and teach its truths. Like a workman (or workwoman!) they must strive to handle the Word of truth accurately, and so be approved of the Lord in their study (2 Tim. 2.15).

This module focuses on the facts, principles, and implications of interpreting the Bible. In our first lesson, *Biblical Inspiration: The Origins and Authority of the Bible*, we will outline the need for biblical interpretation, and what we need to do to prepare for this great task. We will explore both the divine and human dimensions of the Bible, clarify the goal of all interpretation, and lay out clearly our theological assumptions regarding the high place of the Scriptures in the Church. We will especially concentrate on the kind of life and heart preparation necessary to interpret God's Word accurately. We will also look at the Bible's claim to be inspired of God, and its authority and place in theological and spiritual judgments in the Church. In a day where biblical scholarship has exploded, we will also take a brief look at modern biblical criticism, and wrestle with its claims as it relates to our study of Scripture today.

In our second lesson, *Biblical Hermeneutics: The Three-Step Model*, we will introduce an effective method of biblical interpretation designed to help you approach your study of Scripture so as to bridge the gap between our ancient and contemporary worlds. We call it the Three-Step Model: understand the original audience, discover general principles, and make applications to life. In this lesson, too, we will actually examine a passage of Scripture employing this model, looking at a passage in Paul's letter to the Corinthians, in his first epistle, 9.1-14. Using the framework found in your Keys to Bible Interpretation appendix, we will canvass this great text of Scripture looking specifically at how a deliberate, careful, and prayerful approach can yield great knowledge and encouragement to us as we strive to understand God's will through his holy Word.

We focus upon the types of literature found in the Bible and how to interpret them in our third lesson entitled *Biblical Literature: Interpreting the Genres of the Bible*. We will define and outline the concept of genres (pronounced JOHN-ruhs) in biblical

interpretation, laying out an overview of the idea, and giving a few basic assumptions of this kind of special hermeneutics. We will then discuss various forms of biblical genres, but will give special attention to two types of literature which represent the vast majority of the actual material in the Bible, narrative and prophetic. We will give brief but meaty discussions of both narrative study (i.e., story theology) as well as prophetic and apocalyptic literature, showing how attention to genres can help us better interpret Scripture.

Finally, we will close our module study with our fourth lesson, *Biblical Studies: Using Study Tools in Bible Study*. Here we will explore the kind of solid scholarly reference tools available to us as we attempt to understand the meaning of a biblical text. The student of the Bible has access today to many remarkable tools, both written and software, all which can help him or her gain a mastery of the Word. We will concentrate first on the basic tools for solid biblical interpretation: a good translation of Scripture, Hebrew and Greek aids, a Bible dictionary, a concordance, and exegetical commentaries. We will also consider additional tools that may enrich our study of Scripture. These will include cross-reference aids, topical Bibles, cross-reference Bibles, and topical concordances. We will also discuss aids which focus on history and customs of the Bible: Bible dictionaries, Bible encyclopedias, atlases, and other related reference works. Finally, we will briefly look at Bible handbooks, study Bibles, and other helps, and conclude our discussion with the use of Bible commentaries, and the role of tools in general as you interpret your Bible for devotion, preaching, and teaching.

The Bible's own remarkable claim of its transforming power ought to be reason enough to challenge us to master the Word of God. "All Scripture is breathed out by God and profitable for teaching, for reproof, for correction, and for training in righteousness, that the man of God may be competent, equipped for every good work" (2 Tim. 3.16-17). The God-breathed Word of God in the words of humankind is sufficient to enrich us, delight us, and make us competent and equipped for every good work. Truly, the Word of God cannot be broken, will always accomplish its purpose, and will ensure the person of God enjoys good success in all they do to advance the Kingdom of God wherever they are (John 10.35; Isa. 55.8-11; Josh. 1.8).

Objectives for *Capstone* Module 5, Bible Interpretation

*Objectives for Lesson 1
Biblical Inspiration:
The Origins and
Authority of the Bible*

After your reading, study, discussion, and application of the materials in this lesson, you will be able to:

1. Define hermeneutics as the discipline and branch of knowledge which focuses on interpretation, especially the interpretation of texts.

2. Give evidence that the Bible must be interpreted as a divine and human book, with both dimensions to appreciate and fully understand the nature of Scripture.

3. Lay out the critical presuppositions that historically orthodox Christians have believed about the nature of Scripture including their divine origin, Scripture interpreting Scripture, the idea of progressive revelation, the Christ-centered nature of Scripture, and the necessity of the Holy Spirit to understand God's Word.

4. Give an overview of the *Three-Step Model* of biblical interpretation which includes understanding the original situation, discovering biblical principles, and applying the meaning of Scripture to our lives.

5. Recite the various elements involved in preparing the heart for biblical interpretation, including the need for humility and prayer, diligence and determination, and rigorous engagement of the Bible as a workman.

6. Demonstrate a knowledge of the kinds of roles we ought to adopt as we prepare our mind for serious biblical interpretation including the role of an explorer, the role of a detective, and the role of a scientist – seeking the Word diligently, following up on clues, and weighing the evidence carefully before making judgments.

7. Exhibit from Scripture its claim that the Bible is both inspired by God as well as written by human authors.

8. Demonstrate and distinguish between the various theories of inspiration which seek to explain how and in what way the Scriptures can be inspired by the Holy Spirit and also be influenced by human authors.

9. Present carefully the rationale and history of biblical criticism, and how this modern discipline seeks to trace the origins of the Scriptures from the original events spoken of in the Bible to the actual reports of those happenings recorded in the canonical books of Scripture.

*Teaching Objectives for
Capstone, by Module*

10. Give a brief explanation, including the benefits and problems associated with the major subsections of modern biblical criticism, including form, source, linguistic, textual, literary, canonical, redaction, and historical criticisms, as well as translation studies.

*Objectives for Lesson 2
Biblical Hermeneutics:
The Three-Step Model*

After your reading, study, discussion, and application of the materials in this lesson, you will be able to:

1. Give evidence to show how the *Three-Step Model* is an effective method of biblical interpretation designed to help us understand the truth of Scripture and bridge the gap between our ancient and contemporary worlds.

2. Provide a definition of the *Three-Step Model* of biblical interpretation, and recite it without aids: "to so understand the meaning of the original situation that we may discover general principles of truth which may be applied in our personal lives in the Spirit's freedom."

3. Highlight the ways in which all study of the Word of God must unfold the meaning and message of God's final revelation to us in the person and work of Jesus Christ.

4. Demonstrate your knowledge of how the *Three-Step Model* corresponds to the grammatical-historical method of Scripture interpretation, which affirms the plain sense of its meaning, God's progressive revelation in Christ, the unity of the Bible, and the integrity of the text.

5. Reproduce the critical reasons for each step in the *Three-Step Model*, including why each is necessary, the difficulties associated with each, the key attitude required in each step, the activities associated with each one, as well as an example of each step in Scripture.

6. Distinguish between the kinds of attitudes necessary for each phase of study in the *Three-Step Model*: humility, thoroughness, and liberty for each of the phases respectively.

7. Reproduce an example of the *Three-Step Model* using 1 Corinthians 9.1-4 as a case study of its application, employing each step of the method practically as you go through the text.

8. See how the study of a particular passage must be done in light of the message of the entire chapter, section, book of the Bible, and ultimately, in light of the Bible's message to us in Christ.

9. Show through personal use of *Three-Step Model* how each of the key stages focuses on the text in such a way as to credibly discern its purpose of illumination of the text's meaning, and the transformation of our lives through the joy of discovering biblical principles for life.

10. Discern the key elements, cautions, and procedures in investigating the original situation of the text, discovering biblical principles, and making correct applications of the Scripture's teaching to your life.

Objectives for Lesson 3 Biblical Literature: Interpreting the Genres of the Bible

Teaching Objectives for Capstone, by Module

After your reading, study, discussion, and application of the materials in this lesson, you will be able to:

1. Define the term "genre" and its role in biblical interpretation, i.e., that particular kind of literary form which communicates truth and must be interpreted according to the rules of that form.

2. Analyze the basic assumptions of genre study of the Scriptures that make it both an essential and worthwhile discipline, including the Bible as a book of literature, as a book which pays attention to literary rules and principles, and the way in which God employed human literary strategies to communicate his Word.

3. Lay out some of the more important forms of biblical genre, including the use of narrative (both historical and imaginative), the Law (legal writings), epistles (letters), prophecy, wisdom literature (proverbs, monologues, riddles, fables, parables, allegories, etc.), and poetry.

4. Provide the purposes of biblical genres, including to fulfill a particular need, to deepen our understanding of our fundamental human experience, to allow us to image reality in its most concrete from, to display the artistry of the biblical authors as led by the Spirit, and to reveal the richness of the mystery of God and his work in the world.

5. Give evidence of the major benefits of careful genre study, including how it will empower us to discover the author's original intention, edify our souls, enrich our appreciation of life, entertain us, and enlighten our minds as we rigorously pursue the meaning of God in the particular form of literature we are exploring.

6. Define the term "special hermeneutics," i.e., the rules and procedures that enable us to interpret the literary forms of the Bible.

7. Demonstrate a knowledge of narrative form in literature, and the general assumptions of story theology, which include God's providing a record of his work in the story accounts of the Bible, that all theology is reflection on the stories of the Bible, that the stories that refer to historical accounts in Scripture are reliable and accurate, that the stories are written with artistic skill and mastery, that we can encounter God in the story text, and that God often provides his own commentary on the meaning of the biblical story accounts.

8. Lay out the key propositions of story theology: that stories introduce us to sacramental presences, they are more important than facts, they are normative for the Christian community, that Christian traditions evolve and define themselves by stories, and that stories precede and produce community, censure and accountability, and produce theology, ritual, and sacrament. They are history.

9. Provide and explain the general elements of narrative in Scripture, including the setting, characters, author's point of view, plot, and theme of the story.

10. Explain the general principles underlying prophecy as a genre of biblical interpretation, including how prophecy offers truth about God and the universe, that it flows from the Spirit and is a specific mode of revelation from God which manifests itself in personal and literary modes.

11. Define the elements of apocalyptic literature as a biblical genre, including its definition, the types of apocalyptic in the Bible (i.e., Daniel and Revelation), the two main types of Jewish apocalypses, and the most distinctly apocalyptic book in Scripture, the book of Revelation.

12. Reproduce the three interpretive principles for the prophetic and apocalyptic genres of Scripture: the need to focus on the person of Jesus Christ, to refer the prophetic messages to the call of the Kingdom of God, and to emphasize the fulfillment of God's sovereign purposes even in the face of evil, suffering and injustice.

*Objectives for Lesson 4
Biblical Studies:
Using Study Tools
in Bible Study*

After your reading, study, discussion, and application of the materials in this lesson, you will be able to:

1. Identify and understand the role of scholarly tools in our attempt to understand the meaning of the text.

2. Recite the purpose of using tools in biblical interpretation, including their ability to help us bridge the various gaps

between the biblical world and our own contemporary world, to take advantage of the explosion of remarkable tools that have emerged in our day, and their value in helping us be more faithful to the Word of God by enabling us to reconstruct their meaning in its original context.

3. Recognize and explain what are considered the basic and elemental tools to all biblical interpretation including a good translation of the Bible, Greek and Hebrew lexicons keyed to the Strong's numbering system, a solid Bible dictionary, a concordance, and credible exegetical commentaries which focus on the biblical meanings of the passage.

4. Recognize and explain those tools which can provide additional insight into the meaning of biblical texts, including several different translations of the Bible, a Bible atlas and handbook, a topical Bible, a dictionary of theology, and finally theological commentaries which focus on the larger theological context of the passage.

5. Explain the three languages in which the Bible was written (Hebrew, Aramaic, and Greek), and identify the particular challenges associated with making good translations, including the difficulties of word usage, cultural distinctions, contextual considerations, and differences among the translators themselves.

6. Explain the meaning of concordances, lexicons, dictionaries, and commentaries, and show how to use the particular tools in the context of biblical interpretation, as well as offer a suggestion for each that could enhance our exegesis of Scripture.

7. Define the role of cross-reference aids in biblical exegesis (e.g., topical bibles, cross-reference bibles, and topical guides and concordances), define their benefits for study, and lay out some of the major cautions we should be aware of when we use such tools.

8. Lay out the reasons for employing Bible dictionaries, encyclopedias, atlases, and handbooks dealing with customs and history, identifying the benefits of such tools, as well as the caution of what wrong use or over-reliance on them can produce in our own interpretation.

9. Cite the definition, benefits, and cautions associated with the use of Bible handbooks, study Bibles, and guides to biblical imagery, demonstrating their usefulness and our caution in employing them in our study.

Teaching Objectives for Capstone, by Module

10. Outline the major kinds of commentaries that exist as aids to our interpretation (i.e., devotional, doctrinal, exegetical, and homiletic), and carefully articulate the major benefits and cautions associated with their use.

11. Summarize the "best use" protocol for using extra-biblical tools in our biblical interpretation, including our attempt to help us bridge the gap between the two worlds of the text and our contemporary world.

12. Articulate the limits of the tools, i.e., how in the final analysis, all claims are to be rigorously tested against the claims of the Scriptures themselves, and nothing is to be accepted that is found to contradict the plain confession of the Scriptures about the person of Christ and his work of redemption.

Module Description

Capstone **Module 6 – God the Father**

The study of the person of our God, the Father Almighty, is one of the most important and richest of all studies in the Word of God. It affects every part of our discipleship, worship, and ministry; truly, as our Lord Jesus said, "And this is eternal life, that they know you the only true God, and Jesus Christ whom you have sent," (John 17.3).

In our first lesson, *Prolegomena: The Doctrine of God and the Advance of the Kingdom*, we will briefly explore the first things, the *prolegomena*, which undergirds a study of theology, looking at the necessity of God revealing himself to us. We will study the concepts of general and special revelation, and carefully explore the importance of studying the doctrine of God in terms of God's immanence, i.e., his present and active involvement in creation, as well as his transcendence, God's infinite nature and unknowableness.

In our second lesson, *God as Creator: The Providence of God*, we will examine God's supreme authority and providence over all creation and history. God works all things according to his will. The Father Almighty is sovereign over all, the source of all life, and the Sustainer of all through his Son, Jesus Christ. We will also explore how God's providence is expressed in his preservation and governance of all things, and see how a solid, biblical understanding of God's providence resolves major modern errors in philosophy and theology, namely, pantheism, deism, fatalism, and chance.

We take a slightly different turn in our third lesson, *The Triune God: The Greatness of God*. We will look at the biblical evidence for the Trinity, God's triune personhood. The Scriptures teach that there is only one God, and yet this same God reveals himself as God the Father, Son, and Holy Spirit. The members of the Trinity are one, diverse and equal, the one true God, Father, Son, and Holy Spirit. After examining the Trinity, we will then briefly examine the attributes of God's greatness: his spirituality, his life, his personality, his infinite character, and his unchanging essence.

Finally, in lesson four we turn our attention to *God as Father: The Goodness of God*. Here we will discover God's marvelous goodness demonstrated in his moral attributes of his perfect moral purity, absolute integrity, and unbounded love. And, we close our module with a look at the goodness and severity of God, exploring the relationship between God's goodness and severity, his love and justice.

Teaching Objectives for Capstone, by Module

Truly, our God the Father Almighty is the one, true, and glorious God of heaven. Knowing him better will equip us to represent him with honor as his servants. May God bless you as you explore the untold riches of Scripture regarding our great and mighty God!

Objectives for *Capstone* Module 6, God the Father

Teaching Objectives for Capstone, by Module

Objectives for Lesson 1 Prolegomena: The Doctrine of God and the Advance of the Kingdom

After your reading, study, discussion, and application of the materials in this lesson, you will be able to:

1. Recite the first things, the *prolegomena*, associated with the formal study of the doctrine of God the Father, or *theology proper*.
2. Give reasons why is it critically important for God to reveal himself to us *before* we can know him.
3. Highlight the truths connected to *general revelation*, the means by which God reveals himself to all people everywhere, and *special revelation* where God reveals himself to particular human beings at particular times and places.
4. Show how the *Nicene Creed* provides a clear statement of the *greatness* of the one true God, the God and Father of our Lord Jesus Christ.
5. Give evidence of God's *immanence* (i.e., God's present and active involvement in creation) and his *transcendence* (God's infinite nature and unknowableness).
6. Provide an explanation of the meaning of the *attributes of God*, their problem and purpose, as well as their nature and classification.

Objectives for Lesson 2 God as Creator: The Providence of God

After your reading, study, discussion, and application of the materials in this lesson, you will be able to:

1. Explain how God's supreme authority and providence is shown over all creation and history.
2. Show how "providence" means that "God works out his sovereign will in the universe whereby all events are disposed by him to fulfill his purposes for himself and his creation for good."
3. Use the Scriptures to show how the Father is Sovereign over all, the Source of all, and the Sustainer of all through his Son, Jesus Christ. All things are disposed to sync up with his will for himself, so he can receive glory for all things.

4. Demonstrate how God's special work of providence is revealed in his preservation and governance of all things.
5. Make clear how many of the errors associated with modern philosophy and religion come from misunderstanding the providence of God over creation and history.
6. Show an understanding of the key elements of preservation and governance, along with God's intent to restore creation at Christ's return.
7. Provide a brief explanation of how the providence of God resolves some of the modern errors of philosophy and theology, namely, pantheism, deism, fatalism, and chance.

Objectives for Lesson 3
The Triune God:
The Greatness of God

After your reading, study, discussion, and application of the materials in this lesson, you will be able to:

1. Show from Scripture a general outline of the Bible's teaching about the doctrine of the *Trinity*, God's triune personhood.
2. Explain that the Bible teaches us both that there is only one God, and yet this same God reveals himself as God the Father, Son, and Holy Spirit.
3. Demonstrate from the Scriptures how God is spoken of as one God yet also as *plural*, that is, more than one person, which speaks of the Father, the Son, and the Holy Spirit as being persons within the Godhead.
4. Recite some of the major historical understandings of the Trinity.
5. Recognize the meaning of God's trinitarian nature, affirming that the members of the Trinity are one, diverse, and equal, the one true God, Father, Son, and Holy Spirit.
6. Show an understanding of the various aspects of the Father's greatness, i.e., his spirituality, his life, his personality, his infinite character, and his unchanging essence.

Objectives for Lesson 4
God as Father:
The Goodness of God

After your reading, study, discussion, and application of the materials in this lesson, you will be able to:

1. Provide an outline of God's marvelous goodness expressed in his moral attributes of his perfect moral purity, absolute integrity, and unbounded love.
2. Show how God's perfect moral purity is demonstrated through his holiness, righteousness, and justice.
3. Clarify those qualities associated with God's integrity, i.e., his genuineness, veracity, and faithfulness.

4. Recite an overview of the attributes associated with the love of God, his benevolence, grace, mercy, and persistence.
5. Detail the biblical basis for the wrath of God as a moral quality usually associated with God's severity.
6. Explain the relationship between God's goodness and severity, his love and justice.
7. Express the need for an understanding of God's attributes and nature that prevents any confusion or conflict about the Lord and his actions.

Module Description

Capstone Module 7 – Foundations of Christian Leadership

The leaders of the Church of God are his precious gift to his people throughout the ages. The evidence that Jesus loves his people dearly is that he has granted unto them apostles, prophets, evangelists, pastors and teachers to equip his people to represent the Kingdom of God in this fallen and soon-to end world (Eph. 4.9-16). This module highlights the various roles and offices associated with this high and important task in the Kingdom of God.

To begin with, in Lesson 1, *The Christian Leader as Deacon (Diakonoi)* we will probe the foundations of Christian leadership as it relates to the offices and functions of leadership in the local church. We will explore the ministry of deacons, or, in the Greek, *diakonoi*, examining its meaning in the Greek NT, and its probable origins in the Jewish synagogue. We will also look at the diaconate, or ministry of deacons, and comment on the authority and functions of this ministry through three models of the Deacon's role: as a servant, as a steward, and as an assistant.

Next, in our second lesson, *The Christian Leader as Elder (Presbyteroi)* we will trace the notion of elder from its OT root in the tribal system and synagogue, to the Sanhedrin, and to the NT Church. We'll then give careful consideration to the calling of and the criteria for becoming an elder in the NT Church, and will complete our brief study by examining several analogies to help us understand the nature of biblical eldership; that of an overseer, a father or parent, a colleague or team member, and finally a representative. We will consider these in order to discover new ways we can put the principles of eldership into practice in our own lives and ministries.

In Lesson 3, *The Christian Leader as Pastor (Poimenes)*, we will outline the biblical context of the idea of the pastorate, starting with the definition of the Greek term for pastoring, and tracing historically the development of the idea of a formal office of the pastorate. We will then highlight the calling and the criteria for representing God as an undershepherd of the flock. We will close our section with a discussion of pastoral authority, along with a look at three biblical models and analogies of pastoral care: that of a nurturer and care giver, a protector and guardian, and a leader of the flock of God.

Finally, in Lesson 4, *The Christian Leader as Bishop (Episkopoi)*, we will provide a broad definition and overview to this dynamic

Teaching Objectives for Capstone, by Module

Objectives for Lesson 1 The Christian Leader as Deacon: Diakonoi

concept of bishop or overseer. Beginning with a consideration of the NT language, we will trace its probable context from the council of elders in Jewish rulership, including the development of the concept, through the history of the Church. After considering the calling and criteria of the bishop's office, we will examine the concept of bishop through the images of supervisor, apostle, and spiritual director. We hope our study will show how the very nature of Christian leadership and Christian community demands bishop-level oversight and relationship which goes beyond just the local body itself.

It is hard to imagine a more wonderful gift to an assembly or group of assemblies than godly, Christlike leadership, true shepherds who guard and protect the flock of God. May God use this study to inspire you to nurture and care for his people, to emulate the Good Shepherd who laid down his life for his sheep.

Objectives for *Capstone* Module 7, Foundations of Christian Leadership

After your reading, study, discussion, and application of the materials in this lesson, you will be able to:

1. Articulate the foundations of Christian leadership as it relates to the offices and functions of leadership in the local church (deacons, elders, pastors, and bishops).
2. Define one of the foundations of Christian leadership from the standpoint of the ministry of deacons, or, in the Greek, *diakonoi*, giving evidence of the meanings of the term *diakonoi* in the Greek NT.
3. Trace the origins and development of the role of the deacon from its parallel role in the Jewish synagogue, the *hazzan*.
4. Lay out clearly the key issues related to the call to the diaconate, or ministry of deacons, and the various biblical criteria and qualifications connected to being a deacon in the Church of God.
5. Outline the authority of the deacon's office in both Scripture and history, and elaborate on some of the functions of this important ministry among the people of God.
6. Unpack the data on three images or models of the deacon's role, i.e., the roles of servant, steward, and assistant.
7. Define the kinds of issues and concepts involved in equipping deacons for urban congregations, as well as the various principles and practices associated with the office.

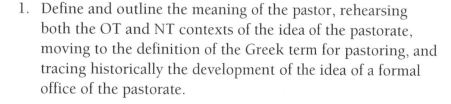

8. Recognize the importance of the diaconate for urban congregations, both in terms of meeting practical needs as well as dividing the labor amongst the leaders to ensure that the congregation's full priorities are not neglected.

Objectives for Lesson 2
The Christian Leader
as Elder: Presbyteroi

After your reading, study, discussion, and application of the materials in this lesson, you will be able to:

1. Recite the meaning of the Greek term *presbyteros* as the translated term for elder in the NT.
2. Narrate the evolution of the concept *elder* from its OT roots in the tribal system of Israel, the development of the concept in the synagogue, to its usage as an official position in the Sanhedrin, and finally to the NT Church.
3. Provide a clear record of the elements involved in the calling of NT elders, as well as the biblical qualifications associated with becoming an elder in the Church.
4. Lay out critically the biblical authority and responsibilities connected with the faithful fulfillment of the office of serving as an elder in the body, and speak of the implications of this authority and responsibility in the affairs of Christian community today.
5. Recreate from memory the key analogies given in Scripture of the *Christian Leader as Elder (Presbyter)*: the Christian elder is imaged as an overseer of the affairs of the community, a father or parent who heads the spiritual family of the Lord, a colleague or team member who contributes to the council of elders in their role as leaders of the congregation, and finally as a representative both of the Lord and the people in the community.
6. Articulate the major assumptions and issues needed to understand the significance of elders for urban congregations, and suggest practical ways in which we can both select and equip elders for our churches in the city.

Objectives for Lesson 3
The Christian Leader
as Pastor: Poimenes

After your reading, study, discussion, and application of the materials in this lesson, you will be able to:

1. Define and outline the meaning of the pastor, rehearsing both the OT and NT contexts of the idea of the pastorate, moving to the definition of the Greek term for pastoring, and tracing historically the development of the idea of a formal office of the pastorate.

2. Detail both the calling of individuals to the pastorate, and highlight the criteria for representing God as an undershepherd of the flock.

3. Lay out the NT contours of the authority and role of the pastor viewed through the lens of the various forms of church government (episcopal, monarchical, and congregational).

4. Recite the functions of the godly biblical pastor as outlined in the NT and Church history.

5. Elaborate the three biblical models and analogies of what a pastor does in relationship to the flock of God, i.e., the pastor as nurturer and care giver, as protector and guardian, and as leader of the flock of God.

6. Give evidence of the particular perils and promise for fulfilling the pastoral role in the inner city, as well as the specific ways we may equip urban pastors for their important duty.

7. Discuss some of the more important principles in the practice of pastoring the urban congregation, as well as the wonderful promises associated with the pastoring of the flock of God.

*Objectives for Lesson 4
The Christian Leader
as Bishop: Episkopoi*

After your reading, study, discussion, and application of the materials in this lesson, you will be able to:

1. Recite the meanings of the term *episkopos* (i.e., bishop) with the Septuagint, its usages in the classic Greek, and within the New Testament itself.

2. Articulate how and in what ways the terms for "pastor," "elder," and "bishop" all refer to the same office, with emphases on different roles and responsibilities of Christian leadership in the Church.

3. Outline possible origins and the development of the office of the bishop through the council of elders in Jewish rulership where an elder could be recognized as one to speak on behalf of and represent the entire council of elders.

4. Elaborate how in the history of the church the office of the bishop expanded to mean an appointed or elected individual given charge over a number of pastors or groups of congregations in a given context.

5. Define both the calling and criteria of the bishop, from the biblical qualifications in 1 Timothy 3 and Titus 1, as well as the example of Jesus.

6. Detail how bishops were selected, and then provide the nature of the bishop's authority and function to give oversight, including the bishop's expanded authority as "pastor of pastors," as well as one given the responsibility to oversee *all the churches* within his area of responsibility.

7. Lay out how all traditions have some version of the *function* of a bishop even though they may not have any *nomenclature* (language, categories) of the bishop. All churches require ongoing oversight and supervision.

8. Reproduce the three biblical images of the role of the bishop: as supervisor, as apostle, and as spiritual director.

9. Show how the bishop as supervisor functions as a super-intendent, coordinating and organizing the outreach, personnel, and resources of churches under his/her care to make maximum impact for the Church's edification and the Kingdom's advancement.

10. Specify the ways in which a bishop functions as an apostle, charged with the ongoing care of new churches and their leaders, doing all they can to ensure the protection, edification and development of the them.

11. Give evidence how the bishop functions as a spiritual director, providing challenge and encouragement to budding ministries and churches as they mature in Christ.

12. Sketch out carefully the importance of pastoral and church association, both as it relates *regionally* through the locale church, and through affinity and shared identity.

13. Argue for the role of the bishop-level oversight being given to urban churches in association with each other, and how that ministry might flesh itself out among urban congregations.

14. Review the blessing, benefit, and reward of faithful obedience to the call of the Christian leader as bishop, with the prospect of exercising authority in the Kingdom of God.

Teaching Objectives for Capstone, by Module

Teaching Objectives for Capstone, by Module

Module Description

Capstone **Module 8 – Evangelism and Spiritual Warfare**

Evangelism is proclaiming and demonstrating to the world that God has visited the world in the person of Jesus of Nazareth, and that this visitation is now accompanied by liberation from the devil and from the effects of sin! To evangelize is to prophesy deliverance in Messiah Jesus.

The lessons of this module are organized to provide you with a solid overview of the critical issues arising from a biblical grasp of evangelism and spiritual warfare. The first lesson, *Spiritual Warfare: Binding of the Strong Man*, outlines the war of the universe that was caused by the disobedience of the devil and humankind. God's good creation was made subject to demonic powers and death, and human-kind is now enslaved by selfishness, disease, alienation, and death. Through the life, death, and resurrection of Jesus Christ, believers are delivered from Satan's dominion, as well as from the effects of the Curse through the power of the Spirit. Evangelism is proclaiming God's deliverance through Jesus Christ to the entire world in the power of the Holy Spirit.

Lesson two deals with *Evangelism: The Content of the Good News of the Kingdom*. Evangelism proclaims and demonstrates God's deliverance in Christ through word as well as love and service to others. This ministry focuses on Christ; evangelism is nothing less than communicating the person and work of Jesus Christ! The Nicene Creed offers a clear useful, and powerful outline of the critical truths associated with Jesus' incarnation, passion, resurrection, ascension, and Second Coming. If we master these truths, we can clearly communicate them in our urban neighborhoods.

Our next lesson, *Evangelism: Methods to Reach the Urban Community*, reveals how evangelism is not only what we say but who we are and what we do. To speak persuasively of the Lord Jesus in our communities, our credibility must be rooted in solid character and genuine spirituality. We will look at communication methods by which to share the Good News, and the importance of preparation for effective urban evangelism through intercessory prayer. We will look at personal soul winning and sharing one's testimony, along with the importance of evangelism through public preaching and discourse. We will also consider the concept of the household network, or *oikos* in urban evangelism.

Finally in lesson four, *Follow-up and Incorporation*, we will explore the idea of conserving the fruit of our evangelism by following up new converts, that act of "incorporating new converts into the family of God so they can be equipped to grow in Christ and use their gifts for ministry." We will look at how the apostles nurtured new converts, and study how we can use the same steps to bring new converts into a local assembly of believers, on the road to spiritual maturity and fruitfulness.

Our Lord Jesus desires that we bear much fruit to the glory and praise of God (John 15.8-16). May the Lord bless your study of his Word so you can join the harvest workers in gathering the fruit of the Lord's own salvation, to the Father's glory!

Objectives for *Capstone* Module 8, Evangelism and Spiritual Warfare

*Objectives for Lesson 1
Spiritual Warfare:
Binding of the
Strong Man*

After your reading, study, discussion, and application of the materials in this lesson, you will be able to:

1. Describe carefully the truths surrounding the voluntary rebellion and disobedience of the devil and the first human pair, and how the universe as a result of this disobedience has been thrown into spiritual war.
2. Show from the Scriptures that although God made the world good, because of the Fall, demonic powers were unleashed in the world, creation was made subject to corruption and death and humankind is now enslaved, subject to disease, death, alienation, and selfishness.
3. Demonstrate from the Bible that salvation essentially is God's deliverance of humankind and creation through the power of the Spirit from the power and effects of sin, from Satan's dominion and tyranny and the fear of death, as well as from the effects of the Curse and sin.
4. Communicate clearly how evangelism is proclaiming God's promised and prophesied deliverance through Jesus Christ to the entire world in the power of the Holy Spirit.

*Objectives for Lesson 2
Evangelism: The
Content of the Good
News of the Kingdom*

After your reading, study, discussion, and application of the materials in this lesson, you will be able to:

1. Recite some of the various biblical terms in the New Testament describing the good news of the Gospel.

2. Articulate how evangelism is seen as proclaiming the message of salvation in Christ as well as demonstrating that message through our love and service to others.
3. Explain Romans 10.9-10 as a clear, simple, and powerful outline of the message of the Gospel.
4. Show clearly how in order to win others to Jesus and train them to do the same, we simply must know the truth concerning Jesus Christ.
5. Detail how evangelism is telling people of the person and work of Jesus Christ, who he is and what he did as the heart of our faith and of the Gospel.
6. Highlight the main points of the Nicene Creed regarding Jesus' incarnation, passion, resurrection, ascension, and Second Coming.
7. Give to others through a biblical use of the Creed a running story of the Gospel message which can be adapted as we share the message in our communities.

*Objectives for Lesson 3
Evangelism:
Methods to Reach
the Urban Community*

After your reading, study, discussion, and application of the materials in this lesson, you will be able to:

1. Share with others the kind of lifestyle and conduct we as leaders must adopt in order to touch our urban communities.
2. Show from Scripture how evangelism is not only what we say but who we are and what we do (i.e., evangelism must be rooted in solid character and genuine spirituality).
3. Recite what kind and quality of spirituality we need to have to be a credible witness to God's grace in Christ (through our walk with God, our relationship with our families, and with outsiders).
4. Demonstrate with Scripture the importance of a lived faith, of being zealous to do good works, especially on behalf of those who are poor and most vulnerable.
5. See how we can prepare for effective evangelism through prevailing intercessory prayer.
6. State from the Bible the importance of the roles of personal soul-winning, public preaching, and discourse in evangelism.
7. Give an overview of the importance of the concept of the household network or *oikos* in urban evangelism.

*Objectives for Lesson 4
Follow-Up and
Incorporation*

After your reading, study, discussion, and application of the materials in this lesson, you will be able to:

1. Defend the idea that the key to successful evangelism is following up new Christians by incorporating them into a local assembly of believers as quickly as possible.
2. Provide a biblical definition of follow-up and incorporation of new believers in the Church as "incorporating new converts into the family of God so they can be equipped to grow in Christ and use their gifts for ministry."
3. Recite the reasons for follow-up: follow-up of new believers is critical because new Christians are vulnerable to attack from the enemy, they need to be reoriented to their new faith in Christ, and they need immediate parental care as little newborns in Christ.
4. Give the five biblical methods of apostolic follow-up: prevailing prayer, immediate personal contact with the new believers, sending representatives for encouragement and challenge, regular personal correspondence, and appointing leaders over them.
5. Lay out the biblical rationale for baptism and membership with a local body as a means of publicly testifying of their new-found faith.
6. Lay out the biblical rationale for baptism and membership with a local body as a means of publicly testifying of their new-found faith.

Teaching Objectives for Capstone, by Module

Module Description

***Capstone* Module 9 – Old Testament Witness to Christ and His Kingdom**

The Spirit-breathed Scripture is anchored on the witness of Jesus of Nazareth. He and he alone provides unity, continuity, and coherence to both the Old and New Testaments, and no one can claim a holistic or accurate view of the Bible without him being central in all phases of exegesis. He is the Bible's theme (John 5.39-40). In this module we trace some of the significant markers of the OT's witness to Messiah, and see how those markers provide us with a strong handle on the meaning of the entirety of Scripture.

In our first lesson, *The Promise Given*, we will examine the relationship of the Old Testament to the New Testament through the idea of progressive revelation. We will look at the complimentary connections which exist in the OT and NT as they relate to the person of Christ and his Kingdom, and consider the unique motif of promise and fulfillment, and how this integrates and makes one the teaching of Scripture on the person of Jesus Christ. This unity of truth is seen in God's marvelous promise to send a redeemer to humanity through whom God's enemy would be destroyed, and humankind would be redeemed. In the *protoevangelium* (i.e., the first telling of the Gospel in Genesis 3.15), through the covenant promise of Abraham and its extensions we see how the Messianic hope is the unifying principle of the OT and the joyous fulfillment of the New, all finding their climax in the person of Jesus Christ. He is both the seed of the woman and the seed of Abraham.

In lesson two, *The Promise Clarified*, we explore the biblical typology that reveals how the experience of Israel, the descendants of Abraham and the people of God, represent an analogy where we can understand the larger relationship of God with all of the redeemed through Jesus Christ. We will look at the roles of types and analogies in our study of Scripture, and explore four distinct moments within Israel's history which can help us understand the OT essentially as a witness to Christ and his kingdom reign (i.e., the Exodus, the conquest of Canaan, the entering into the Promised Land, and the restoration of Israel from the Babylonian Captivity). In this lesson we will also see further how the OT provides witness to Christ in the OT sacrificial system. Jesus of Nazareth is the substance and fulfillment of the Tabernacle, the Levitical Priesthood, the Temple sacrifices, and the feasts and festivals of Israel. In a real way, all of these personages, events, and institutions prefigure the person and work of Jesus Christ as the fulfillment of God's promise to Abraham.

Lesson three focuses on *The Promise Personalized*, whose aim is to see how many of the character types in the OT point to and illustrate the ministry of Jesus Christ in the NT. We will explore the types in the OT which point to Jesus' roles as a prophet, priest, and king, considering Moses as a type of Christ in his prophetic role, Melchizedek as a type of Christ in his priestly order, and David as a type of Christ in his role as King of God's people. We will also look at several cases of character types which deserve special mention because of their significance in understanding Christ's role as head of humanity, redeemer of his kinsmen, and warrior in God's conquest. These characters represent the person of Adam, Joseph, and Joshua. In these figures the promise of God for redemption and restoration are made personal and visible for all to see.

Finally, we will close our module with lesson four, *The Promise Universalized*. Here we will consider the nature and scope of OT Messianic prophecy as it relates to providing us with a clear OT witness to Christ and his Kingdom. We will provide the rationale of OT Messianic prophecy, and quickly outline the OT Messianic predictions which are repeated in the NT, specifically predictions fulfilled in Jesus Christ concerning his birth, his person and life, his death, his resurrection, and coming glory. We will also consider the significant issue of how God has extended the promise and blessings of Abraham, a promise extended in the apostles' teaching, to include all peoples. We will also look carefully at the OT predictions about the Messiah in Acts and the Epistles, and a picture will emerge for us–that God Almighty, the true and living God, has not only fulfilled his promise for salvation to Abraham, but he has also included Gentiles in that salvation.

No greater work can be done on earth than becoming a workman or work woman of the Lord in regard to his sacred text: "Do your best to present yourself to God as one approved, a worker who has no need to be ashamed, rightly handling the word of truth" (2 Tim. 2.15). The accurate handling of the text demands a Christo-centric orientation that discovers and cherishes the OT witness to Jesus Christ. My sincere desire is that the Holy Spirit will reveal to you the glory and majesty of the picture of Jesus in the OT text, and that this picture will transform us, even as Paul suggests: "And we all, with unveiled face, beholding the glory of the Lord, are being transformed into the same image from one degree of glory to another. For this comes from the Lord who is the Spirit" (2 Cor. 3.18).

Teaching Objectives for Capstone, by Module

Objectives for Lesson 1
The Promise Given

Objectives for *Capstone* Module 9, The Old Testament Witness to Christ and His Kingdom

After your reading, study, discussion, and application of the materials in this lesson, you will be able to:

1. Define the relationship of the Old Testament to the New Testament through the idea of *progressive revelation*, which affirms that God has revealed himself progressively and definitively throughout the history of his people, and finally through Jesus Christ.

2. Lay out the various aspects of progressive revelation, including God's continuous revelation of himself to us through creation, through specific manifestations and occasions, and in these last days through his Son

3. Show how the OT explains and reveals the NT through the person of Christ, and how both testaments focus upon God's final and full revelation of himself in Jesus Christ and his kingdom reign.

4. Reproduce Augustine's epigram (saying) on the relationship between the two testaments: "In the OT the NT lies hidden; in the NT the OT stands revealed."

5. Highlight the complimentary concepts which connect and explain the relationship of the Old and New Testaments, including the OT providing the introduction to the NT's conclusion about Christ, the OT as anticipation of Christ and the NT as its climax, the OT as the shadow (prefiguring) of the person and work of Christ and the NT as the embodiment of those figures, the OT as the ineffective former revelation of God's salvation and the NT revelation in Christ as the consummated latter, and the OT as the particularized form of God's salvation universalized to all nations in the NT.

6. Lay out the definition and elements of the *promise and fulfillment* motif in OT revelation, which affirms the promise of God for his own chosen one to redeem humankind and to destroy the devil's work, a promise fulfilled in the person of Jesus of Nazareth.

7. Identify the central texts in Scripture which affirm how the OT's work is to provide a compelling and definitive witness to the person of Messiah fulfilled in the person of Jesus Christ (cf. Luke 22.25-27, 44-48; Matt. 5.17-18; John 1.45; 5.39-40; Heb. 10.5-10 with Ps. 40.6-8).

8. Describe the implications of the *promise-fulfillment* motif for OT study, especially the way in which it suggests that a clear picture of Messiah can be seen in the history of the patriarchs, the nation of Israel, the Messianic prophecies, and the moral standards of the Law.

9. List the ways in which the *promise and fulfillment* motif affirms the unity of the Old and New Testaments, in terms of God's intention to reveal himself, to redeem his people, and to do this through the promise made to Abraham and his descendants fulfilled in the person of Jesus of Nazareth.

10. Define and explain the concept of the *protoevangelium*, the first telling of the Gospel in Genesis 3.15, laying out the specifics of the promise including hostility between the serpent and the woman and their respective "seeds," the bruising of the heel of the woman's seed, and the crushing of the serpent's head by the seed.

11. Recite the theological implications of the *protoevangelium*, namely that God would provide humanity with a Savior through the woman's lineage who would destroy the serpent, albeit having his heel bruised; Jesus of Nazareth is this divine seed commissioned to destroy the devil's work.

12. Trace the covenant promise of Yahweh with Abraham as the continuation of this divine promise, including the fact that Abraham and his "seed" would be the means whereby redemption and restoration would come to God's people as well as to the nations of the earth in him; Jesus of Nazareth is declared to be the seed of Abraham in the NT apostolic witness.

Objectives for Lesson 2 The Promise Clarified

After your reading, study, discussion, and application of the materials in this lesson, you will be able to:

1. Give a clear and simple definition of *type*, as an object, event, happening, image, or reality that prefigures in the OT a reality in the NT, usually focused on Jesus Christ (as its *antitype*).

2. Outline the major justifications for a typological approach of the study of the Scriptures, including Jesus' and the apostles' use of the method, and the implicit connection in many of the same representations and images mentioned throughout Scripture.

3. List the major aspects of biblical types: that they are historically real, they illumine the person and work of

Teaching Objectives for Capstone, by Module

Christ, are contained in the NT, are connected to God's redemptive work in Christ, and they illumine the teaching of God on the matter they cover.

4. Articulate the principles for using typology properly in biblical hermeneutics, including the need to believe that God has placed correspondences in the Bible, to focus on Christ in drawing connections between the Old and New Testaments, to concentrate on the major links suggested in the types themselves and not on the details, to appreciate the relevance of the type *through the antitype*.

5. Explain how the experience of Israel, the descendants of Abraham and the people of God, represent an analogy where we can understand the larger relationship of God with all of the redeemed through Jesus Christ.

6. Highlight specifically how God's deliverance of his people during the Exodus prefigures specific dimensions of God's deliverance of his people through Jesus of Nazareth; our Passover, manna, and spiritual water from the Rock.

7. Demonstrate how the conquest of the nation of Canaan, the entering into the Promised Land and the establishment of Israel's kingdom reign pictures the conquest of God's enemies through Christ whom God will establish as King and Lord forever, and the blessing of God's kingdom people, the Church, who will rule with Christ as co-regents with him.

8. Show how God's restoration of his people after the captivity is a type of study of Scripture, and how the three distinct moments within Israel's history help us understand the OT essentially as a witness to Christ and his kingdom reign. These three moments are the Exodus, the conquest of Canaan and entering into the Promised Land, and the restoration of Israel from the Babylonian Captivity.

9. Summarize these three moments in Israel's history as parallel to the new life given to us by faith in Christ, which is a *New Exodus*, a new deliverance from the powers which oppress us spiritually; the fight against the devil and the world by the Church in spiritual warfare which represents a *New Conquest of Canaan*, and the ministry of the Gospel of Christ as a *New Restoration of God*, leading eventually to the new heavens and new earth under the sovereign authority of Jesus Christ.

10. Show how the various elements and activities associated with the Tabernacle is a type of the salvation provided in Jesus Christ, including how the Tabernacle was a copy or shadow

of the true dwelling place of God in the heavenlies, a symbol of God's presence among his people, and a way for God to reveal through type the one true salvation in Jesus.

11. Describe how the Tabernacle's dimensions and compartments made access available to God, so Jesus Christ makes access to God available through his blood sacrifice.

12. Show how the various articles of the Tabernacle represent distinctive aspects of Jesus Christ and his work: the *Brazen Altar* represents sacrificial redemption in Christ, the *Laver* represents the cleansing we receive through the blood of Jesus Christ, the *Table of Shewbread* represents Jesus Christ as the Bread of Life, the *Golden Candlestick* represents Christ as the Light of the world, the *Altar of Incense* represents Jesus' ministry of intercession on behalf of his people, the *Veil* represents the body of Jesus torn and broken for us on Calvary, the *Ark of the Covenant* represents the communion with God we share by faith in Jesus Christ.

Teaching Objectives for Capstone, by Module

13. Highlight the elements of the priesthood which show how Jesus Christ perfects in every way the pattern and meaning of the high priesthood of Aaron, and yet surpasses it through the priesthood in the order of Melchizedek, whose order was eternal, unchangeable, perfect, and final.

14. Give knowledge of how Jesus Christ fulfills in meaning and substance all the offerings associated with the Temple sacrifices: the *whole burnt offering* is a type of Jesus' own free will offering of himself to God; the *meal offering* is a type of Jesus' own presentation and dedication of his life and sufferings to God acceptable to him in every respect; the *peace offering* is a type of Jesus Christ himself who is our peace with God and with one another; the *sin offering* is a type of Jesus Christ who became sin for us by bearing our offense and penalty on the Cross; the *trespass offering* is a type of how Jesus is both propitiation for our sins as well as cleansing and provision for us to live a new life.

15. Explain how Jesus is the *antitype* in terms of the meaning of Israel's feasts, festivals, and convocations: in the *Feast of the Passover*, Jesus is our Paschal Lamb whose blood cleanses and redeems us; in the *Feast of Unleavened Bread*, Jesus is the one who inspires our walk in holiness before him, and not in malice or evil living; in the *Feast of First Fruits*, Jesus is the first fruits of the coming harvest of new humanity to be redeemed for God; in the *Feast of Pentecost*, Jesus is the one who with the Father pours out his Holy Spirit upon the

Church in this present age; in the *Feast of Trumpets*, Jesus is the one who will return and regather his people for redemption and blessing; in the *Day of Atonement*, Jesus is both the High Priest and the sacrifice offered to God in the heavenly Tabernacle for our sin; in the *Feast of Tabernacles*, Jesus is the one who will regather his people at his Second Coming for glorification and rest.

*Objectives for Lesson 3
The Promise Personalized*

After your reading, study, discussion, and application of the materials in this lesson, you will be able to:

1. Recognize and articulate the importance of character types in the stories and journeys of Israel: how they provide us with a full and rich presentation of the truth about Christ, spurring great interest in the craftsmanship of the OT stories, causing us to worship God because of the richness of his salvation plan, and enabling us to see the Bible as a whole, especially the connections between the testaments.

2. Lay out the elements of a character-type study, including getting a general outline of the character's life, searching for links and resemblances between the character and Jesus as the antitype, avoiding over-concentration on details that fail to connect the type to its antitype, and seeking to expand one's knowledge of the antitype *through* the understanding of the type.

3. Recognize the benefits of character-type investigations: gain an increased knowledge of the Scriptures, learn to communicate the Word to others at higher levels of interest, relevance, and entertainment, regain a sense of wonder at the inspiration of the Scriptures, and discover a more comprehensive picture of Jesus Christ through the types.

4. Give knowledge of how the character types in the OT point to and illustrate the ministry of Jesus Christ in the NT in his roles as prophet, priest, and king. While Christ is illumined in the character types, the nature of his own roles is infinitely greater in both glory and significance.

5. Show how Moses, the Prophet of the Lord, is an OT character type of Jesus Christ, who as an infant was sought by a king, was hidden in Egypt for a time for his protection, was sent by God to deliver God's people and God's message, was rejected at his own "first coming," chose a Gentile bride during the period of his rejection, and learned obedience through suffering. Show further how he mediated a covenant

between the people and God, reflected the glory of the Father (by contrast), and was messenger of the Lord, both to God's people and his enemies.

6. Outline how Melchizedek, the Priest of the Most High God, is an OT character type of Jesus Christ, whose name resonates with the title of Christ (King of righteousness, King of peace), who was both a priest and a king, who possessed no genealogy, who was called the Priest of the Most High God, who received tithes from God's people, who blessed faithful Abraham, and whose priesthood is eternal and unchanging.

7. Articulate how David, the King of Israel, is an OT character type of Jesus Christ, who was born in Bethlehem, grew in lowly reputation, was chosen and anointed by God to rule over God's people Israel, who was a shepherd (risking his life for his sheep), was sent to his brothers who derided him, and who as God's warrior defeated God's enemy who had oppressed God's people. Articulate further how prophetic promises were given regarding his future reign, how God made a covenant with him that the Kingdom would never depart from his heart, and how his reign was an administration of justice and equity to all the people.

8. Show how special cases of character types in the OT deserve special mention because of their significance in understanding Christ's role as head of humanity, redeemer of his kinsmen, and warrior in God's conquest. These characters represent the person of Adam, Joseph, and Joshua.

9. Detail the various aspects of Adam, the Source of humankind, as an OT character type of Jesus Christ by contrast. Show how both Adam and Jesus are the source and head of all those connected to them by birth and rebirth, with Adam as the head of the old creation, and Christ of the *new creation*, Adam being of the earth, Christ as the *Lord from heaven*, Adam being made a living soul, and Christ a *life-giving Spirit*. As in Adam all die, in Christ all are made alive, and as Adam brought pride and disobedience into the world, so the righteousness of Christ justifies those who believe in him.

10. Lay out how Joseph, redeemer of his kinsman, is an OT character type of Jesus, beloved of his father, sent by his father to his kinsman, hated by his brothers who plotted to kill him, rejected by his brothers the "first time," and was sold for "blood money" (pieces of silver). Further show how he was imprisoned with two criminals (one who "died" and

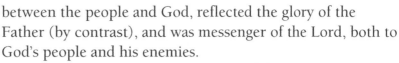

Teaching Objectives for Capstone, by Module

Teaching Objectives for Capstone, by Module

the other "lived"), was considered dead but lived as one alive to the Gentiles. Show how he was raised from the dungeon and exalted to a place of authority, and power, and took a Gentile bride. Finally, show how, like Christ, he gave all honor to the king, and delivered all glory and treasure into the king's hand, brought his people to repentance and self-knowledge, was reconciled to his kinsman and received back into fellowship, and was acknowledged to be the savior of his people and their ruler.

11. Give evidence of how Joshua, the captain of the Lord's armies is an OT character type of Christ, his name resonates with Jesus' name (Joshua=Jehovah is salvation; Jesus=Jehovah saves), he alone was chosen by God to lead the people into the Promised Land, his commitment was to utterly destroy God's enemies in Canaan, and he was accompanied by a special manifestation of the presence of the Lord throughout his fight with God's enemies. Show, too, how he subordinated himself to the leading of God, dying to his own will, how his warfare was rooted in his relationship with Yahweh, leading God's people personally into battle, fighting alongside them in combat against God's enemies, and won complete victory, dividing the spoils among those who fought beside him in the battle.

12. Explain how the roles of prophet, priest, and king, are the special character types of Adam, Joseph, and Joshua are seen in the life of Jesus. While such roles and types are tremendously helpful in providing our OT witness to Christ, they give comprehensive not exhaustive pictures of the life and ministry of Christ. Only by linking the *prefiguring in the OT* to the *revelation of Christ in the NT* do we get the fullest picture and meaning of these roles and types together in the life and ministry of Jesus.

Objectives for Lesson 4 The Promise Universalized

After your reading, study, discussion, and application of the materials in this lesson, you will be able to:

1. Define the term for Messiah in the Greek *messias*, the Aramaic form of the Hebrew mashiach, which means "to anoint"; *Christos* is the equivalent NT terminology meaning "anointed one."

2. Provide a general overview of the basic characteristics of OT Messianic prophecy, including its focus on the deliverance of God's people, its strong use of figurative language, its

predictions in the "prophetic perfect" tense (as if they were already accomplished), and their lack of easy-to-understand timetables as to their precise fulfilment. The main characteristic is its linkage of the testaments to Jesus Christ as the fulfillment of its prophetic descriptions.

3. Outline the lineage of the Messiah as given in the OT literature, which includes the seed of the woman in Genesis, of the line of Seth, the seed of Abraham, the lineage of Isaac, through the house of Jacob, of the tribe and clan of Judah, through Boaz, Obed, Jesse and David, down to the person of Jesus of Nazareth.

4. Show how OT Messianic prophecy is key to understanding the OT witness to Christ: it is the way that Jesus and the apostles applied the OT to his life, these prophecies illumine our understanding of the way Jesus used the OT, they directly connected the testaments (in the way Augustine suggested, that theOTis revealed in the NT), and finally, that Jesus of Nazareth fulfills the prophetic predictions of the expected Messiah.

5. Give a brief sketch of the main points included in the OT Messianic prophecies which give witness to Christ and his Kingdom, including prophecies about his birth at Bethlehem, his prophetic forerunner, and his identity as Immanuel.

6. Include in the sketch the main prophetic predictions about Messiah's person and life, i.e., his introduction by the coming "voice in the wilderness," his divine status as Wonderful, Counselor, Mighty God, Everlasting Father, and Prince of peace, his anointing as the Servant of Yahweh, and his anticipated Kingship and reign. Further, the sketch should include his role as the cornerstone of God's salvific work, his role as light for the Gentiles, and his role as prophet priest and king.

7. Articulate the major elements concerning the *Passion* of Christ, i.e., the suffering and death of Messiah, including (but not limited to) his brutal treatment and death, his vicarious (substitutionary) wounding and bruising for the sins of the world, his great agony, his betrayal, his feet and hands being pierced, his false trial and verdict, and his death.

8. Lay out the major texts and their content regarding his resurrection, including Peter's sermon at Pentecost and Paul's preaching at Antioch, as well as the predictions made in the Gospels of his resurrection.

9. Provide a general outline of some of the OT Messianic texts which predict the coming glory of Messiah, including the exaltation of Messiah as the King of glory, the terrifying judgment upon God's enemies, his return for his people, the majesty, beauty, and glory of creation's transformation that will occur under his reign, and the everlasting and universal dominion that will be given to him.

10. Show how God has extended the promise and blessings of Abraham to the Gentiles, to all who believe in Jesus Christ as Messiah.

11. Give evidence of the three movements in the NT's use of OT Messianic prophecy, including 1) Jesus' explanation of the OT predictions about himself, 2) the apostles' commentary on Jesus' meaning in the NT writings, especially in the preaching of the book of Acts, and 3) the Church's application of the apostles' commentary of Jesus' understanding of the OT.

12. Detail how the promise was universalized to all nations by the inclusion of Gentile salvation in the Messianic hope, including the revealed mystery of Gentiles as fellow heirs of the covenant and heirs of salvation, and the prophetic clues given that pointed to Gentile salvation (e.g., the seed of the woman destroying the serpent, all the families of the earth being blessed in Abraham, and how the Messiah would be a light to all the Gentiles).

13. Show how the various strands of OT Messianic prophecy were progressively understood by the apostles to represent God's salvation for all peoples, including the outpouring of the Spirit on all flesh, and full inclusion of Gentiles as fellow heirs of the Abrahamic promise.

14. List some of the key ways OT Messianic prophecies were used by the apostles in the Acts and the Epistles, including the outpouring of the Spirit on all flesh, the rejection of Messiah by the builders (Jewish generation), Jesus as light for the Gentiles, the rebuilding of the tent of David including Gentile salvation, and the Messianic blindness of God's people (the Jews) due to their hardness of heart. Also, they mention the global proclamation of the Gospel, the provoking of the Jews to jealousy, and the blessing of Abraham on the Gentiles.

15. Summarize the OT Messianic prophecy regarding the Gentiles as God not only fulfilled his promise for salvation to Abraham, but his inclusion of Gentiles in that salvation promise.

Teaching Objectives for Capstone, by Module

Teaching Objectives for Capstone, by Module

Module Description

Capstone Module 10 – God the Son

The identity of the person and work of Jesus of Nazareth is arguably the most critical subject in all Christian reflection and ministry. Indeed, it is impossible to minister in the name of the Lord Jesus Christ if that ministry is based upon false and ignoble views of who he was (and is), what his life signified, and what we are to make of him today. Everything is at stake in our right conception of his life, death, resurrection, ascension, and return. This module highlights his majestic person and deeds, and mastering the biblical material on him is the task of all responsible discipleship and ministry.

In the first lesson, *Jesus, the Messiah and Lord of All: He Came*, we consider the significance of the Nicene Creed for Christological studies. We will look specifically at how the Nicene Creed helps frame our thinking as urban ministers about a study of the biblical materials on Jesus, especially in the sense of helping us view Christ's work as two movements: his humiliation (i.e., his becoming human and dying on the cross for our sakes) and his exaltation (his resurrection, ascension, and the hope of his return in power). We will also discover the biblical teaching on Jesus's nature before he came to earth, as preexistent Word or Logos. We will consider his divinity as well as two historical heresies regarding Christ's divinity, and close our discussion by commenting on the significance of Jesus' divinity for our faith and discipleship.

Next, our second lesson, *Jesus, the Messiah and Lord of All: He Lived*, explores the humanity of Christ. We will focus on his dual reasons for coming to earth: to reveal to us the Father's glory and redeem us from sin and Satan's power. We will also look at the creedal language regarding Jesus' humanity, his conception by the Holy Spirit and birth to the Virgin Mary, and investigate some of the historical errors connected with denying either Jesus' divinity or humanity. We close this lesson by considering three important aspects of Jesus' life and ministry on earth. These include his identity as the Baptized One who identifies with sinners, the Proclaimer of the Kingdom of God, reasserting God's right to rule over creation, and as the Suffering Servant of Yahweh who would give his soul as a ransom for many.

In our third lesson, *Jesus, the Messiah and Lord of All: He Died*, we will explore the theological implications of Jesus' humiliation and death, his descent in his divine person on our behalf. We will consider Jesus' humiliation in the Incarnation, his life and ministry, as well as his death. In considering his sacrifice on Calvary, we will explore some of the historical models for understanding his work on the cross. These include the perspective of his death as a ransom for us, as a propitiation (divine satisfaction) for our sins, as a substitutionary sacrifice in our place, as a victory over the devil and death itself, and as a reconciliation between God and humankind. We will also explore some of the historical alternative views of Jesus' death. These include his death as 1) a moral example, 2) a demonstration of God's love, 3) a demonstration of God's justice, 4) a victory over the forces of evil and sin, and 5) a satisfaction of God's honor.

Finally, in our fourth lesson, *Jesus, the Messiah and Lord of All: He Rose and Will Return*, we begin with a consideration of the various aspects and implications of two events which mark the exaltation of Christ. The resurrection serves as a vindication of Jesus' Messiahship and sonship, and his ascension grants to our Savior a position of dignity and authority that allows him to fill all things with his glory. We explore these in light of the biblical teaching of the Creedal language, enabling us to understand God's intent to exalt Jesus of Nazareth to supreme heir of all things as a result of his death on the cross. We will close our study by looking at the last three statements regarding Christ's person in the Nicene Creed. We will consider his coming in glory, his judgment of the nations, and discuss briefly the nature of his coming reign of the Kingdom of God.

Perhaps no study of doctrine can compare with the thrill of understanding from a biblical and creedal way the richness, wonder, and mystery of God's Son, Jesus of Nazareth. His humiliation and ascension is the heart of the Gospel, and the center of our devotion, worship, and service. May God use this study of his glorious person to enable you to better love and serve him who alone has been given the preeminence by the Father. To him be the glory!

Objectives for *Capstone* Module 10, God the Son

Objectives for Lesson 1 Jesus, the Messiah and Lord of All: He Came

After your reading, study, discussion, and application of the materials in this lesson, you will be able to:

1. Articulate the significance of the Nicene Creed for Christological studies.

Teaching Objectives for Capstone, by Module

Teaching Objectives for Capstone, by Module

2. Define carefully the topic of Christology and speak of its general importance in our training as leaders in the Church.

3. Show precisely how the Nicene Creed helps frame our thinking about a study of the biblical materials on Jesus, especially in the sense of helping us view Christ's work as two movements, his humiliation (i.e., his becoming human and dying on the cross for our sakes) and his exaltation (his resurrection, ascension, and the hope of his return in power).

4. Outline the ways in which a study of Christology can be of very special help today for those like us who work in urban communities, seeing how a new understanding of Christ can enable us to better communicate God's love to humankind, and his glorious kingdom promise.

5. Detail precisely the key elements of the nature of Jesus before he came to earth, as preexistent Word or *Logos*, using the Nicene Creed as a key to understanding Jesus' deity.

6. Lay out the three different ways in which Jesus' preexistence is seen in the Scriptures, first as God the Son, a divine person equal with God, as the Expected One in OT Messianic prophecy, and then as the Incarnate, the Word of God made flesh, God in human form.

7. Provide details and refute two of the central historical heresies regarding Christ's divinity, and comment on the significance of Jesus' divinity for our faith and discipleship.

*Objectives for Lesson 2
Jesus, the Messiah and
Lord of All: He Lived*

After your reading, study, discussion, and application of the materials in this lesson, you will be able to:

1. Articulate the general purpose for Jesus' coming to earth: to reveal to us the Father's glory and redeem us from sin and Satan's power.

2. Outline the creedal language regarding Jesus' humanity, his conception by the Holy Spirit and birth to the Virgin Mary.

3. Summarize two of the prominent historical errors that have arisen from contesting Jesus' becoming a human being: Nestorianism – *that Christ was two distinct persons*, and Eutychianism – *that Christ has one blended nature*. The Councils of Nicea (325) and Chalcedon (381) settled these questions, affirming that Jesus was *fully God and fully human*.

4. Evaluate and refute errors associated with misreading Jesus' humanity: *Docetism* which asserted that *Jesus was not human*

and *Apollinarianism* which asserted that *Jesus was not fully human.*

5. Restate the practical implications of the unity of Jesus' divine and human nature, and the significance of Jesus' humanity for us: Jesus, our high priest, can empathize with our needs and represent us before God. As our Second Adam, we will be conformed to his image in our future glorification with him.

6. Identify and biblically defend the concept of Jesus as the Baptized One who identified with the plight and peril of the sinners he came to save, as well as the concept of Jesus as the Proclaimer of the Kingdom of God – Jesus reasserting God's right to rule over creation, showing through his person, miracles, healings, and exorcisms the signs of the Kingdom present in his own person on earth.

7. To analyze and unpack the idea of Jesus as the Suffering Servant of Yahweh, sketching his Messianic mission from the public announcement of his ministry, and the way in which Jesus revealed himself as the expected Servant of Yahweh through his proclamation of good news to the poor, his demonstration of justice among God's people, and his vicarious sacrifice on behalf of God's people as a "ransom for many."

Teaching Objectives for Capstone, by Module

Objectives for Lesson 3 Jesus, the Messiah and Lord of All: He Died

After your reading, study, discussion, and application of the materials in this lesson, you will be able to:

1. Articulate with Scripture and concrete examples the significance of the humiliation of Jesus Christ, that is, his descent in his divine person and glory to come to earth and die on our behalf.

2. Illustrate and state the major points of Jesus' humiliation in his Incarnation and in his life and ministry.

3. Elaborate with Scripture and clear reasons how this humiliation of Jesus is specifically revealed in his death.

4. Expand upon some of the key historical perspectives on Jesus' death and the way in which these dimensions enable us to understand the blessing our Lord's death was for humankind.

5. These include the view of his death as a ransom for us, as a propitiation for our sins, as a substitutionary sacrifice in our place, as a victory over the devil and death itself, and as a reconciliation between God and humankind.

6. Elaborate on how the Nicene Creed unequivocally confesses that our Lord Jesus Christ died and was buried, and how this act was the culmination of our Lord's humiliation upon earth in his descent from his heavenly, preexistent glory.

7. Lay out theories of the atonement which have emerged through history, including his death: 1) as an example, 2) as a demonstration of God's love, 3) as a demonstration of God's justice, 4) as a victory over the forces of evil and sin, and 5) as a satisfaction of God's honor.

8. Argue how no one historical theory of the atonement by itself can explain the richness of the meaning of Jesus' death, but rather they each contain dimensions of truth which can help us gain a comprehensive understanding and appreciation of the significance of Jesus' death for us.

Objectives for Lesson 4
Jesus, the Messiah
and Lord of All:
He Rose and Will Return

After your reading, study, discussion, and application of the materials in this lesson, you will be able to:

1. Explain with Scripture and worthy arguments the various aspects and implications of two events which mark the exaltation of Christ, the resurrection and the ascension.

2. Elaborate the key points which show how the resurrection serves as a vindication of Jesus' Messiahship and position as God's Son.

3. Articulate the importance and significance of Jesus' ascension which grants to our Savior a position of dignity and authority that allows him to fill all things with his glory.

4. Show how the Nicene Creed and its confession gives a clear and persuasive summary of the teaching of the Scriptures on both the resurrection and the ascension, and give the major implications of these great events.

5. Outline the final three Christological events referred to in the Nicene Creed on the present and coming ministry of the exalted Christ.

6. Argue from both the Scriptures and the Creed about the Second Coming of Christ in glory, and lay out its character and its significance for us in ministry.

7. Defend the biblical and creedal affirmations about Jesus' judgment of the nations, and the main elements in the coming reign of Jesus.

8. Elaborate the key issues and implications of Christ's return and reign for us as we do ministry in the city.

Module Description

Capstone Module 11 – Practicing Christian Leadership

In Module 11 in our *Capstone Curriculum* series, entitled Practicing Christian Leadership, we demonstrate our devotion to our Savior by practicing a kind of leadership that both honors and glorifies our Lord and edifies and builds up his people. We explore these important concepts and practices throughout this important study.

The first lesson, *Effective Worship Leading*, considers the idea of representation of the Lord Jesus as fundamental in practicing every dimension of Christian leadership as his agents and servants. Closely connected to this important idea, we will also consider carefully the role of ministering the Word and Sacrament among the people of God. Throughout this lesson we will see how we as Christian leaders may lead God's people to experience his grace and direction through an effective ministry of the Word of God and a faithful practice of the sacraments of the Church.

In our second lesson, *Effective Christian Education*, we will explore the idea of bringing new believers into our churches, dealing specifically with how we welcome and integrate new believers into our community life together. We will also explore the concept of parenting new Christians and discipling them in the Church. We will look carefully together at the meaning of spiritual parenthood, seeking to biblically define and practically outline how we can enable new and growing believers in the Lord to mature in Christ.

Next, lesson three deals with an important aspect of Christian leadership, *Effective Church Discipline*. The practice of Christian leadership involves our thorough knowledge of the principles of biblical exhortation, and here we will explore reasons why this ministry is so necessary for Christian leaders among God's people. In this lesson we will also address the question of the practice of church discipline. We will look at both the biblical definitions and practical guidelines of godly rebuke and restoration in the context of God's community.

Finally, in lesson four we will focus on *Effective Counseling: Preparing, Caring, and Healing*. Here we will define effective biblical counseling, starting with a general explanation of it and its implications for us as urban Christian leaders. Our goal will be to understand both the therapeutic and pastoral implications of counseling and leading God's people. Together we will discover how we can become better care givers for those encountering the dark side of life, trials, tribulations, and distress. As God's servants and under-shepherds of his people, we will discover how we may come to bear the burdens of those who are experiencing trouble or stress, and do all we can in order to edify the flock of God, even as he gives us opportunity.

What an adventure it is to serve the living God by caring for his dear people! My prayer for you is that you become that Christian leader God desires you to be, all for his glory!

Objectives for *Capstone* Module 11, Practicing Christian Leadership

Objectives for Lesson 1 Effective Worship Leading: Worship, Word, and Sacrament

After your reading, study, discussion, and application of the materials in this lesson, you will be able to:

1. Recite the different ways in which leadership is a form of representation, i.e., representing the Lord, his person, his people, and his purposes in the community.
2. Give reasons why in leadership we do not represent our own purposes or interests in our lives and ministries, but the Lord's purposes and interests in all we say and do.
3. Outline the importance of the role of worship in bringing glory and honor to God in the midst of his people.
4. Detail the importance of liturgy by worshiping God in the spirit, in truth, in order, and in faith.
5. List the key reasons behind the role of the Word and Sacrament in practical Christian leadership.
6. Give the key principles involved in nourishing the people of God on a full and steady diet of the Word of God and helping them experience genuine body life through a joyous celebration of Baptism and the Lord's Supper.

Objectives for Lesson 2 Effective Christian Education: Incorporating, Parenting, and Discipling

After your reading, study, discussion, and application of the materials in this lesson, you will be able to:

1. Identify the critical steps in welcoming and integrating new believers into the Church.
2. Define the meaning of incorporation from a biblical point of view, and recite some of its key implications as it relates to practicing Christian leadership.
3. Articulate the key elements of incorporation, including bringing new believers into the body of believers, accepting new believers on the basis of their repentance and faith,

grounding new believers in the truth of Jesus, guiding them into body life, and finally the importance of introducing them to pastoral care.

4. Outline the concept of spiritual parenthood, biblically defining what precisely is the definition of parenting new and growing believers in the Lord.

5. Explain the nature of spiritual parenthood in the framework of the Apostle Paul in the New Testament.

6. Lay out carefully the elements of spiritual parenthood and relate how these elements relate to the spirituality and growth of new and immature urban disciples of Christ.

Objectives for Lesson 3 Effective Church Discipline: Exhorting, Rebuking, and Restoring

After your reading, study, discussion, and application of the materials in this lesson, you will be able to:

1. Define the concept of biblical exhortation, and explore reasons why this ministry is so necessary for Christian leaders among God's people.

2. Distinguish the difference between the standing and the state of a Christian's position and discipleship, and apply that knowledge to the issue of Christian exhortation.

3. Connect the practice of exhortation to the challenge of believers remaining faithful to the Lord in their walks with God, each other, and in the world.

4. List the basic reasons why it is necessary to exhort one another to remain faithful, including the devil's opposition, the nature of our adoption in Christ, avoiding judgment from God, maintaining our integrity, and being conformed to the model of Christ.

5. Understand the basic principles associated with the theology and practice of exhorting others in a God-honoring way.

6. Recite the basic biblical definitions of practicing discipline in the Church, and outline the nature of what it means to rebuke and restore members of God's community.

7. Exegete Matthew 18 with an eye to discover Jesus' instruction regarding carrying out discipline in the Church.

8. Outline the critical cautions associated with carrying out discipline in the Church, including pride, acting on uncorroborated accusations, and a neglect of genuine authority in discipline.

9. Detail the benefits of discipline, i.e., a sound faith, a strong community, a safe family, a solid testimony, and a glorified Savior.

Objectives for Lesson 4
Effective Counseling:
Preparing, Caring
and Healing

After your reading, study, discussion, and application of the materials in this lesson, you will be able to:

1. Understand the practicing Christian leader as one who provides counsel to the people of God by providing effective spiritual direction through a careful, relevant application of the Word of God.

2. Define the connection between Christian leadership and godly counseling.

3. Correlate the concept of Christian leadership to that of God's physician of the soul and spirit, i.e., a Christian counselor is God's Physician, that is, in the same way a compassionate physician cares for the body of a patient, so a spiritual counselor seeks to care for the soul and life of the person he cares for.

4. Trace the importance biblically of the relationship of the Holy Spirit to that of the godly counselor who uses the Word of God to meet the deepest needs of his people.

5. Argue how the Word of God can outfit us for the task of biblical counseling, along with the Holy Spirit and good advice from others.

6. Envision the Christian leader as shepherd, as one who provides care for and seeks healing for the flock of God during their times of trial and distress to reestablish them on their faith journey with the Lord and his people.

7. Recite the ways in which the Word of God sees tribulation as an inevitable reality for all God's people, and the unique role that pastoral care plays in interceding for them, protecting them, and caring for their specific needs in a responsive way.

8. Outline some of the special problems associated with offering care to souls in distress, i.e., the problem of evil, of care giving, of anger against God, and of vengeance and forgiveness.

Module Description

Capstone **Module 12 – Focus on Reproduction**

As 21st century disciples of Jesus in the cities of America, we desire to be fruitful in the work of God–ministering to the lost, and advancing the Kingdom of Christ (John 15.8,16). In Module 12, *Focus on Reproduction*, we concentrate our attention on the need to evangelize, equip, and empower the lost in order that they might become salt and light in the communities where they live and work.

In our first lesson, *Church Growth: Reproducing in Number and Quality*, we affirm the single most critical concept in understanding mission in the city: the lordship of Jesus Christ. As risen Lord and God's Anointed Messiah, Jesus has been exalted to the position of head over all things to the Church and Lord of the harvest. In this lesson we survey his call to make disciples of all nations, to *Evangelize*, as well as to affirm that radical discipleship is proven in Christian community. Jesus has called us to evangelize the lost, equip new disciples to live the Christian life, and to empower his Church to reproduce itself, all for the glory of God.

Next, in our second lesson, *Planting Urban Churches: Sowing*, we introduce the important concept of *oikos* in urban evangelism. Here we show how an *oikos* is that web of common kinship relationships, friendships, and associations that make up a person's larger social circle. Beginning with an outline of *oikos* in the NT, we then explore the meaning of this critical idea for urban cross-cultural evangelism.

In lesson three we further outline the second main phase of church planting, *Equipping*, through the idea of follow-up, or incorporating new disciples into the Church. Arguing that the Church is God's means of bringing new Christians to maturity, we provide key elements and tips in the practice of following up new believers in Christ. In this lesson we will also look closely at the practice of discipling growing believers. Examining the role of the discipler as model, mentor, and friend, we will offer practical advice in how to help new Christians grow to maturity.

Finally, in lesson four, we will consider our role in helping new churches progress toward independence through *Empowerment* and the final phase of urban church planting: transition. We will define the purpose, plan, and perspectives related to empowering through four biblical aspects of godly urban church leadership. Without a doubt, godly, servant leadership is critical to ensure a dynamic growing church in the city. We conclude our module study with a blueprint of a godly urban church, those characteristics that represent a healthy, reproducing church in the city that is an agent of change and freedom in its community, in Jesus' name.

My sincere prayer is that God will grant you grace to understand his will for reproducing fruit and making disciples of the Kingdom in the city. May his Spirit grant you the power and desire to make disciples where you live, and so multiply his Church, to the glory of his great name!

Objectives for *Capstone* Module 12, Focus on Reproduction

Objectives for Lesson 1 Church Growth: Reproducing in Number and Quality

After your reading, study, discussion, and application of the materials in this lesson, you will be able to:

1. Defend the idea that the single most critical concept in understanding evangelism, discipleship, and church planting is the lordship of Jesus Christ.
2. Show biblically how Jesus as the risen Lord and God's Anointed Messiah has been exalted to the position of head over all things to the Church and Lord of the harvest.
3. Recite Scripture that supports that Jesus himself serves as the ground of all missionizing activity, who alone is the Lord who calls his servants to the field and empowers them with his Spirit, determining where he will send them.
4. Explain how Jesus as Lord determines what his servants must endure for his name's sake, and how Jesus promises to stand with them to the end of their task.
5. Affirm how in all mission, teaching, preaching, and outreach, we must appeal to our Lord Jesus, for he alone enables us to win souls and plant churches in the city.
6. Demonstrate from the Bible the way in which radical discipleship is produced and authenticated in Christian community.
7. Articulate the three integrated steps of urban church planting: evangelizing the lost, equipping the new disciples to live the Christian life in the context of Christian community – the Church, and empowering the leaders and the community to reproduce itself and associate with other like-minded churches.

8. Highlight the ten critical principles drawn from a church planting model from Acts, and apply them to your own church planting efforts in the city.

Objectives for Lesson 2
Planting Urban
Churches: Sowing

After your reading, study, discussion, and application of the materials in this lesson, you will be able to:

1. Recite and defend with Scripture the most significant concept in urban evangelism today: *the principle of oikos*, or household evangelism, including the idea of an *oikos* as that web of common kinship relationships, friendships, and associations that make up a person's larger social circle.
2. List out clearly the more difficult challenges involved in urban evangelism (including broken family units, economic underdevelopment, alienation and loneliness, drug abuse, violence, housing shortages, and general despair)
3. Demonstrate the concept of *oikos* in the NT, and explain how this concept was critical in the early church's conception of penetrating larger social units with the Gospel.
4. Explore the relationship of *oikos* to identity as members of the family of God, and examine the significance of the relationship of *oikos* to evangelism and church planting in the New Testament.
5. Detail the kind of *oikos* relationships (i.e., that web of common kinship relationships, friendships, and associations that make up a person's larger social circle) that exist in our urban communities, and how critical this concept is for penetrating the circle of influence of city residents today.
6. Articulate the central benefits for *oikos* evangelism in the city, and relate these strategies to our evangelistic methods as we launch incarnationally into the community with the Gospel.

Objectives for Lesson 3
Planting Urban
Churches: Tending

After your reading, study, discussion, and application of the materials in this lesson, you will be able to:

1. Defend and articulate from Scripture the idea of the importance of following up new converts and discipling new believers in urban church planting.
2. The act of discipleship is welcoming new believers into the Church, i.e., incorporating new believers and equipping them in the local assembly of believers, which is God's agent of the Kingdom in this world.

3. Define follow-up of new believers as "incorporation into the family of God for the purpose of edification and fruitfulness, to the glory of God." This includes the notion of welcome and introduction into the body, building up in the body to the fullness of Christ, and using one's gifts to contribute to fulfilling the Great Commission, all to the glory of God.

4. List the reasons why follow-up of new Christians is so essential to their spiritual well-being, including their need for protection, for new identity, for ongoing instruction and feeding, for the cultivation of new friends and life patterns, and the need for regular pastoral care.

5. Articulate the dynamics of follow-up, including baptism and membership in a local assembly, worship, befriending, pastoral care, preaching and teaching, discovery and use of one's spiritual gifts, and service and sharing of one's faith.

6. Explain the steps in practicing biblical follow-up: understanding the goal of discipleship as maturity, grounding the new believer in their assurance of salvation, teaching the new Christian to share their faith, and feed upon the Word of God. This also included equipping them to walk with the Lord, introducing them to other members of the body, and connecting them to a small group as the building block of their faith.

7. Show how follow-up is an essential dimension of equipping believers in the *Assemble and Nurture phases* of church planting.

8. Discuss carefully the role of the local church in effective discipling of new and growing Christians, especially in the sense that the Church is the place which incorporates new converts into the faith, establishes them in their walk and doctrine, and equips them for the work of the ministry.

9. Inform others as to the biblical examples of discipleship (e.g., Moses and Joshua, Jesus and the Twelve, Paul and Timothy), as well as the elements involved in the apostles' investment in others' lives (through personal example, pastoral care, prayer, personal contact, sending representatives, correspondence, and delegation of authority).

10. Outline the roles of the disciple-maker in the church as model, mentor, and friend.

11. Understand the practical ways in which we begin to disciple other Christians in the context of the Church, i.e., through nurturing new believers, growing Christians, and potential leaders.

12. Defend the notion that as we assemble believers in the church and nurture them through follow-up and discipleship, we can see growth occur which will lead to a strong, healthy, and dynamic church being planted in the city.

Objectives for Lesson 4 Planting Urban Churches: Reaping

After your reading, study, discussion, and application of the materials in this lesson, you will be able to:

1. Articulate the concept of *Empowerment*, as it relates in the urban church planting process. This process seeks to help the emerging church become sufficient to work with other congregations as leadership authority is given over to the church in order that it may become a self-governing, self-supporting, and self-reproducing church.
2. Support biblically and logically the notion that raising up godly leaders who can shepherd and protect the church is the single greatest responsibility of effective urban church planting. Without godly gifted leaders taking responsibility for the well being of the newly formed church, the likelihood that it will survive, let alone thrive, are nil to none.
3. Give evidence of the kinds of investments that are necessary in order for the leadership team of a church to have the authority, character, competence and membership support necessary to ensure a dynamic healthy church.
4. List out some of the major challenges involved in empowering an emerging church for maturity and reproduction. These include the issue of authority, avoiding dependence while ensuring friendship and connection, and encouraging the church to not merely survive but reproduce itself for Christ.
5. Outline the four central aspects of godly church leadership: the godly leader must be *commissioned*, i.e., a person of distinct recognized call; the godly leader must be a person of *character*, i.e., a person of proven experience; the godly leader must be a person of *competence*: a person of gifting and skill; finally, the godly leader must be a person of *community*: a person who lives to serve and sacrifice on behalf of others.
6. Provide an overview, a snapshot, a blueprint of the three concepts and seven criteria related to empowerment which ensure the kind of church that effective urban church planters seek to empower and reproduce. These concepts include striving to ensure the church's independence,

Teaching Objectives for Capstone, by Module

ensuring godly association with other churches, and encouraging ongoing reproduction in service and mission.

7. Outline the seven criteria which define an empowered urban church. A newly planted urban church is empowered for reproduction when 1) a faithful group of converted, gathered, and maturing disciples of Jesus are in assembly; 2) it has selected its own pastors and leaders; 3) it has redefined the relationship it has with missionaries and workers who help to found it; 4) it encourages unique, burden-driven, gift-oriented ministries from its members; 5) it generates its own resources and income for operations, ministry and missions; 6) it faithfully stewards its resources and facilities, and 7) it is focused on reproducing itself, in service to the Lord and advance of the Kingdom in mission.

8. Be able to recognize what a focus on reproduction will demand: pouring into the leaders who share the vision, sacrificing on behalf of the vision God gave, and doing your part in fulfilling the Great Commission, starting where we live and from there, to the ends of the earth.

Capstone Module 13 – The New Testament Witness to Christ and His Kingdom

Module Description

There can be no question that the most critical and important subject to master in the life of a Christian leader is the actual person and teachings of Jesus of Nazareth. No other subject is as significant or controversial as the meaning of his life and ministry. This module is designed to introduce you to a "life of Jesus" survey that concentrates on the historical accounts in the Gospels, beginning at the announcement of his birth to his ascension after his death at Calvary. No other study can yield a greater intellectual and spiritual harvest than a concentrated focus upon the historical facts surrounding Jesus' life, ministry, passion, death, resurrection, and ascension. Jesus of Nazareth is Messiah and Lord of all!

Our first lesson, *The Messiah Announced*, will concentrate on a brief first look at the critical perspectives and processes associated with a profitable study of the life of Christ. We'll then proceed to look at the birth, infancy, and childhood narratives of the Messiah. We will see that the New Testament reveals in the Gospel accounts of the Apostles that Jesus of Nazareth is the Messiah who fulfills the promise of God for salvation, redemption, and revelation. We will also look carefully at the one chosen by God to announce Messiah's ministry, John the Baptist, attending both the baptism of Jesus, and his temptation in the wilderness. We end our first lesson by considering two important incidents concerning Jesus' announcement of his Messiahship: his inaugural sermon at Nazareth, and his first public miracle attesting his Messiahship at the wedding at Cana.

In our second lesson, *The Messiah Opposed*, we begin by looking at the historical context which surrounded Jesus at the time of his appearing in his public ministry. We will survey the nature of Rome's domination of the first century world, and see how the different Jewish sects and parties responded to Rome and to Jesus. We will look at the Sadducees, Pharisees, Essenes, Zealots, and Herodians. In the second segment of this lesson we will explore the Jewish concept of the Kingdom of God at the time of Jesus. We'll see how the nation of Israel, oppressed by political powers, believed that when Messiah came, the Kingdom of God would come in power, restoring the material universe and saving humankind from the control of Satan. Of course, Jesus proclaimed the Kingdom present, and demonstrated its reality in his healings and exorcisms, revealing the Kingdom's presence in his own person and ministry.

Lesson three deals with *The Messiah Revealed*, which aims to understand that in the person of Jesus, the promised Messiah is powerfully revealed through his perfect life and character, his masterful leadership of the Apostles, and his submissive sonship to his Father. Jesus' Messiahship is made plain through his prophetic teaching ministry, as well as in the mighty demonstrations of power, both in signs and wonders (miracles) and dramatic encounter with spiritual demons. Here we will also briefly consider the suffering and death of Jesus (i.e., his Passion). His death provides us with a clear revelation of the promised Messiah. We will also consider Peter's confession of Jesus' true identity, accompanied by Jesus' prediction of his death, and his resolve to go toward Jerusalem. We will look at Jesus' triumphal entry into Jerusalem, his final week encountering the Jewish leaders, and his Passover with the disciples. Finally, we will look at the events surrounding his crucifixion and death, his agony in prayer in the Garden to his burial after his death on the cross. Undoubtedly, Jesus' suffering and death give strong and undeniable testimony of his identity as the Son of God, as God's anointed Christ, the one who can reassert God's right to rule over his creation and over all humankind.

Finally, lesson four discusses *The Messiah Vindicated*. This lesson considers both the significance of the resurrection of Messiah Jesus, and its importance in our theology, faith, and ministry. Once we consider the evidence for the resurrection, we will then survey the various appearances of Jesus, beginning with his resurrection at the tomb up until his appearance to the Apostles at the Sea of Galilee. Nothing provides a clearer witness to the vindication of the Messianic identity of Jesus Christ than this one unequivocal fact: Jesus Christ has been raised from the dead.

We will close this module with a critical study of the Great Commission as a continuing vindication of Jesus' identity as Messiah, and the importance of this commission as it relates to the fulfillment of prophecy as well as to global mission. For forty days after his resurrection, Jesus demonstrated its truthfulness to the Apostles, and gave his promise to send them the Holy Spirit to fulfill that commission. We close our study of the life of Jesus with a look at the Ascension, the final historical sign which gives evidence of Jesus' vindication as Messiah. Jesus of Nazareth is the Messiah of God.

Again, there can be little doubt that the depth of our ministry and leadership can proceed no further than the depth of our knowledge of Jesus Christ, the Messiah of God and Lord of all. Therefore, may our God and Father provide you with both the hunger, passion, and discipline to master the life and ministry of Jesus. In so doing, you will be able to be his disciple and make disciples of Jesus in your church, in your ministry, and wherever else God may lead.

Objectives for *Capstone* Module 13, The New Testament Witness to Christ and His Kingdom

Objectives for Lesson 1
The Messiah Announced

After your reading, study, discussion, and application of the materials in this lesson, you will be able to:

1. Explain the critical perspectives and processes associated with a profitable study of the life of Christ.
2. Give an outline of the key stories associated with the Birth narratives, infancy, and childhood of Jesus.
3. Defend the idea that the New Testament reveals in the Gospel accounts of the Apostles the person of Jesus of Nazareth, who is the Messiah who fulfills the promise of God for salvation, redemption, and revelation.
4. Provide a concise explanation of the ministry of John the Baptist as the one chosen by God to announce Messiah's ministry to the nation of Israel.
5. Describe the temptation of Jesus in the wilderness, as well as his calling of his disciples, and two important incidents concerning the announcement of the Messiah: his public announcement of his Messiahship at Nazareth, and his first public miracle attesting his Messiahship at the wedding at Cana.

Objectives for Lesson 2
The Messiah Opposed

After your reading, study, discussion, and application of the materials in this lesson, you will be able to:

1. Explain the historical context which surrounded Jesus at the time of his appearing in his public ministry, including the various details which defined Rome's domination of the world and their relationship to Jesus' contemporaries.

2. Describe the way in which the various groups in Israel at the time of Jesus reacted differently to the Roman occupation, and show how these reactions of the different Jewish sects and parties largely determined their response to Jesus.

3. Give a brief overview of the Sadducees, Pharisees, Essenes, Zealots, and Herodians, their response to the Roman occupation, and their corresponding reaction to the ministry of Jesus.

4. Detail the Jewish concept of the Kingdom of God at the time of Jesus, influenced as it was by their oppression from political powers, including their belief that the Kingdom of God would come in power, restoring the material universe and saving humankind from the control of Satan.

5. Defend the biblical evidence that supports the idea that Jesus proclaimed the Kingdom present, and demonstrated its reality in his person, and works of healings and exorcisms.

Objectives for Lesson 3
The Messiah Revealed

After your reading, study, discussion, and application of the materials in this lesson, you will be able to:

1. Demonstrate your understanding of the richness of Jesus as Messiah in his personal revelation spoken of in the Gospel accounts.

2. Show how from the New Testament Scriptures that Jesus' Messianic identity is powerfully revealed through his perfect life and character, his masterful leadership of the Apostles, and his submissive sonship to his Father.

3. Describe how the Bible makes plain Jesus' Messianic identity in his prophetic teaching ministry, as well as in the mighty demonstrations of power, both in signs and wonders (miracles) and dramatic encounter with spiritual demons.

4. Outline the episodes which make up the suffering and death of Jesus (i.e., his Passion), and show how his death provides a clear biblical revelation of his role as Messiah.

5. Explain how Peter's confession of Jesus' true identity, accompanied by Jesus' prediction of his death, underwrites Jesus' Messiahship.

6. List and briefly give commentary on the final events of Jesus' life on earth: his triumphal entry into Jerusalem, his Passover with his disciples, as well as the events surrounding his crucifixion and death, from his agony in prayer in the Garden to his burial after his death on the cross.

Objectives for Lesson 4
The Messiah Vindicated

After your reading, study, discussion, and application of the materials in this lesson, you will be able to:

1. Recite the basic facts related to the significance of the resurrection of Messiah Jesus, and how the entire credibility of our theology, faith, and ministry is based on the historical certainty of Jesus having been raised from the dead.
2. Provide a listing of the various appearances of Jesus, beginning with his resurrection at the tomb up until his appearance to the Apostles at the Sea of Galilee.
3. Cite biblical evidence to show the vindication of the Messianic identity of Jesus Christ through the apostolic testimony that he has been raised from the dead.
4. State briefly how the Great Commission serves as a continuing vindication of Jesus' identity as Messiah, and the importance of this commission as it relates both to the fulfillment of prophecy as well as to global mission.
5. Show how the Great Commission was repeated in Jesus' post-resurrection appearances, and how Jesus demonstrated his resurrection to the Apostles during a forty-day period of manifestation.
6. Argue for the importance and relevance of the ascension of Christ as the final historical sign which gives evidence that Jesus of Nazareth is the Messiah of God.

Teaching Objectives for Capstone, by Module

Module Description

Capstone Module 14 – God the Holy Spirit

There are few theological truths in the history of the Church that have sparked as much controversy, disagreement, and schism as the doctrine of the Holy Spirit. From ancient disagreements about Trinity and "procession" to modern disagreements about the baptism and gifts of the Holy Spirit, there is much that might cause us to approach this module with caution; but, I sincerely hope that this is not the case. The doctrine of the Holy Spirit lies at the very heart of the way that we understand who God is and how we experience his living presence in our midst. The Spirit is sent to empower and lead the Church of God and to give new life to all those who respond in faith to its message about Jesus. Our hope is that the truths you learn about the Holy Spirit will not only be "formal theology" which helps you to understand God better, but will be also "practical theology" which allows you to depend on the Holy Spirit in ever increasing measure as you minister in God's Church and witness in the world.

The first lesson, *The Person of the Holy Spirit*, focuses upon God the Spirit as the third person of the one Trinitarian God. We will explore the biblical portrayal of the Spirit as a divine person who both is God and who consciously acts as God. We will also discuss the relationship of the Spirit to the Father and the Son as the one who is the "bond of love" between them and their "gift of love to the world." We will talk about the Spirit as the "Life-giver" and show how the names, titles, and symbols of the Spirit in the Scriptures portray him as the source and sustainer of physical and spiritual life and as the one who is at work to renew all things.

In our second lesson, *The Prophetic Work of the Holy Spirit*, we will explore the nature of prophetic revelation and come to understand the Spirit as the one who both inspires and illuminates the Word of God. We will also see that the prophetic role of the Spirit includes his ministry of conviction. He is the one who overcomes the deception caused by sin and leads us to true repentance. The prophetic work of the Holy Spirit is both the means by which God reveals himself and the means by which he enables us to believe that revelation.

Lessons three and four deal with *The Powerful Presence of the Holy Spirit (Part One)* and *The Powerful Presence of the Holy Spirit (Part Two)*, respectively. Here the focus is on what the Holy Spirit does in the lives of those who repent and believe. We will speak about the role of the Spirit in regeneration, adoption, baptism, gifting, indwelling, sealing, and sanctification. We will come to understand that the powerful work of the Spirit enables the Church to fulfill its mission in the world.

The person of the Holy Spirit is as real and vital as God the Father and God the Son. The Spirit is sent by the Father and the Son into the world so that we can experience loving fellowship with them and so that we can be empowered to obey God's commands and accomplish his mission. Our prayer is that your dependance on the Spirit will grow as you study the Scriptures together.

Objectives for *Capstone* Module 14, God the Holy Spirit

*Objectives for Lesson 1
The Person of
the Holy Spirit*

After your reading, study, discussion, and application of the materials in this lesson, you will be able to:

1. Describe the essential Christian understanding of God as Trinity.
2. Use the Scriptures to defend the truth that the Holy Spirit is fully God.
3. Use the Scriptures to defend the truth that the Holy Spirit is a Divine Person.
4. Explain the *filioque* and briefly describe the theological disagreements which have resulted from it.
5. Understand and defend the theological reasons for believing that the Spirit proceeds from the Father and the Son.
6. Explain Augustine's definition of the Holy Spirit as the "bond of love" between the Father and the Son.
7. Explain why the Holy Spirit must be worshiped and glorified along with the Father and the Son.
8. Understand why the theological study of the Holy Spirit is called *Pneumatology*.
9. Summarize the Old Testament view of the Spirit of God.
10. Use the Scriptures to describe the life-giving role of the Spirit in creating and sustaining the world.
11. Identify the major symbols associated with the Holy Spirit in the Scriptures and show how they contribute to our understanding of him as the Life-giver.
12. Explain how the names and titles of the Holy Spirit in the Scriptures contribute to our understanding of him as the Life-giver.
13. Explain why the ministry of the Spirit is a source of hope.

*Objectives for Lesson 2
The Prophetic Work
of the Holy Spirit*

After your reading, study, discussion, and application of the materials in this lesson, you will be able to:

1. Describe the biblical concept of prophecy.
2. Understand that all Scripture is a "prophetic" word from the Spirit of God.
3. See that all prophecy involves "forthtelling" a message from God, while some prophecy also involves "foretelling" a future event in God's plan.
4. Demonstrate from Scripture that prophecy is a ministry given to women as well as men.
5. Prove from Scripture that prophecy comes through the ministry of the Holy Spirit.
6. Verify the biblical claim that the Holy Spirit is the author of the Scriptures.
7. Define the doctrines of *inspiration* and *illumination* and explain the relationship between them.
8. Recognize that human beings are deceived about their sinful condition (its seriousness and consequences) and unwilling and unable to truly seek God and his righteousness.
9. Explain the meaning of conviction and describe the Spirit's role in bringing people to a knowledge of their sinful condition.
10. Define the key Hebrew and Greek words for repentance.
11. Describe the kinds of change that accompany true biblical repentance.
12. Demonstrate from the Scriptures that repentance is produced by the work of the Holy Spirit.

*Objectives for Lesson 3
The Powerful Presence
of the Holy Spirit, I*

After your reading, study, discussion, and application of the materials in this lesson, you will be able to:

1. Use the acrostic "RABBIS" to remember the work of the Holy Spirit in the lives of believers.
2. Explain the meaning and theological significance of the Spirit's role in the regeneration, adoption, and baptism of believers in Christ.
3. Understand agreements and differences among Christians over the meaning of "baptism in the Holy Spirit."
4. Use the Scriptures to show that the work of the Holy Spirit is the means by which God regenerates, adopts, and baptizes those who place their faith in Christ Jesus.

*Objectives for Lesson 4
The Powerful Presence
of the Holy Spirit, II*

After your reading, study, discussion, and application of the materials in this lesson, you will be able to:

1. Use the *RABBIS* acrostic to remember the work of the Holy Spirit in the lives of believers.
2. Explain the meaning and theological significance of the Spirit's role in gifting, indwelling, sealing, and sanctifying believers in Christ.
3. Identify key Scriptures which show that the work of the Holy Spirit is the means by which God gifts, indwells, seals and sanctifies believers in Christ.

*Teaching Objectives for
Capstone, by Module*

Module Description

Capstone Module 15 – The Equipping Ministry

The ministry of the Word of God lies at the heart of the equipping ministry. Paul tells the Ephesians that God has given the Church apostles, prophets, evangelists, and pastors and teachers in order that they might equip the saints for the work of ministry, for building up the body of Christ (Eph. 4.11-12). There is no precedent for seeing a church as having a single minister: as believers we hold to the universal priesthood of believers (1 Pet. 2.8-9), in the universal ministry of the gifts of the Spirit (1 Cor. 12.1-11), and the universal functioning of the members of the body of Christ (Romans 12.3-8). This module focuses on your role through preaching and teaching to equip believers to fulfill their God-given ministries in Christ.

In the first lesson, *The Ministry of Proclamation: Kerygma (1)*, we will define and provide an overview of the concept of preaching. We will look briefly at the distinctiveness of the preaching ministry to teaching, and speak about the development of preaching in the ministry of Jesus and the apostles. We will then look at some of the difficulties we will have to overcome if we are to be the kind of messengers of the Lord we need to be in our very needy day and time. In the second segment of this important lesson we will also examine the call to preach, suggesting that God sends men and women to be his messengers to proclaim his Word. We will then look carefully at the kind of character that we need to have for effective preaching, and look at the content of effective biblical preaching – the biblical truth regarding Jesus Christ and his Kingdom.

Next, we will explore in our second lesson, *The Ministry of Proclamation: Kerygma (2)*, how the Holy Spirit affects every dimension of an effective preaching ministry. We will consider the kind of vessel or preacher the Spirit is most likely to use, and then look at some of the key aspects of the Spirit's work in the proclamation of the Word. We will also examine the three steps of planning out, delivering, and following up on the preached Word. As communicators of the Word of God, we must first establish contact with hearers, communicate the content of the Word clearly and boldly, and make connections with the truth of the message and the lives of the audience, proclaiming all in dependence on the Holy Spirit.

In the third lesson we will turn our attention to the ministry of teaching. In that teaching session, *The Ministry of Teaching: Didache (1)*, we will provide a definition and overview of the biblical concept of teaching. We will canvass the principles in the teaching ministry recorded in the NT, beginning with Jesus and the apostles, and outline the benefits of the teaching ministry in the Church. We will consider both the distinctives and difficulties associated with the ministry of teaching, and make a plea for us to recover the ministry of teaching in our urban churches in order to build the Kingdom in our communities. As with the preaching ministry, we will analyze the call, character, and content of the teaching ministry, highlighting the central virtues needed for a fruitful ministry. As those entrusted with the Word of God, we must recognize our call to teach, be humble enough to be clear in our presentation of Jesus Christ and his Kingdom, and teach for maturity and fruitfulness in the Church. By understanding the call, the character and the content of the teaching ministry, we will be better able to lead others into the truth.

Finally, in lesson four, *The Ministry of Teaching: Didache (2)*, we will carefully examine how the Holy Spirit impacts and leads us in our ministry of teaching in the Church. The Holy Spirit selects particular members in the Church of Jesus Christ and supplies them with his own anointing, gifting, and call to teach. The called teacher is responsible for using his or her gift with all their energy, being faithful and teachable, while the Holy Spirit employs their gift for the sake of building up the body. We will close our module with a focus on the three steps in designing, delivering, and applying a teaching presentation. To teach our students well we must first establish contact with our students, then communicate the content of the Word of God in our lesson with clarity and boldness. Finally, we strive to make connections with the lives of the students and the truth of the Word of God. To teach is to strive to see individuals obey all that Christ has commanded us, through the leading of the Spirit.

A revolution can occur in urban ministry when gifted and available men and women minister the Word of God in such a way as to raise up a new generation of laborers in the city – those who can care for the hurting, share the truth of God, and declare the Kingdom to their neighbors. Your role in this ministry is urgent and needed.

Teaching Objectives for Capstone, by Module

*Objectives for Lesson 1
The Ministry of
Proclamation:
Kerygma, I*

Objectives for *Capstone* Module 15, The Equipping Ministry

After your reading, study, discussion, and application of the materials in this lesson, you will be able to:

1. Define the preaching ministry according to the various terms used in the NT translated "preaching," "preach," etc., all of which contain an element of *announcing a message to an audience, to proclaim a message publicly*.

2. Outline the various models of preaching informed by the meanings of preaching in the NT, i.e., the preacher as herald (one who announces a message on behalf of another as a *herald* or *messenger*), the preacher as *ambassador* (i.e., the preacher as a representative of the Kingdom of God, speaking its message in a foreign land); the preacher as *delivery man* (i.e., in ways similar to the prophetic office, the preacher functions as one meant to ensure that a message gets safely and clearly to a predetermined audience).

3. Lay out some of the major distinctives of the preaching ministry, including its focus on mixed audiences, even sometime, wholly non-religious ones, its intimate connection to the Gospel of Christ and evangelistic activity, its focus on preaching to those who have never heard of the Good News of Christ before, and its concentration on *public* address, whether to those who are saved or lost.

4. Explain some of the major features of preaching in the ministry of Christ and the apostles, i.e., Jesus' clear and compelling proclamation of the Kingdom of God come in his person in fulfillment of the OT Messianic hope, and the apostolic proclamation of Jesus of Nazareth as the Messiah, and the call to repentance and faith to both Jew and Gentile in his name.

5. Give evidence of your understanding of the ways in which the Church historically has broadened the ministry of preaching, including views of preaching as the manifestation of the Incarnate Word from the written Word through the spoken word, as proclamation of divine truth, as a retelling of the biblical story, and as a spoken word that builds bridges between the hearer and Scripture.

6. List out some of the major difficulties in the preaching ministry, including the inability of people to understand God's Word due to satanic interference, the weakness of the human vessels who proclaim the message, the number of

issues seen as critical to preaching, and the ever present need to rediscover God's power as the key to effective preaching.

7. Demonstrate a knowledge of the call to the preaching ministry, including the call of a divine unction and compulsion to proclaim God's Gospel in Christ, Paul's selection as Christ's chosen instrument to carry his name to the nations, the Holy Spirit's movement in the heart and life of the one so called, understanding preaching as a response to the divine call, not as a job, and its association with God's gifts, endowments, and direction.

8. Outline the importance of the role of character in the preaching ministry, especially the idea that "who we are is more important than what we do," the cardinal virtue of preaching being courage and its cardinal vice being *cowardice.*

9. Detail the content of the preaching ministry which includes the Good News of Jesus Christ, i.e., salvation and life through faith in his name, the message of Christ crucified for the sins of the world, the Kingdom of God in Jesus Christ, and the whole counsel of God about the Messiah and the rule of God in him.

*Objectives for Lesson 2
The Ministry of
Proclamation:
Kerygma, II*

After your reading, study, discussion, and application of the materials in this lesson, you will be able to:

1. Detail the ways in which the Holy Spirit affects every dimension of an effective preaching ministry.

2. Outline critically the kind of individual that the Holy Spirit uses to preach the Word effectively, including those who are obedient to the call of God to preach who are convinced of the power of the Word of God for salvation and change, and who have a command of the Word of God yet who retain a mind to study its treasures, and who are free in Christ to become all things to all to save some.

3. Explain specifically how the Holy Spirit oversees and influences the entire process of the preaching event, thwarting the devil's veiling of the Gospel to the lost, illuminating the message for the preacher and their audience, anointing and inspiring the preacher in their presentation while convicting the audience of the truth, and confirming the spoken word with signs and wonders of its veracity.

4. Lay out the particular things that occur as a result of the Holy Spirit's work in the preaching ministry, including deep

Teaching Objectives for Capstone, by Module

conviction of sin, righteousness, and judgment before the Lord, solid conversions through repentance and faith in Jesus Christ, and true incorporation into the body of Christ.

5. Recite the three central steps in planning out, delivering the content, and making connection with the audience through the preached Word.

6. Lay out the ways in which we establish contact with our hearers as we spotlight issues, concerns, ideas, or experiences that resonate in the lives of the audience, which can also be used as a springboard into our preaching content.

7. List key principles as to how we can paint a picture through our words in the spiritual eyes of our hearers so as to show them our themes (not merely tell them about it), preaching messages which focus on Christ and his Kingdom, using the Bible's methods of images, symbols, and stories, being organized in a plain and simple manner.

8. Explain how use of the liturgy and the Church calender allow us to provide our audiences with a continuous retelling of the Story of God in the life and work of Jesus, and thus highlight the whole counsel of God annually through his story.

9. Gain skill in making connections in our preaching with the audience by inviting them to specific and particular responses, helping them to understand their spiritual condition before God by making clear appeals and bold invitations for repentance and change, and when responses are made, gaining insight as to how these should be followed up on quickly and thoroughly.

Objectives for Lesson 3
The Ministry of
Teaching: Didache, I

After your reading, study, discussion, and application of the materials in this lesson, you will be able to:

1. Define the various terms given for *teacher*, *teaching*, and to *teach* in the NT.

2. Outline the teaching ministry according to the various models offered of it in the NT, including the model of the teacher as a *scribe of the Kingdom* (one who teaches or instructs in the revelation of Jesus Christ and his Kingdom), the teacher as a *master builder* (one who builds on the teaching of Jesus, the apostles and prophets to make their meaning clear for others to teach others), the teacher as a *master craftsman* (one who equips apprentices who will be able to train others also), and the teacher as *seer* (in modern

terms, a *color commentator* on the game of the Lord, one explaining the working of God in the world, and our response to it).

3. Lay out some of the major distinctives of the teaching ministry, including its focus on building up disciples in Jesus Christ to maturity, and fulfilling the teaching clause of the Great Commission, to equip the saints for the work of the ministry, and to protect growing disciples from the threat of heresy, schism, dead orthodoxy, and spiritual immaturity.

4. Explain some of the major features of the teaching ministry in Jesus' clear and compelling teaching of the Kingdom of God, and the apostles' focus on the teaching ministry in the Messianic community, the Church, and thus how teaching played a critical role in credentialing and empowering leaders, defending the apostolic faith, and offering an apology for the Christian hope.

5. Highlight some of the central difficulties associated with the teaching ministry, including the tendency to follow modern trends rather than the historic Christian faith, over-dependence on highly analytical and technical approaches to biblical truth, undue focus on methods and gimmicks rather than the heart of the Christian message, and the tendency to substitute academic performance rather than dependence on the anointing of the Holy Spirit.

6. Show how that in urban ministry there is a need for us to recover the ministry of teaching (i.e., the ministry of equipping the saints for the work of the ministry) in our urban churches in order to build the Kingdom in our most vulnerable and neglected urban communities.

7. Demonstrate with use of the Scriptures the ingredients of a legitimate call to the teaching ministry, including an under-standing of the teaching ministry as a call to *equip the saints for the work of the ministry*. Show that teaching is not a matter of scholarship alone, but spiritual gifting and enablement from Christ – the ability to lead others to discover the truth through dialogue and study, and above all else, the anointing and enablement of the Holy Spirit in the one teaching and those who are being taught.

8. Outline the way in which the "principle of character" (i.e., who a teacher is in his or her character will sooner or later impact what they as a teacher say and do) impacts the fruitfulness of the teacher.

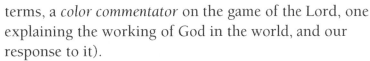

Teaching Objectives for Capstone, by Module

9. Reproduce and defend with Scripture that the cardinal virtue of the teaching ministry is *clarity*, rightly dividing the Word of truth and relating that meaning to the lives of the students, and show the same with the cardinal vice of the teaching ministry being *pride and hypocrisy*, knowledge puffs up, and, it is easy to lay standards on others that you yourself are unwilling to apply and keep.

10. Detail the *content* of the teaching ministry which includes the teaching clause of the Great Commission, i.e., to *instruct disciples of Jesus to obey everything that he commanded*, to make plain the person and work of Jesus Christ for the purpose of Christlikeness in character and life, to make plain the teaching regarding the Kingdom of God and the promise and the righteousness associated with it, and understanding and defending the *apostolic tradition*, i.e., the historic orthodox faith and how it relates to their life and witness where they live.

Objectives for Lesson 4
The Ministry of
Teaching: Didache, II

After your reading, study, discussion, and application of the materials in this lesson, you will be able to:

1. Detail the ways in which the Holy Spirit uses a person who through discipline and spiritual brokenness has prepared himself for the Spirit's teaching ministry. These traits include the teachers' faithfulness (i.e., their reliability and trustworthiness as a steward of God's mysteries), their teachableness (i.e., their ability to be taught daily by the Lord and their leaders), and their hunger and thirst for the Lord and his wisdom (i.e., their seeking the Lord's wisdom like treasure).

2. Outline some of the other characteristics of an effective teacher, including their rigorous and disciplined obedience to the Word (i.e., doing what they ask others to do), their teaching of Jesus Christ and his Kingdom (the King and his authority), and their devotion to constantly excel at the teaching craft (i.e., building up their ability to teach the Word with skill and power).

3. Explain specifically how the Holy Spirit oversees and influences the entire process of the teaching event. This includes his giving the gift of teaching to the select members of Christ's body, guiding both teacher and student into the truth, providing continuous insight into the Word of God, anointing the teacher in their ministry, making intercession

for us, providing illumination into specific inquiries of the truth, and supplying power to obey the Word of God.

4. Lay out the particular effects that occur as a result of the Holy Spirit's work in the teaching ministry, including enabling us to obey everything Jesus commanded, being insulated against the lies and deception of false teachers so as to reach stability in our personal faith, maturing as disciples of Jesus in the Church, and becoming solid enough so as to teach others to teach others.

5. Recite and outline with Scripture the three central steps in planning out, delivering the content, and making connection with the audience through the preached Word: establishing contact with the life situation of our audience, communicating content of the Word of God clearly and boldly, and making connections through the disciplined application of the Word to our lives.

6. Reproduce the ways in which we establish contact with our hearers in the teaching situation specifically as we prepare and teach lessons that pay careful attention to the culture and life situation of the students–their language, the ways in which they understand, process, and communicate ideas and truths.

7. Give evidence that you understand the key principles related to communicating the Word of God effectively in the teaching lesson, including the many ways in which we can paint a picture and engage our students in such a way as to make the meaning of the text come alive for them, as directly and concretely as possible.

8. See how use of Jesus' method of teaching stories, metaphors, images, and symbols with passion and clarity can make the communication of the Word dramatically more effective, especially with urban cultures which tend to take these elements more seriously than others.

9. Explain how to address specific subjects that are appropriate to the audience and the situation, but keep the focus on the continuous retelling of the Story of God in the life and work of Jesus, and our application of his will for our lives as citizens of the Kingdom.

10. Gain skill in making connections in your teaching situations, i.e., learning to interconnect the content of your communication of the biblical message with the practical concerns, needs, and challenges of your students' lives.

Teaching Objectives for Capstone, by Module

11. Demonstrate how to draw out key principles which summarize the teaching imaged and spoken forth during the content section of the teaching, learning to allow room for the Holy Spirit to challenge the students, while constantly admonishing the students to relate the truth of God to their lives in a specific and particular way.

12. Learn and apply some practical suggestions in designing an effective teaching session, including how to build the entire lesson around teaching aims, developing a clear outline of your ideas, communicating in new ways, keeping your teaching focused on obeying the words of Jesus from different dimensions. All is to be done in conscious dependence upon the Holy Spirit.

13. Show from Scripture how all effective teaching strives to see individuals obey all that Christ has commanded us, through the leading of the Spirit.

Teaching Objectives for Capstone, by Module

Capstone **Module 16 – Doing Justice and Loving Mercy: Compassion Ministries**

Module Description

As disciples of the Lord Jesus Christ, we are responsible to display in our words and deeds the life of the Kingdom to Come in the midst of our churches, and through our lifestyles and ministries of compassion to others. This module, *Doing Justice and Loving Mercy: Compassion Ministries*, highlights the ways in which we as Christian leaders both conceive and practice generosity in the body of Christ and in the world. As leaders of the church in the city, it is critical that we understand the richness of the biblical insights around this subject, as well as explore the possible ways in which we as believers and Christian ministers can demonstrate the love and justice of the Kingdom where we live.

The first lesson, *Let Justice Roll Down: The Vision and Theology of the Kingdom*, focuses on the first word, or prolegomena toward an understanding of doing justice and loving mercy. We will define the structure of the world from a biblical point of view, and assess the different ways in tradition that church/world relationships have been viewed, and highlight a theology of God that can help us understand the critical role that doing justice and loving mercy plays in our kingdom testimony. We will also look carefully at the *imago Dei* (i.e., the image of God) in Scripture. We will see the uniqueness of humankind, and explore its implications for viewing all individuals, families, peoples, and nations as precious and irreplaceable.

Our second lesson, *Doing Justice and Loving Mercy: The Urban Congregation*, explores the priority of demonstrating justice and mercy in the Church of Christ. As the people of God, we must understand the "home grown" quality of Christian love, and in this lesson we will consider the significance of God's grace in sustaining ministries of mercy and love, and the implications of experiencing God's grace in our approaches to justice and mercy. We will observe, too, the practices of justice and mercy in God's OT community as well as in the Church, God's kingdom community today. We will also observe the "two-four-six" rules of God's love and justice through the Church. We will begin by looking at the two objects which can receive God's justice and mercy, members of the Church and those outside. We will then consider the four channels through which God manifests his love: the family, the Church, care societies, and the state. We will finish our study by looking at six principles which should inform our care-giving as local congregations.

In lesson three, *Doing Justice and Loving Mercy: Urban Community and Neighborhood*, we will discuss the two critical truths underlying our understanding of serving in the world: God as creator and Jesus as Lord of all. The Church responds to the lordship of Jesus Christ, serving both as the locus (place) of God's working as well as his agent (ambassador) through whom he works. We will look at the four classic ways that church/world relations have been understood in Church history, and then look at four models which can help us understand better just how the urban church should interact with its neighborhood and community. We will here also introduce a simple yet effective approach to organize our efforts together as we seek the Lord's will to minister mercy and justice in our urban neighborhoods. Prepare, Work, and Review, (PWR) is a simple but exciting process of seeking the Lord's wisdom in ministry. And in this lesson we will provide some practical advice on how to organize in order to provide effective care to others as we address the needs of those in our community.

Finally, in lesson four, *Doing Justice and Loving Mercy: Society and World*, we will seek to expand this notion of doing justice and loving mercy to the very ends of the earth. Here we will look to comprehend our calling to live as world Christians, striving to think globally but to act locally. We will look critically at the issues of poverty and oppression, and the protection of the environment. After considering these weighty issues, we close this module's discussion with a focus on one of the great issues of our time, the concept of difference. We will explore the oft-misunderstood notion of diversity from a kingdom perspective. We will explore the ways in which wrong concepts of difference can fuel bigotry and hatred among people, lead to violence, war and the loss of life and destruction of property. Here we will explore three Christian approaches to mass violence and war, and end our time with a plea for us to embrace a dynamic ministry of Christian peacemaking.

In a world torn by violence, cruelty, and injustice, we desperately need representatives of the Kingdom who can demonstrate both the justice and mercy of our Lord Jesus Christ. Only the Church can reveal the righteousness, unity, and grace of the Kingdom of God in the midst of a world torn by malice, vengeance, and disunity. Only in Christ can we pursue a peace that is authentic and that will last. Until our Lord returns, we are called to display his righteousness in the earth.

Objectives for *Capstone* Module 16, Doing Justice and Loving Mercy: Compassion Ministries

Teaching Objectives for Capstone, by Module

Objectives for Lesson 1 Let Justice Roll Down: The Vision and Theology of the Kingdom

After your reading, study, discussion, and application of the materials in this lesson, you will be able to:

1. Recite the elements of a valid first word, or *prolegomena*, for an understanding of doing justice and loving mercy.
2. Outline and define the system of the world from a biblical point of view, and show the different ways in Church tradition that church/world relationships have been viewed.
3. Highlight a biblical theology of God that can help you understand the critical role that doing justice and loving mercy plays in our kingdom testimony.
4. Explain carefully and precisely the image of God and its basis in the teachings of the Bible.
5. Lay out the ways in which the Scriptures portray humankind as unique and precious because of God's special gift of creation, forming human beings in his own image and likeness.
6. List the reasons why we ought to view all individuals, families, peoples, and nations as precious and irreplaceable.
7. Detail the theological implications of the teaching regarding the *imago Dei*, especially how this high view of humankind justifies our best and most dedicated effort at the preservation and care for human life, wherever it exists and wherever we find people in distress.

Objectives for Lesson 2 Doing Justice and Loving Mercy: The Urban Congregation

After your reading, study, discussion, and application of the materials in this lesson, you will be able to:

1. Outline the priority of justice and mercy for the ministry and work of the Church of Christ.
2. Show from Scripture how the Church has been granted the sober responsibility of demonstrating God's justice and mercy in the world today, called to demonstrate this first to its own members, in a kind of "home grown" quality of Christian love.
3. Recite how the grace of God underpins and shapes our theologies of justice, mercy, and love, and lay out the

Teaching Objectives for Capstone, by Module

implications of experiencing God's grace in our approaches to justice and mercy.

4. List the basic elements involved in the rationale and practices of justice and mercy in the life of Israel, God's OT community.

5. Give the basic theological rationale for the Church as God's kingdom community, and its call to justice and mercy in this age, and specifically for the urban church.

6. Give evidence of the significance of the two objects of God's justice and mercy, i.e., the members of the Church and those outside.

7. Discuss the four channels through which God manifests his love: the family, the Church, care societies, and the state.

8. Recount the six key principles which should inform our care-giving as local congregations as we seek to demonstrate God's justice and mercy in our urban communities.

*Objectives for Lesson 3
Doing Justice and
Loving Mercy:
The Urban Community
and Neighborhood*

After your reading, study, discussion, and application of the materials in this lesson, you will be able to:

1. Reaffirm the two critical truths in the Nicene Creed that underlie our understanding of serving in the world: God as *creator* and Jesus Christ as Lord of all.

2. Acknowledge the primary ways in which Scripture acknowledges how the Church responds to the lordship of Jesus Christ, serving both as the *locus* (place) of God's working as well as his *agent* (ambassador) through whom he works.

3. Recite the four different and classic ways in Church history that Christians have understood the Church's relationship to the world: to withdraw from the world and its affairs, to transform the world through direct oversight, to live in tension with the world, being in it but not of it, and finally to live as prophetic witness to the world in our model and proclamations.

4. Outline four of the biblical models of the Church which have immediate bearing on church/world relationships for urban life: we are called to be neighbors, the salt of the earth, the light of the world, and a royal priesthood of God in the city.

5. Detail the specific elements of ministry management to maximize opportunities in urban Christian outreach and justice: Prepare, Work, and Review or PWR.

6. Lay out in Scripture the foundation of all solid ministry management, i.e., the theology of God's purpose and wisdom, and identify and refute the major barriers and objections that some might raise to planning ministry processes.

7. Give clearly and persuasively the key benefits to adopting a flexible but disciplined approach to urban ministry management.

8. Know how to mobilize gifted available team members for ministry using the specific items of the PWR process, highlighting the kinds of attitudes and actions necessary for aggressive and credible outreach in urban communities.

9. Identify some of the key problems and challenges associated with outreach in urban neighborhoods, and provide practical advice on how to handle these issues as you engage in proclaiming the Good News and doing good works in the city.

*Objectives for Lesson 4
Doing Justice and
Loving Mercy:
Society and World*

After your reading, study, discussion, and application of the materials in this lesson, you will be able to:

1. Discuss the ramifications of applying a kingdom ethic of doing justice and loving mercy to the very ends of the earth.

2. Explain our responsibility as disciples of Christ in today's society to live as world Christians, striving to think globally but act locally.

3. Lay out the ways in which the Church is both an outpost and beachhead of the Kingdom, called to demonstrate freedom, wholeness, and justice in its engagement with the world, responding in love, obeying the leading of its head, the Lord Jesus Christ.

4. Provide a basic knowledge of four of the critical issues pertaining to world justice today: poverty and oppression, the human environment, ethnocentrism and difference, and war and violence.

5. Rediscover our roles as representatives of Christ and his Kingdom, and our duty to be aware of and engage with clarity the great issues of our time, and lead our congregations to act consistent with our calling to be salt and light in them.

6. Outline the biblical understanding of the concept of difference from a kingdom perspective, and detail how wrong uses of the categories of difference can fuel bigotry and hatred among people.

7. Explore the three historic models of Christian approaches to mass violence and war, and the rationale behind each model.

8. Give evidence of the need for Christian disciples to embrace a dynamic ministry of Christian peacemaking that will bring forgiveness, reconciliation, and grace to communities and societies torn by malice, vengeance, and disunity.

Appendix 5
Professor's Guide

Professor's Guide

This appendix is aimed at those who are interested in preparing and teaching original courses for leaders in the urban church.* Much of the information in the front part of this Mentor's Guide will be useful to you, however, as a professor you will create the course content as well as teach it.

* In the terminology used at The Urban Ministry Institute, a Mentor is someone who teaches a class where the core content is delivered by video or audio using TUMI's published distance-education courses. In contrast to this, a Professor actually develops a new course for use at the local ministry site.

Qualifications
Professors must fully support the vision of *The Urban Ministry Institute*. They must be in agreement with World Impact's Affirmation of Faith Statement (see page 265). They must show expertise in the field(s) related to the courses they teach or the seminars they lead (normally an academic degree and/or ordination plus substantive ministry experience).**

** The Site Coordinator will make the final determination of qualifications. The rule of thumb is that the Professor must have sufficient academic background and ministry experience to train pastors who are already engaged in the practice of ministry. Cross-cultural experience and urban ministry experience may also be factors considered in evaluating whether a person can be considered for this position.

Job Description
Professors are responsible for developing and teaching courses, tutoring students, and/or leading seminars and conferences that fulfill the goals and objectives of *The Urban Ministry Institute*. As you teach your course, your job responsibilities include:

- Delivering the course content
- Evaluating student progress
- Helping students to apply the learning to their specific ministry situations

Our focus is on developing leaders in the urban context and so we expect that your courses will be developed with this end goal in mind.

Steps to Developing a Course

1. For your information and orientation, please take time to study Section I of this *Mentor's Manual* to provide an overview of *The Urban Ministry Institute*, our curriculum, pedagogy, and programming. Please pay special attention to the role of the Great Tradition in TUMI's across-the-curricula strategy (i.e., our *Sacred Roots* emphasis), especially the commitment to creedal theology informed by the historic Nicene Creed. Also, comprehending the rationale and steps on our projects (both the

Please visit
www.tumi.org/mentor
for more information.

Ministry and Exegetical Projects) as well as our thinking in Section II, *Understanding the Role of the Mentor*. This entire section can enable you to ascertain our strategy of classroom learning and educational programming, and may contribute in your own particular design of your course.

2. Work with your Site Coordinator to:

   a. Choose a course topic

   b. Schedule the dates and times for the course

   c. Choose the appropriate department (Biblical Studies, Theology and Ethics, Christian Ministry, or Urban Mission) for the course and to understand the key departmental goals that may apply

   d. Receive an assigned course number

   e. Have your course textbooks ordered and made available

A Course Syllabus template is available at www.tumi.org/mentor.

3. Create a course syllabus* that includes the following elements:

   a. Course description

   b. Course objectives

   c. Assigned readings for the course

   d. Scripture memorization

   e. Ministry Project Guidelines

   f. Exegetical Paper Guidelines

   g. Grade Requirements

   h. Course Schedule

Work with you Site Coordinator to have the course syllabus copied and available for students.

Guidelines for Photocopying Materials for Student Handouts and/or for Classroom Presentation

The Urban Ministry Institute respects the rights of authors and publishers and adheres to the educational fair use standards as outlined in Section 107 of the Copyright Law of the United States of America and Related Laws Contained in Title 17 of the United States Code Title. Your Site Coordinator can give you guidelines that assist you in making informed decisions about when photocopying of copyrighted materials is appropriate.

Professor's Guide

Appendix 6
Fast Facts on the Capstone Curriculum

4	Average number of years to complete *Capstone Certificate* (one class per quarter)
4	Subject areas: Biblical Studies, Theology and Ethics, Christian Ministry, Urban Mission
8	Years to write and produce the *Capstone Curriculum*
16	Modules with 16 student exegetical papers, and 16 ministry projects completed by student
41	Textbooks are required reading for students
72	Lessons: 16 modules x 4 lessons/module
128	Video segments: 16 modules x 8 segments/module
166	Verses memorized by students
217	Recommended supplemental textbooks
256	Classroom hours (8-week format)
380+	Case Studies
8,080	Scripture Passages
10,000+	Pages in the *Capstone Curriculum*

Fast Facts on the Capstone Curriculum

Appendix 7

Comparing the Scripture Memorization Lists in the Capstone Curriculum and Master the Bible System

- Arranged by department area
- Total verses: 188 with repeats; 166 without repeats

Module and Lesson	Memory Verse	MTB System
Biblical Studies		
Conversion and Calling Module 1, Lesson 1 • *The Word That Creates*	2 Pet. 1.19-21	2.10.1a (v. 19) 2.1.1a (vv. 20-21)
Conversion and Calling Module 1, Lesson 2 • *The Word That Convicts*	John 16.7-11	1.7.4a
Conversion and Calling Module 1, Lesson 3 • *The Word That Converts*	Rom. 10.8-13	1.2.3a (vv. 9-10) 4.2.1a (vv. 11-13)
Bible Interpretation Module 5, Lesson 1 • *Biblical Inspiration: The Origins and Authority of the Bible*	2 Pet. 1.19-21	2.10.1a (v. 19) 2.1.1a (v. 20-21)
Bible Interpretation Module 5, Lesson 2 • *Biblical Hermeneutics: The Three-Step Model*	Ezra 7.10 Acts 17.11 Ps. 1.1-3	
Bible Interpretation Module 5, Lesson 3 • *Biblical Literature: Interpreting the Genres of the Bible*	2 Tim. 3.14-17	1.6.1b (vv.15-17)
The Old Testament Witness to Christ and His Kingdom Module 9, Lesson 1 • *The Promise Given*	Gen. 3.15; 12.1-3	1.1.2a (v. 3.15) 1.1.2b (vv. 12.1-3)
The Old Testament Witness to Christ and His Kingdom Module 9, Lesson 2 • *The Promise Clarified*	Luke 24.44-48	2.2.1b
The Old Testament Witness to Christ and His Kingdom Module 9, Lesson 3 • *The Promise Personalized*	Deut. 18.15-19	3.1.2a (v. 15)
The New Testament Witness to Christ and His Kingdom Module 13, Lesson 1 • *The Messiah Announced*	John 1.14-18	2.6.2a
The New Testament Witness to Christ and His Kingdom Module 13, Lesson 2 • *The Messiah Opposed*	John 15.18-20	4.1.5b
The New Testament Witness to Christ and His Kingdom Module 13, Lesson 3 • *The Messiah Revealed*	Luke 24.44-49	2.2.1b (vv. 44-48) 2.7.2a (vv. 49-53)

Scripture Memorization in Capstone and MTB

Scripture Memorization in Capstone and MTB

Module and Lesson	Memory Verse	MTB System
Theology and Ethics		
The Kingdom of God Module 2, Lesson 1 • *God's Reign Challenged*	Isa. 14.12-17	2.3.5a (vv. 12-15)
The Kingdom of God Module 2, Lesson 2 • *God's Reign Inaugurated*	Luke 11.15-20	4.5.5a
The Kingdom of God Module 2, Lesson 3 • *God's Reign Invading*	1 Pet. 2.9-10	1.4.5b
God the Father Module 6, Lesson 1 • *Prolegomena: The Doctrine of God and the Advance of the Kingdom*	Ps. 19.1-3	1.1.1b
God the Father Module 6, Lesson 2 • *God as Creator: The Providence of God*	1 Chron. 29.11-12	
God the Father Module 6, Lesson 3 • *The Triune God: The Greatness of God*	Matt. 3.16-17	3.3.2b
God the Son Module 10, Lesson 1 • *Jesus, the Messiah and Lord of All: He Came*	John 1.14-18	2.6.2a
God the Son Module 10, Lesson 2 • *Jesus, the Messiah and Lord of All: He Lived*	Heb. 2.14-17	
God the Son Module 10, Lesson 3 • *Jesus, the Messiah and Lord of All: He Died*	1 Pet. 2.21-24	
God the Holy Spirit Module 14, Lesson 1 • *The Person of the Holy Spirit*	Rom. 8.15-17	1.8.2a (vv. 14-17)
God the Holy Spirit Module 14, Lesson 2 • *The Prophetic Work of the Holy Spirit*	Rom 8.18-21	
God the Holy Spirit Module 14, Lesson 3 • *The Powerful Presence of the Holy Spirit, I*	Rom. 8.22-25	

Module and Lesson	Memory Verse	MTB System
Christian Ministry		
Theology of the Church Module 3, Lesson 1 • *The Church Foreshadowed in God's Plan*	1 Pet. 2.9-10	1.4.5b
Theology of the Church Module 3, Lesson 2 • *The Church at Worship*	Heb. 10.19-22	
Theology of the Church Module 3, Lesson 3 • The Church as Witness	Matt. 28.18-20	4.10.1a
Foundations of Christian Leadership Module 7, Lesson 1 • *The Christian Leader as Deacon*	Mark 9.35-37	
Foundations of Christian Leadership Module 7, Lesson 2 • *The Christian Leader as Elder*	1 Pet. 5.1-4	
Foundations of Christian Leadership Module 7, Lesson 3 • *The Christian Leader as Pastor*	Acts 20.26-28	
Practicing Christian Leadership Module 11, Lesson 1 • *Effective Worship Leading: Worship, Word, and Sacrament*	John 4.21-24	
Practicing Christian Leadership Module 11, Lesson 2 • *Effective Christian Education: Incorporating, Parenting, and Discipling*	2 Tim. 2.1-2	4.10.3a (v. 2)
Practicing Christian Leadership Module 11, Lesson 3 • *Effective Church Discipline: Exhorting, Rebuking, and Restoring*	Heb. 12.5-8	
The Equipping Ministry Module 15, Lesson 1 • *The Ministry of Proclamation: Kerygma I*	Eph. 4.11-16	3.8.1a (vv. 15-16)
The Equipping Ministry Module 15, Lesson 2 • *The Ministry of Proclamation: Kerygma II*	2 Tim. 2.1-3	4.10.3a (v. 2)
The Equipping Ministry Module 15, Lesson 3 • *The Ministry of Teaching: Didache I*	Heb. 5.11-6.3	

Scripture Memorization in Capstone and MTB

Scripture Memorization in Capstone and MTB

Module and Lesson	Memory Verse	MTB System
Urban Mission		
Foundations for Christian Mission Module 4, Lesson 1 • *The Vision and Biblical Foundation for Christian Mission I*	Heb. 6.17-18	
Foundations for Christian Mission Module 4, Lesson 2 • *The Vision and Biblical Foundation for Christian Mission II*	Eph. 5.25-27 Eph. 6.10-13	4.7.2a
Foundations for Christian Mission Module 4, Lesson 3 • *Christian Mission and the City*	Heb. 11.13-16	
Evangelism and Spiritual Warfare Module 8, Lesson 1 • *Spiritual Warfare: Binding of the Strong Man*	Heb. 2.14-15 2 Cor. 11.3	
Evangelism and Spiritual Warfare Module 8, Lesson 2 • *Evangelism: The Content of the Good News of the Kingdom*	Rom. 10.9-10	1.2.3a
Evangelism and Spiritual Warfare Module 8, Lesson 3 • *Evangelism: Methods to Reach the Urban Community*	2 Tim. 2.24-26	
Focus on Reproduction Module 12, Lesson 1 • *Church Growth: Reproducing in Number and Quality*	Matt. 28.18-20 Acts 1.8	4.10.1a 1.10.5a
Focus on Reproduction Module 12, Lesson 2 • *Planting Urban Churches: Sowing*	Acts 16.30-34	1.10.4a (vv. 30-31)
Focus on Reproduction Module 12, Lesson 3 • *Planting Urban Churches: Tending*	2 Tim. 2.1-2	4.10.3a (v. 2)
Doing Justice and Loving Mercy Module 16, Lesson 1 • *Let Justice Roll Down: The Vision and Theology of the Kingdom*	Amos 5.20-24	
Doing Justice and Loving Mercy Module 16, Lesson 2 • *Doing Justice and Loving Mercy: The Urban Congregation*	Eph. 2.8-10	1.3.3a
Doing Justice and Loving Mercy Module 16, Lesson 3 • *Doing Justice and Loving Mercy: Urban Community and Neighborhood*	James 1.5-8	

Appendix 8
Ways to Schedule Your Training Programs

Each Capstone module is designed to be taught in 12 classroom hours (concentrated), whereas each Foundations for Ministry course or other created courses are 8-16 classroom hours. Both are consistent with the standards for continuing education across the country. Listed here are several sample formats you can use to schedule the training opportunities (using the 12-hour format) at your Institute. Be flexible to your student body, your faculty, and your situation.

Ways to Schedule Your Training Programs

Format	Description	Possible Dates and Schedule
Weekend Session	Meet four times within two days, 3 hours per meeting	Friday: 7:00pm - 10:00pm Saturday: 8:00am - 11:00am 1:00pm - 4:00pm 6:00pm - 9:00pm
3-Day Session	Meet four times within three days, 3 hours per meeting	Thursday: 6:00pm - 9:00pm Friday: 6:00pm - 9:00pm Saturday: 9:00am - 11:30am 1:30pm - 5:00pm
4-Day Session	Meet four times within four days, 3 hours per meeting	Monday: 6:00pm - 9:00pm Tuesday: 6:00pm - 9:00pm Wednesday: 6:00pm - 9:00pm Thursday: 6:00pm - 9:00pm
5-Day Session	Assign classroom sessions however you desire over the 5-day period	Tuesday: 7:00am - 9:00am Wednesday: 7:00am - 9:00am Thursday: 7:00am - 9:00am Friday: 7:00am - 9:00am Saturday: 8:00am - noon
2-Week Session	Meet twice a week for two weeks, 3 hours per meeting	Tuesdays: 6:30pm - 9:30pm Thursdays: 6:30pm - 9:30pm
4-Week Session	Meet once a week for four weeks, 3 hours per meeting	Tuesdays: 7:00pm - 10:00pm (4x)
6-Week Session	Meet once a week for six weeks, 2 hours per meeting	Wednesdays: 7:00am - 9:00am (6x)
8-Week Session	Meet once a week for eight weeks, 1.5 hours per meeting	Fri: 6:30pm - 8:00pm (8x)

Appendix 9

Sample Weekly Class Schedule

Module or Course Name: _____   Module or Course Number: _____

	1	2	3	4	5	6	7	8
Date								
Session #								
Theme								
Opening (5-10 min)								
Devotional (10-15 min)								
Recite Creed, Pray, Review Last Week's Concepts (15-20 min)								
Contact (15-20 min)								
Break								
Content (30-40 min)								
Connection (20 min)								
Assignments								

Appendix 10

Sample Course Schedule

Here we combine the weekly schedule with any overall class announcements.

Class	Date	Subject
Class Schedule for God the Father (T2-506)		
Hope School of Ministry • Session 1, Spring 2012 • Rev. Dr. Don L. Davis • January 24 - March 20, 2012		
Session 1	Tuesday, Jan. 24	God the Father *Session 1, Introduction*
Session 2	Tuesday, Jan. 31	The Doctrine of God and the Advance of the Kingdom *Does God Exist, and Does He Reveal Himself?* *Session 2, Lesson 1, Segment 1*
Session 3	Tuesday, Feb. 7	The Doctrine of God and the Advance of the Kingdom *Can God Be Known to Us?* *Session 3, Lesson 1, Segment 2*
Session 4	Tuesday, Feb. 14	God as the Creator: The Providence of God *Nicene Affirmation of God the Father Almighty* *Session 4, Lesson 2, Segment 1* Reading Assignments for Lesson 1 Due, Quiz for Lesson 1
Session 5	Tuesday, Feb. 21	God as the Creator: The Providence of God *Implications of the Nicene Affirmation* *Session 5, Lesson 2, Segment 2*
Session 6	Tuesday, Feb. 28	The Triune God: The Greatness of God *God's Greatness (Natural Attributes)* *Session 6, Lesson 3, Segment 1* Reading Assignments for Lesson 2 Due, Quiz for Lesson 2, Exegetical Project Topic Due
Session 7	Tuesday, Mar. 6	The Triune God: The Greatness of God *God's Triune Glory: The Trinity* *Session 7, Lesson 3, Segment 2*
Session 8	Tuesday, Mar. 13	God as Father: The Goodness of God *Moral Qualities of Goodness* *Session 8, Lesson 4, Segment 1* Reading Assignments for Lesson 3 Due, Quiz for Lesson 3
Session 9	Tuesday, Mar. 20	God as Father: The Goodness of God *Moral Qualities of Severity* *Session 9, Lesson 4, Segment 2*
	Tuesday, Apr. 3	All Assignments Due

Sample Course Schedule

News and Notes

1. Our textbooks are designed to be a part of your ongoing pastoral library; please obtain copies of all texts as tools for ministry in the church.

2. In order to maximize our class time together, please ensure that all reading and homework assignments are turned in before class. (Find the assignments on the separate sheets handed out in class.)

3. If you cannot make a class session, please notify me *in advance* (whenever possible). Make-up work will then be scheduled at your/my convenience.

4. Below is a list of all of the assignments that need to be turned in for this class on [Date]. (Remember ALL of the assignments need to be turned in at one time.)
    a. Reading Assignment, Lesson 1
    b. Reading Assignment, Lesson 2
    c. Reading Assignment, Lesson 3
    d. Scripture Memory, Lesson 1
    e. Scripture Memory, Lesson 2
    f. Scripture Memory, Lesson 3
    g. Exegetical Project Paper
    h. Ministry Project
    i. Final Exam
    j. Final Exam essay question 1 (stapled to final exam)
    k. Final Exam essay question 2 (stapled to final exam)

5. **Registration deadline for our next class, [*Class Title*], is [Date]. Register by that date in order to receive scholarship prices for your student workbooks.**

Appendix 11
The Three-Step Model

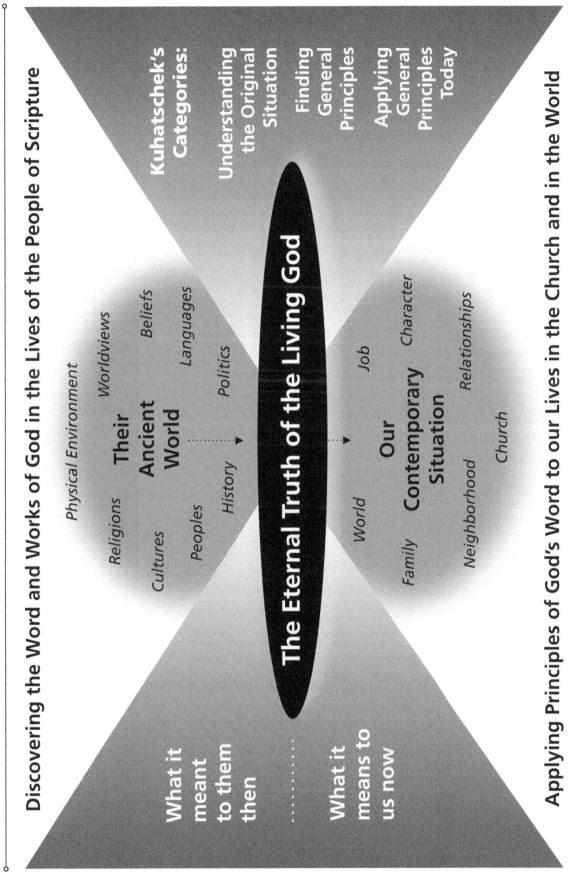

Discovering the Word and Works of God in the Lives of the People of Scripture

Kuhatschek's Categories:

Understanding the Original Situation

Finding General Principles

Applying General Principles Today

Their Ancient World

Physical Environment
Worldviews
Beliefs
Languages
Politics
History
Peoples
Cultures
Religions

The Eternal Truth of the Living God

Our Contemporary Situation

Job
Character
Relationships
Church
World
Family
Neighborhood

What it meant to them then

What it means to us now

Applying Principles of God's Word to our Lives in the Church and in the World

The Three-Step Model

The Exegetical Project

Appendix 12

The Exegetical Project:
Using the Three-Step Model to Exegete Scripture

Please also read pages 8-10 in your Capstone student workbook before starting, or refer to the course syllabus in Foundations.

Introduction

Start with a one-paragraph introduction which states the passage you are studying, and the main idea in it.

STEP ONE – Original Situation

What was God saying to the people in the text's original situation?

1. Who? When? Where? Why? What? (Observe passage carefully.)

    a. Read chapter around passage and discuss insights.

    b. Identify and discuss historical, literary, and cultural issues.

2. Do a verse-by-verse study of each verse in your passage. Make a simple verse-by-verse outline.

    a. Read in other translations and discuss insight.

    b. Study and discuss unique words.

3. Summarize the original meaning of the passage. Don't talk about general principles or applications yet.

Key Tools

Bible Dictionary, Study Bible, Additional Translations, Word Dictionary, Commentaries and Concordance.

STEP TWO – Finding General Principles

What principles does the text teach that is true for all people, in all places, at all times?

1. Finish Original Situation then find General Principles.

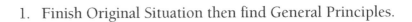

2. State what the General Principles are.

3. Check against other Scripture and discuss.

4. Check against commentaries and discuss.

5. Draw out key general principles (1-3).

Key Tools
Concordance, Commentaries, and Topical Bible

STEP THREE – Applying General Principles
What is the Holy Spirit asking me to do with these principles in my life and ministry?

The Exegetical Project

1. Do this section after completing the Original Situation and General Principles sections. This is where you address the issues which surfaced in the previous sections and apply them to your life and to those you are teaching.

2. How? How is this passage "Good News" to me and others? How does this passage affect my relationship to God, others, the church and culture?

3. So what? "What am I to believe?" and "What am I to do?" "Now that I have studied this passage, what difference does it make?"

4. Relate key general principles to your life and ministry.

Key Tools
Newspapers, News, Listening, Praying

- Include parenthetical notes in your paper.
- Include a *Works Cited* page at the end of your paper. (See the following appendix, *Documenting Your Work*.)

Appendix 13

Documenting Your Work
A Guide to Help You Give Credit Where Credit Is Due
The Urban Ministry Institute

Documenting Your Work

Avoiding Plagiarism

Plagiarism is using another person's ideas as if they belonged to you without giving them proper credit. In academic work it is just as wrong to steal a person's ideas as it is to steal a person's property. These ideas may come from the author of a book, an article you have read, or from a fellow student. The way to avoid plagiarism is to carefully use "notes" (textnotes, footnotes, endnotes, etc.) and a "Works Cited" section to help people who read your work know when an idea is one you thought of, and when you are borrowing an idea from another person.

Using Citation References

A citation reference is required in a paper whenever you use ideas or information that came from another person's work.

All citation references involve two parts:

- Notes in the body of your paper placed next to each quotation which came from an outside source.
- A "Works Cited" page at the end of your paper or project which gives information about the sources you have used

Using Notes in Your Paper

There are three basic kinds of notes: parenthetical notes, footnotes, and endnotes. At The Urban Ministry Institute, we recommend that students use parenthetical notes. These notes give the author's last name(s), the date the book was published, and the page number(s) on which you found the information. Example:

> In trying to understand the meaning of Genesis 14.1-24, it is important to recognize that in biblical stories "the place where dialogue is first introduced will be an important moment in revealing the character of the speaker . . ." (Kaiser and Silva 1994, 73). This is certainly true of the character of Melchizedek who speaks words of blessing. This identification of Melchizedek as a positive spiritual influence is reinforced by the fact that he is the King of Salem, since Salem means "safe, at peace" (Wiseman 1996, 1045).

Creating a Works Cited Page

A "Works Cited" page should be placed at the end of your paper. This page:

- lists every source you quoted in your paper
- is in alphabetical order by author's last name
- includes the date of publication and information about the publisher

The following formatting rules should be followed:

1. **Title**

   The title "Works Cited" should be used and centered on the first line of the page following the top margin.

2. **Content**

   Each reference should list:
   - the author's full name (last name first)
   - the date of publication
   - the title and any special information (Revised edition, 2nd edition, reprint) taken from the cover or title page should be noted
   - the city where the publisher is headquartered followed by a colon and the name of the publisher

3. **Basic form**

   - Each piece of information should be separated by a period.
   - The second line of a reference (and all following lines) should be indented.
   - Book titles should be underlined (or italicized).
   - Article titles should be placed in quotes.

   Example:

   Fee, Gordon D. 1991. *Gospel and Spirit: Issues in New Testament Hermeneutics.* Peabody, MA: Hendrickson Publishers.

Documenting Your Work

4. **Special Forms**

A book with multiple authors:

> Kaiser, Walter C., and Moisés Silva. 1994. *An Introduction to Biblical Hermeneutics: The Search for Meaning.* Grand Rapids: Zondervan Publishing House.

An edited book:

> Greenway, Roger S., ed. 1992. *Discipling the City: A Comprehensive Approach to Urban Mission.* 2nd ed. Grand Rapids: Baker Book House.

A book that is part of a series:

> Morris, Leon. 1971. *The Gospel According to John.* Grand Rapids: Wm. B. Eerdmans Publishing Co. The New International Commentary on the New Testament. Gen. ed. F. F. Bruce.

An article in a reference book:

> Wiseman, D. J. "Salem." 1982. In *New Bible Dictionary.* Leicester, England - Downers Grove, IL: InterVarsity Press. Eds. I. H. Marshall and others.

Electronic sources (i.e. Internet sources):

> James, Henry. *The Ambassadors.* Project Gutenberg, 1996. ftp://ibiblio.org/pub/docs/books/gutenberg/etext96/ambas10.txt.

An article in a periodical:

> Cook, Alison. "Phoenix Rising." *Gourmet*, April 2000, 62-64. A review of Restaurant Hapa.

(An example of a "Works Cited" page is located at the end of this appendix.)

For Further Research

Standard guides to documenting academic work in the areas of philosophy, religion, theology, and ethics include:

Atchert, Walter S., and Joseph Gibaldi. 1985. *The MLA Style Manual.* New York: Modern Language Association.

The Chicago Manual of Style. 1993. 14th ed. Chicago: The University of Chicago Press.

Turabian, Kate L. 1987. *A Manual for Writers of Term Papers, Theses, and Dissertations.* 5th edition. Bonnie Bertwistle Honigsblum, ed. Chicago: The University of Chicago Press.

Example of a "Works Cited" listing

Works Cited

Cook, Alison. "Phoenix Rising." *Gourmet,* April 2000, 62-64. A review of Restaurant Hapa.

Fee, Gordon D. 1991. *Gospel and Spirit: Issues in New Testament Hermeneutics.* Peabody, MA: Hendrickson Publishers.

Greenway, Roger S., ed. 1992. *Discipling the City: A Comprehensive Approach to Urban Mission.* 2nd ed. Grand Rapids: Baker Book House.

James, Henry. *The Ambassadors.* Project Gutenberg, 1996. ftp://ibiblio.org/pub/docs/books/gutenberg/etext96/ ambas10.txt.

Kaiser, Walter C., and Moisés Silva. 1994. *An Introduction to Biblical Hermeneutics: The Search for Meaning.* Grand Rapids: Zondervan Publishing House.

Morris, Leon. 1971. *The Gospel According to John.* Grand Rapids: Wm. B. Eerdmans Publishing Co. The New International Commentary on the New Testament. Gen. ed. F. F. Bruce.

Wiseman, D. J. "Salem." 1982. In *New Bible Dictionary.* Leicester, England-Downers Grove, IL: InterVarsity Press. Eds. I. H. Marshall and others.

Documenting Your Work

Appendix 14
Sample Student Information Sheet

An editable version of this document can be found at **www.tumi.org/mentor***.*

God the Father: T2-506				
Rev. Dr. Don L. Davis • Spring 2012, Session 1 • January 24 - March 20, 2012				
Student Name	Evening Phone	Day Phone	Email Address	Church
Allen, Larry				
Anderson, Fairy Dean				
Andrews, Kevin				
Andrews, LaTonia				
Asher, Zoe				
Berrios, Gerson				
Berrios, Mayra				
Boatwright, Betty				
Butler, Nathan				
Caleb, Carey				
Cheung, Michael				
Clausen, Patty				
Collins, Taullesa				
DeShazer, Roosevelt				
Duncan, Heath				
Eustache, Jean				
Graham, Joe				
Graham, Sue				
McMillian, Linda				
Wendt, Debbie				

Appendix 15
Sample Attendance Record Sheet

*An editable version of this document can be found at **www.tumi.org/mentor**.*

God the Father: T2-506									
Rev. Dr. Don L. Davis • Spring 2012, Session 1 • January 24 - March 20, 2012									
Student Name	1/24	1/31	2/7	2/14	2/21	2/28	3/6	3/13	3/20
Allen, Larry									
Anderson, Fairy Dean									
Andrews, Kevin									
Andrews, LaTonia									
Asher, Zoe									
Berrios, Gerson									
Berrios, Mayra									
Boatwright, Betty									
Butler, Nathan									
Caleb, Carey									
Cheung, Michael									
Clausen, Patty									
Collins, Taullesa									
DeShazer, Roosevelt									
Duncan, Heath									
Eustache, Jean									
Graham, Joe									
Graham, Sue									
McMillian, Linda									
Wendt, Debbie									

Sample Attendance Record Sheet

Appendix 16

Sample Reading Assignment Handout

Taken directly from the Satellite Gateway at www.tumi.org, this document is a summary of the reading assignments and edited with dates when those assignments were due.

God the Father, *Capstone* Module 6
Reading Assignment

Each *Capstone* module has assigned textbooks which are read and discussed throughout the course. We encourage you to read, reflect upon, and respond to these with your professor and fellow learners.

Students: Part of our course work requires that you purchase, read, and reflect upon the textbook(s) for the course. The assignment is to read each required textbook and write a precis (concise summary) of its main point, as you see it. Please summarize its major theme and argument, and then give your concise evaluation for **each** reading. Although the Student Workbook only shows space for two readings, the student must write a summary for each reading by using the back of the form. It is of utmost importance to us for our students to analyze a text, that is, to read it, understand its thesis (main point), articulate its argument in a respectful way (whether you agree with the author or not), and then respond as to why you agree or disagree with the thesis. This practice helps strengthen your ability to engage different opinions in a respectful way, and learn to listen to others and respond with clarity and respect. In this way, you learn to dialogue with and discuss with others whose beliefs differ from your own.

*Mentors: The reading assignments are keyed specifically to the lesson format of each module. **Please note that, depending on how you are structuring your course sessions, you have complete flexibility to break up the reading assignments to match your actual class sessions. In other words, if you are running an eight-week course, simply break up the reading assignments to match your sessions.** (See Appendix 8 in* **For the Next Generation, TUMI Mentor Manual** *for sample course schedule options.) What is critical is that you focus on the lesson as the basic unit of teaching in your Capstone courses.*

Lesson 1

For this lesson, please read the following (due Tuesday, February 14):

- Erickson, *Introducing Christian Doctrine*, pp. 130-136, 138-146
- Packer, *Knowing God*, pp. 17-72
- Tozer, *The Knowledge of the Holy: The Attributes of God: Their Meaning in the Christian Life*, chapters 1-10, pp. 1-58
- Dodd, *Dictionary of Theological Terms in Simplified English: A Resource for English-Language Learners* (Please refer to the dictionary throughout this course as needed.)

Lesson 2

For this lesson, please read the following (due Tuesday, February 28):

- Erickson, *Introducing Christian Doctrine*, pp. 92-97, 107-115
- Packer, *Knowing God*, pp. 75-175
- Tozer, *The Knowledge of the Holy: The Attributes of God: Their Meaning in the Christian Life*, chapters 11-17, pp. 59-89
- Dodd, *Dictionary of Theological Terms in Simplified English: A Resource for English-Language Learners* (Please refer to the dictionary throughout this course as needed.)

Lesson 3

For this lesson, please read the following (due Tuesday, March 13):

- Erickson, *Introducing Christian Doctrine*, pp. 99-105, 148-153
- Packer, *Knowing God*, pp. 179-279
- Tozer, *The Knowledge of the Holy: The Attributes of God: Their Meaning in the Christian Life*, chapters 18-23, pp. 90-117
- Dodd, *Dictionary of Theological Terms in Simplified English: A Resource for English-Language Learners* (Please refer to the dictionary throughout this course as needed.)

PLEASE NOTE: The final due date for all reading assignments is Tuesday, April 3 with the rest of your completed assignments.

Appendix 17
Sample Reading Completion Sheet

Sample Reading Completion Sheet

*Part of our coursework requires that you purchase, read, and reflect upon the textbook(s) for the course. The assignment is to read each required textbook and write a precis (concise summary) of its main point, as you see it. Please summarize its major theme and argument, and then give your concise evaluation for **each** reading. Although the Student Workbook only shows space for two readings, the student must write a summary for each reading by using the back of the form. It is of utmost importance to us for our students to analyze a text, that is, to read it, understand its thesis (main point), articulate its argument in a respectful way (whether you agree with the author or not), and then respond as to why you agree or disagree with the thesis. This practice helps strengthen your ability to engage different opinions in a respectful way, and learn to listen to others and respond with clarity and respect. In this way, you learn to dialogue with and discuss with others whose beliefs differ from your own. A printable form of this document can be found at www.tumi.org/mentor.*

The Capstone Curriculum   **Name** _____
God the Father, Module 6
Reading Completion Sheet   **Date** _____

For each assigned reading, write a brief summary (one or two paragraphs) of the author's main point. (For additional readings, use the back of this sheet.)

Reading 1
Title and Author: _____ Pages: _____

Reading 2
Title and Author: _____ Pages: _____

Reading 3

Title and Author: _____   Pages: _____

Reading 4

Title and Author: _____   Pages: _____

Appendix 18

Sample Grade Recording Sheet

An editable form of this document can be found at *www.tumi.org/mentor.*

Sample Grade Recording Sheet

T2-506
God the Father, Module 6
Spring 2012, Session 1

Name	90 Pts Attendance	10 Quiz 1	10 Quiz 2	10 Quiz 3	15 Mem 1	15 Mem 2	15 Mem 3	10 Rdg 1	10 Rdg 2	10 Rdg 3	45 Exeg Prj	30 Min Prj	30 Final Exam	300 Total Points	Final Grade
Allen, Larry														0	
Anderson, Fairy Dean														0	
Andrews, Kevin														0	
Andrews, LaTonia														0	
Asher, Zoe														0	
Berrios, Gerson														0	
Berrios, Mayra														0	
Boatwright, Betty														0	
Butler, Nathan														0	
Caleb, Carey														0	
Cheung, Michael														0	
Clausen, Patty														0	
Collins, Taullesa														0	
DeShazer, Roosevelt														0	
Duncan, Heath														0	
Eustache, Jean														0	
Graham, Joe														0	
Graham, Sue														0	
McMillian, Linda														0	
Newman, Brenda														0	
Oldfather, Jason														0	
Nichols, Susan														0	
Peggs, Penny														0	
Perry, Liz														0	
Talbott, Steven														0	
Turner, Cathy														0	
Valdez, Angie														0	
Wendt, Debbie														0	

Appendix 19
TUMI Grade Scale

Percent/GP		Grade	300	260	245	150	100	70	65	60	50	45	40	35	30
100%	4.2	A+	300	260	245	150	100	70	65	60	50	45	40	35	30
96%	4.0	A	288-299	250-259	235-244	144-149	96-99	67-69	62-64	58-59	48-49	43-44	38-39	34	29
90%	3.8	A-	270-287	234-249	221-234	135-143	90-95	63-66	59-61	54-57	45-47	41-42	36-37	32-33	27-28
88%	3.2	B+	264-269	229-233	216-220	132-134	88-89	62	57-58	53	44	40	35	31	26
84%	3.0	B	252-263	218-228	206-215	126-131	84-87	59-61	55-56	50-52	42-43	38-39	34	30	25
80%	2.8	B-	240-251	208-217	196-205	120-125	80-83	56-58	52-54	48-49	40-41	36-37	32-33	28-29	24
78%	2.2	C+	234-239	203-207	191-195	117-119	78-79	55	51	47	39	35	31	27	23
74%	2.0	C	222-233	192-202	181-190	111-116	74-77	52-54	48-50	44-46	37-38	33-34	30	26	22
70%	1.8	C-	210-221	182-191	172-180	105-110	70-73	49-51	46-47	42-43	35-36	32	28-29	25	21
65%	1.0	D	195-209	169-181	159-171	97-104	65-69	46-48	42-45	39-41	33-34	29-31	26-27	23-24	20
64%		F	194	168	158	86	64	45	41	38	32	28	25	22	19

The chart above uses the following formula: Grade = Percentage x Total Possible Points
For example, out of 150 points possible, A+ = 1.00 x 150; A = .96 x 150; A- = .90 x 150; B+ = .88 x150; B = .84 x 150, and so on.

TUMI Grade Scale

Appendix 20
Scripture Memory Grading Form

Scripture Memory Grading Form

A pdf version of this document can be found at www.tumi.org.

This form is to be used for the Scripture Memory assignments for each module or course. There are 45 total possible points for Scripture memory for each Capstone module. The "Memory Verse Review" section on each Final Exam is for review only. Students have already completed their Scripture Memory assignments from the course and will not receive additional points for this review.

The following ARE counted as errors:
- *A wrong word (each wrong word is an error)*
- *A missing word (each missing word is an error)*
- *A word or words out of order (each word out of order is an error)*

The following SHOULD NOT be counted as errors:
- *Missed or wrong punctuation*
- *A misspelled word*

* This may not be wise in jail or prison settings.

Name: _____ **Credit:** _____

Translation: _____ **Passage Memorized:** _____

In most situations, it is the student's responsibility to grade his/her own Scripture Memory work.* As a reminder, please memorize Scripture only from a translation (ex. ESV, NIV, NASB, RSV, KJV, etc.) and not a paraphrase (ex. *The Living Bible*, *The Message*). Please follow the process below in order to grade your work:

1. Put away any helps you may have (including your Bible), and on a blank sheet of paper, write out your Scripture Memory passage in its entirety.

2. Write the translation on the top of your page along with your name.

3. Using your Bible, check your work, word for word, and put a line through any errors you may have.

4. Count up the number of errors and write them here: _____

5. How many verses were there in this memorized passage? _____

6. You are allowed the equivalent of one mistake per verse to receive full credit for your memory work. If your passage was three verses and you scored perfect on two of the verses and had three errors in the third verse, you will receive full credit for this passage.

7. You are allowed the equivalent of two mistakes per verse to receive half credit for the passage. If your passage was three verses and you made four to six mistakes, you will receive half credit for this passage.

8. If you made more than the equivalent of two mistakes per verse, you will receive no credit for this passage.

9. Write "full credit," "half credit," or "no credit" at the top of this page, depending on how you scored, and give this page to your instructor.

Proctoring

Proctoring

A TUMI Proctor is responsible for proctoring TUMI mentors who also want credit for the classes they are mentoring. Certified proctors have mentored several modules themselves and have completed the TUMI proctor-approval process.

The mentor is assigned a certified TUMI Proctor. The mentor scans and e-mails all reading assignments, memorizations, quizzes, the final, the ministry project, and the exegetical project to the Proctor. Attendance and class participation points are based the mentor's having taught the class, and will be awarded when the mentor completes all assignments on time. The Proctor will grade all assignments via e-mail. At the completion of each module, the Proctor will send the mentor/student a copy of his/her transcript.

Once the mentor finishes all sixteen modules of the Capstone Curriculum, the Proctor will submit an official transcript to TUMI National, and the mentor will receive his TUMI Certificate. Mentors may then participate in any local TUMI graduation ceremony.

Mentors are expected to complete and submit their assignments at the same pace they require of their students. Also, the same Capstone assignment weights apply to the mentors. Keeping the Capstone standards identical for mentors and students is crucial. Mentors are proctored in order to maintain the same excellent standard they require of their students.

Proctors will make themselves available by e-mail, phone, or other social media avenues to provide a reasonable amount of guidance and assistance to mentors as they successfully complete this process.

Appendix 22

World Impact's Affirmation of Faith Statement

1. There is one living and true God, infinitely perfect in glory, wisdom, holiness, justice, power and love, one in His essence but eternally existing in three persons: God the Father, God the Son and God the Holy Spirit. God sovereignly created the world out of nothing, so that His creation, while wholly dependent upon Him, neither comprises part of God, nor conditions His essential perfection.

2. The books which form the canon of the Old and New Testaments are verbally inspired by God, inerrant in the original writings, the only infallible rule of faith and practice.

3. God created humankind in His own image, in a state of original righteousness, from which humanity subsequently fell by a voluntary revolt, and consequently is guilty, inherently corrupt and subject to divine wrath.

4. Jesus Christ, the eternal Son, became human without ceasing to be God by uniting to His divine nature a true human nature in His incarnation, and so continues to be both God and man, in two distinct natures and one person, forever. He was conceived by the Holy Spirit, born of the virgin Mary, exhibited His deity by manifold miracles, fulfilled the requirements of the Law by His sinless life, shed His blood as a vicarious and propitiatory atonement for humanity's sin, was resurrected from the dead in the same body, now glorified. He ascended into heaven and now intercedes in glory for His redeemed as our great High Priest and Advocate, and as the Head of the Church and Lord of the individual believer.

5. The Holy Spirit convicts the world of sin, righteousness and judgment, through the ministry of regeneration and sanctification applies salvation and places believers into the Church, guides and comforts God's children, indwells, directs, gifts and empowers the Church in godly living and service in order to fulfill the Great Commission, and seals and keeps the believer until Christ returns.

6. Every human being, regardless of race or rank, who receives the Lord Jesus Christ by faith is born into the family of God and receives eternal life. This occurs solely because of the grace of God and has no ground in human merit.

7. The Holy Church is the one institution specifically ordained of God to function in the furthering of the Kingdom until Christ comes again. It consists of all those regenerated by the Spirit of God, in mystical union and communion both with Christ, the Head of the Body, and with fellow-believers. Neighborhood congregations are the local manifestation of the Church universal. In obedience to the command of Christ, these congregations preach the Word of God, equip God's people for the work of ministry, and administer the Lord's Supper and Baptism.

8. The Lord Jesus Christ will return bodily, visibly and personally to receive His own, to conform believers to His own image and to establish His millennial Kingdom. He will judge the quick and the dead and will effect a final separation of the redeemed and the lost, assigning unbelievers to eternal punishment and believers to eternal glory, enjoying conscious fellowship with Him.

9. Humanity's chief end in life is to honor and glorify Almighty God. Personal salvation is a means to this end.

World Impact's Affirmation of Faith

Creedal Theology

Appendix 23

Creedal Theology as a Blueprint for Discipleship and Leadership
A Time-Tested Criterion for Equipping New Believers and Developing Indigenous Leaders

Rev. Dr. Don L. Davis

"Creed" derives from the Latin credo, "I believe." The form is active, denoting not just a body of beliefs but confession of faith. This faith is trust: not "I believe that" (though this is included) but "I believe in." It is also individual; creeds may take the plural form of "we believe," but the term itself comes from the first person singular of the Latin: "I believe."

~ G. W. Bromiley. "Creed."
Elwell's Evangelical Dictionary Software, 1998-99.

I. **What Is the Biblical Basis for Creedal Theology?**

A. Creeds in the technical sense are not present in the Bible, but creeds do mean to express essential biblical data and truth.

B. Creedal forms in Scripture

1. The Shema of the Old Testament, Deuteronomy 6.4-9

2. Little credo in Deuteronomy 26.5-9

   Deut. 26.5 (NKJV) – "And you shall answer and say before the Lord your God: `My father was a Syrian, about to perish, and he went down to Egypt and sojourned there, few in number; and there he became a nation, great, mighty, and populous. [26.6] `But the Egyptians mistreated us, afflicted us, and laid hard bondage on us. [26.7]`Then we cried out to the Lord God of our fathers, and the Lord heard our voice and looked on our affliction and our labor and our oppression. [26.8] `So the Lord brought us out of Egypt with a mighty hand and with an outstretched arm, with great terror and with signs and wonders. [26.9]`He has brought us to this place and has given us this land, "a land flowing with milk and honey."

3. New Testament references and occurrences to creedal material

    a. Sources of creedal material

        (1) Traditions, 2 Thessalonians 2.15

        (2) Word of the Lord, Galatians 6.6

        (3) Preaching (Rom. 16.25) (In the technical sense, creeds are not present in the Bible, but they nevertheless express essential biblical data and truth.)

    b. Baptismal creedal confessions, Acts 8.37; Matt. 28.19; Rom. 10.9-10

    c. The Christological confession, Phil. 2.5-11

II. What Is the Instructional Basis for Creedal Theology?

A. Serves as *a syllabus for catechetical teaching* in Christian belief and doctrine in order to ground new believers in the faith

    1. Creed allows for variation (from "simple exposition to advanced theological presentation")

    2. E.g., from recitation of the Creed itself to the treatment of Langdon Gilkey's systematic theology based on the Creed (cf. the Catecheses of Cyril of Jerusalem in the fourth century)

    3. Sources show that candidates for baptism had to display some understanding of the profession they made in baptism (i.e., demanded intellectual comprehension as well as sincere heart commitment).

B. Serves as *a basis for doctrinal and theological education* for the Christian community at large, regardless of level of maturity

Creedal Theology

1. Creeds forged out of theological controversy, the rise of heresies, and the need to protect the apostolic confession from admixture with falsehood

2. The ministry of heresies: enabled early Christian pastors to expand their first rough confessions into more developed formulas

3. Examples of creedal defense

   a. "Maker of heaven and earth": probably to fight Gnostic idea of separation of the True God from creator

   b. Teaching on the Virgin birth and Jesus' death: combats Gnostic claims against Jesus' authentic human nature

   c. The Arian idea of Jesus as less than divine added to affirm Christ's absolute divinity

4. Creed slowly grew to function as both a proper understanding of the Scriptural story as well as test of the orthodoxy of the clergy.

C. Serves as *an important ingredient of the worship (liturgy)* of the community of believers (teaching in and through our worship)

   1. Confession of faith, in song and sermon, is an essential part of all true Christian worship.

   2. Nicene Creed was incorporated in the Eucharistic sequence (i.e., the Lord's Supper service), first in the East, then in Spain, and finally in Rome

   3. Often was placed after the reading of the Scripture as a congregational response of faith to the Word of God

III. What Creeds Have Been Recognized as Prominent and Significant in the Church?

A. In Christian history, three creeds have taken superior place: The Apostles' Creed, the Nicene Creed, and the Athanasian Creed.

1. The Apostles' Creed

   (Traditional English Version) I believe in God the Father Almighty, Maker of heaven and earth, and in Jesus Christ his only Son our Lord; who was conceived by the Holy Ghost, born of the Virgin Mary, suffered under Pontius Pilate, was crucified, dead, and buried; he descended into hell; the third day he rose again from the dead; he ascended into heaven, and sitteth on the right hand of God the Father Almighty; from thence he shall come to judge the quick and the dead. I believe in the Holy Ghost; the holy catholic Church; the communion of saints; the forgiveness of sins; the resurrection of the body; and the life everlasting. AMEN.

   a. Supposedly written by the apostles under inspiration, and therefore came to be called the Apostles' Symbol or Creed (Synod of Milan, 390 A.C.E.)

   b. Lorenzo Valla refuted the apostolic origin (which the East never accepted).

   c. Scholars attribute its origin to the Old Roman Creed (expounded by Rufinius in 404).

   d. Present form originates from the 8th century, and has been made of regular use in the West, especially by the Reformers in liturgies, confessions, and catechisms.

2. The Nicene Creed

   We believe in one God, the Father Almighty, Maker of heaven and earth and of all things visible and invisible.

   We believe in one Lord Jesus Christ, the only Begotten Son of God, Begotten of the Father before all ages, God from God,

Creedal Theology

Light from Light, True God from True God, Begotten not created, of the same essence as the Father, through whom all things were made.

Who for us men and for our salvation came down from heaven and was incarnate by the Holy Spirit and the virgin Mary and became human. Who for us too, was crucified under Pontius Pilate, suffered and was buried. The third day he rose again according to the Scriptures, ascended into heaven and is seated at the right hand of the Father. He will come again in glory to judge the living and the dead, and his Kingdom will have no end.

We believe in the Holy Spirit, the Lord and life-giver, Who proceeds from the Father and the Son. Who together with the Father and Son is worshiped and glorified. Who spoke by the prophets.

We believe in one holy, catholic, and apostolic Church.

We acknowledge one baptism for the forgiveness of sin, and we look for the resurrection of the dead and the life of the age to come. Amen.

Note: The word "catholic" as used in the creed means "universal." It is significant because it reminds believers that there are many congregations but only one Church. No congregation is an end in itself, rather it is organically connected to the whole Church and must understand itself to be in unity with other believers both locally and around the world.

a. Despite its name, it should be distinguished from the creed of Nicea (325), has been debated whether it was recognized at Constantinople I (381), but was recognized by Chalcedon council in 451, and at Constantinople II in 553.

b. The West has added the one Latin clause called the "filioque clause" (i.e., and from the Son) as to the statement on the Holy Spirit, but the East never conceded the orthodoxy of the original drafts.

c. This is the undisputed primary confession of the Church in both the East and West; it is the primary Creed used in Eucharistic and catechetical contexts.

d. A concise, elegant, and beautiful statement of what the earliest pastors, theologians, and leaders of the Church considered to be the elemental essentials of Christian orthodoxy.

e. TUMI's most critical test of historic orthodoxy: fidelity to the teachings of the Nicene Creed.

What Is the Nicene Creed?

The original Nicene creed came out the first worldwide gathering of Christian leaders at Nicaea in Bithynia (what is now Isnik, Turkey) in the year 325. It was called to deal with a heresy called Arianism which denied that Jesus was God and taught that he was instead the greatest created being. The council at Nicaea hammered out language that bishops could use to teach their churches who Jesus was.

A little over fifty years later new challenges were being faced. A modified form of the Arian heresy was making a comeback. And a new problem had also emerged. Some bishops and pastors had begun teaching that the Holy Spirit was not God (was not of the same substance as the Father) and was not really even a creature. He was thought of as a kind of power but not as a person of the Godhead.

To resolve this problem, a council of 150 bishops of the Eastern Church were gathered in 381 at Constantinople (modern day Istanbul, Turkey). This council reaffirmed the fact that Jesus was fully God and then turned their attention to the question of the Holy Spirit which the Nicene council had left untouched (the original Nicene Creed read simply, "We believe in the Holy Spirit."). The council turned this simple statement into a paragraph which explained more fully the person and work of the Holy Spirit.

This expanded version of the original Nicene creed is what is most commonly known as "The Nicene Creed" today, (although it is more technically correct to call it the "Niceno-Constantinopolitan Creed" or the "Creed of the 150 Fathers") It is universally acknowledged by Christians of all denominations1. And it is used as a part of the worship service in many traditions, as well.

~ Terry Cornett, "What Is the Nicene Creed?"
T2-105 Christian Theology: God the Holy Spirit.
The Urban Ministry Institute, 1997.

3. The Athanasian Creed

(Early Fifth Century) Whoever wills to be in a state of salvation, before all things it is necessary that he hold the catholic [apostolic/universal] faith, which except everyone

shall have kept whole and undefiled without doubt he will perish eternally. Now the catholic faith is that we worship One God in Trinity and Trinity in Unity, neither confounding the Persons nor dividing the substance. For there is one Person of the Father, another of the Son, another of the Holy Spirit. But the Godhead of the Father, of the Son, and of the Holy Spirit, is One, the Glory equal, the Majesty coeternal. Such as the Father is, such is the Son, and such is the Holy Spirit; the Father uncreated, the Son uncreated, and the Holy Spirit uncreated; the father infinite, the Son infinite, and the Holy Spirit infinite; the Father eternal, the Son eternal, and the Holy Spirit eternal. And yet not three eternals but one eternal, as also not three infinites, nor three uncreated, but one uncreated, and one infinite. So, likewise, the Father is almighty, the Son almighty, and the Holy Spirit almighty; and yet not three almighties but one almighty. So the Father is God, the Son God, and the Holy Spirit God; and yet not three Gods but one God. So the Father is Lord, the Son Lord, and the Holy Spirit Lord; and yet not three Lords but one Lord. For like as we are compelled by Christian truth to acknowledge every Person by himself to be both God and Lord; so are we forbidden by the catholic religion to say, there be three Gods or three Lords. The Father is made of none, neither created nor begotten. The Son is of the Father alone, nod made nor created but begotten. The Holy Spirit is of the Father and the Son, not made nor created nor begotten but proceeding. So there is one Father not three Fathers, one Son not three Sons, and Holy Spirit not three Holy Spirits. And in this Trinity there is nothing before or after, nothing greater or less, but the whole three Persons are coeternal together and coequal.

a. Creed often attributed to Athanasius around the 4th or 5th century

b. Direct statement on the nature on the Trinity, more thorough

c. Became a test of the orthodoxy and competence of the clergy in the West from the 7th century

d. Differences between Apostles' and Nicene

(1) More complex doctrinal character

(2) More prosaic, less poetic

(3) More as a plumb line of orthodoxy, less as a credo of faith

e. Reformers highly accepted, some use among Anglicans, but the East did not recognize it; of significantly less importance in catechesis and liturgy.

Creedal Theology

The dangers of creed-making are obvious. Creeds can become formal, complex, and abstract. They can be almost illimitably expanded. They can be superimposed on Scripture. Properly handled, however, they facilitate public confession, form a succinct basis of teaching, safeguard pure doctrine, and constitute an appropriate focus for the church's fellowship in faith.

~ G. W. Bromiley. "Creed."
Elwell's Evangelical Dictionary Software, 1998-99.

IV. Why Can a Creedal Theology Be Critical for Establishing New Believers and Developing Indigenous Urban Christian Leaders?

While no commitment to any Creed can ever take away our responsibility to search the Scriptures daily in order to nurture and build our faith, nonetheless, a commitment to using the Creed as a safeguard for historic orthodoxy has great importance in grounding believers in the faith as well as training leaders for the urban church.

A. It represents *a historic, clearly defined outline summary* of the earliest Christian leaders' view of the Apostles' doctrine.

1. It is historic: the Nicene is nearly seventeen centuries old.

2. It is universally respected among traditions as an authoritative summary of the heart of the Apostles' teaching.

3. It has been used successfully throughout Church history as the curricula to ground new Christians and test emerging leaders as faithful disciples of Jesus Christ.

B. It can provide *a simple, memorable, and concise statement* of the substance of historic Christian belief.

1. Simple: not very wordy, provides essential summary

2. Memorable: becomes an easy instrument to serve as core of one's orthodox commitment

3. Concise: although abstract, it is extremely compact in its style but meaningful in its weight and concept

C. It lays *a foundation for determining an evangelical ecumenism*, a plumb line whereby we can judge what is essential for mutual fellowship and service.

1. The Nicene is a kind of universal statement of what Christians have believed on the core issues from the beginning.

2. Probably the most celebrated document that is recognized by virtually every tradition of Christian faith

3. It deals with the essential truths that Christians have historically counted to be bedrock truths of the faith.

D. It defines *the apostolic deposit that represents the defense of the Gospel* and full explication of Kingdom theology.

1. Focuses on the core teachings of the apostles about God and Christ

2. Deliberately drafted to deal with anti-Christ heresies of the day

3. Highlights the core teachings of the Church, especially against its fundamental Christ-centered background

E. It provides *the content of Christian multiplication and reproduction*, the bare minimum for equipping new leaders and giving catechesis for new members in the church.

1. A test of essential biblical conviction, accessible to everyone; the Nicene core is easily contextualized for both liturgy, confession of faith, and the Lord Supper

2. May be adapted easily as a standard for orthodoxy for Christian workers, ministers, pastors, and missionaries

3. Allows us to use a time-tested, Church endorsed rule for determining the doctrinal and theological credential for developing and emerging leaders

V. What Are the Implications for Church Plant Team Leaders?

A. *Embrace the Creed as a kind of shorthand for the biblical Story*; not a replacement for the Story but a concise summary and brilliant highlighting of its most salient points.

1 Timothy 3.14-16 (ESV) – I hope to come to you soon, but I am writing these things to you so that, [15] if I delay, you may know how one ought to behave in the household of God, which is the Church of the living God, a pillar and buttress of truth. [16] Great indeed, we confess, is the mystery of godliness: He was manifested in the flesh, vindicated by the Spirit, seen by angels, proclaimed among the nations, believed on in the world, taken up in glory.

1. The Creed is *essential*; it provides a summary of the Christian Narrative in bold relief.

2. The Creed is *Christo-centric*: the story of Jesus of Nazareth is the key to the entire self-consciousness of Christianity, and the key to understanding the hope of all twenty-first century disciples today.

3. The Creed is *confessional*: the Creed is meant to become a part of our conscience and hope, a statement of our deepest convictions regarding how we understand the nature of the world, God, life, and the afterlife.

Creedal Theology

4. The Creed is *celebratory*: it affirms in concise language we believe about God and Jesus, the Spirit, the Church, and the Age to Come we place ourselves in the sacred stream of men and women throughout history who have bled, suffered, and died on behalf of the biblical story.

B. Recognize *the sophistication of the Creed's teaching*: it can easily be adapted to ground the new believer to empowering the sophisticated theologian, pastor, or bishop.

1. Determine your audience and their need.

2. Relate your teaching to their context.

3. Link your presentation to the readiness and grittiness of the hearts and lives of your people.

   a. Show them why theology makes all the difference.

   b. Connect doctrine to attitude and to perspective.

   c. Use case studies to show how theological perspective bleeds into all fabrics of our psychological and social frameworks.

C. Allow the Creed to squire to help you *defend the Apostles' witness to Jesus Christ* against falsehood: the Creed is not as equal to Scripture, but serves as a historical statement of what the Church has contended for and defended for centuries.

   Jude 1.3-4 (ESV) – Beloved, although I was very eager to write to you about our common salvation, I found it necessary to write appealing to you to contend for the faith that was once for all delivered to the saints. [4] For certain people have crept in unnoticed who long ago were designated for this condemnation, ungodly people, who pervert the grace of our God into sensuality and deny our only Master and Lord, Jesus Christ.

   1. Connect the struggles of your people with the struggles of Christians all over the world, and throughout all history.

2. Relate the teaching of the Creed in its big panoramic vision to what is taking place today.

3. Ground your people in the historical, worldwide, trans-cultural, multi-ethnic and multi-national movement of Jesus.

D. Be diligent *to consistently rehearse historic orthodoxy* with your church plant team, with your fledgling community, and with your developing leaders through the Creed.

2 Tim. 4.1-5 (ESV) – I charge you in the presence of God and of Christ Jesus, who is to judge the living and the dead, and by his appearing and his Kingdom: [2] preach the word; be ready in season and out of season; reprove, rebuke, and exhort, with complete patience and teaching. [3] For the time is coming when people will not endure sound teaching, but having itching ears they will accumulate for themselves teachers to suit their own passions, [4] and will turn away from listening to the truth and wander off into myths. [5] As for you, always be sober-minded, endure suffering, do the work of an evangelist, fulfill your ministry.

1. Do not hesitate to emphasize the critical, life-and-body shaping role of theology; show how theological perspective ultimately determines life outcome.

2. Challenge mentors always to connect specific details and issues to the great biblical narrative, which the creed summarizes and outlines.

3. Use the Creed to connect the faith and works of your people to the historic works of faith done from the apostles onward.

Eph. 4.4 – There is one body and one Spirit, just as you were called in one hope of your calling; [4.5] one Lord, one faith, one baptism; [4.6] one God and Father of all, who is above all, and through all, and in you all.

Creedal Theology

4. Tell the stories which breathe life into the Creed, and allow the Creed to become a means by which you can ground the new believer, encourage the disciple, and enrich the tested soldier.

E. Finally, make *the study, recitation, and discussion of the Creed* a critical part of your church-planting life.

1. Use the Creed in your devotions and corporate worship.

2. Preach on the topics included in the Creed in the community of believers, and emphasize it within your Christian education.

3. Develop studies and curricula for your growing disciples and emerging leaders on the Creed as a criterion of doctrinal and theological necessity.

Rev. Dr. Don L. Davis

Appendix 24
There Is a River
Identifying the Streams of a Revitalized Christian Community in the City *

Ps. 46.4 (ESV) - There is a river whose streams make glad the city of God, the holy habitation of the Most High.

Tributaries of Authentic Historic Biblical Faith			
Recognized Biblical Identity	Revived Urban Spirituality	Reaffirmed Historical Connectivity	Refocused Kingdom Authority
The Church Is One	*The Church Is Holy*	*The Church Is Catholic*	*The Church Is Apostolic*
A Call to Biblical Fidelity Recognizing the Scriptures as the anchor and foundation of the Christian faith and practice	**A Call to the Freedom, Power, and Fullness of the Holy Spirit** Walking in the holiness, power, gifting, and liberty of the Holy Spirit in the body of Christ	**A Call to Historic Roots and Continuity** Confessing the common historical identity and continuity of authentic Christian faith	**A Call to the Apostolic Faith** Affirming the apostolic tradition as the authoritative ground of the Christian hope
A Call to Messianic Kingdom Identity Rediscovering the story of the promised Messiah and his Kingdom in Jesus of Nazareth	**A Call to Live as Sojourners and Aliens as the People of God** Defining authentic Christian discipleship as faithful membership among God's people	**A Call to Affirm and Express the Global Communion of Saints** Expressing cooperation and collaboration with all other believers, both local and global	**A Call to Representative Authority** Submitting joyfully to God's gifted servants in the Church as undershepherds of true faith
A Call to Creedal Affinity Embracing the Nicene Creed as the shared rule of faith of historic orthodoxy	**A Call to Liturgical, Sacramental, and Catechetical Vitality** Walking in the holiness, power, gifting, and liberty of the Holy Spirit in the body of Christ	**A Call to Radical Hospitality and Good Works** Expressing kingdom love to all, and especially to those of the household of faith	**A Call to Prophetic and Holistic Witness** Proclaiming Christ and his Kingdom in word and deed to our neighbors and all peoples

* This schema is an adaptation and is based on the insights of the *Chicago Call* statement of May 1977, where various leading evangelical scholars and practitioners met to discuss the relationship of modern evangelicalism to the historic Christian faith.

There Is a River

Appendix 25
The Nicene Creed

We believe in one God, the Father Almighty, Maker of heaven and earth and of all things visible and invisible.

We believe in one Lord Jesus Christ, the only Begotten Son of God, begotten of the Father before all ages, God from God, Light from Light, True God from True God, begotten not created, of the same essence as the Father, through whom all things were made.

Who for us men and for our salvation came down from heaven and was incarnate by the Holy Spirit and the Virgin Mary and became human. Who for us too, was crucified under Pontius Pilate, suffered and was buried. The third day he rose again according to the Scriptures, ascended into heaven, and is seated at the right hand of the Father. He will come again in glory to judge the living and the dead, and his Kingdom will have no end.

We believe in the Holy Spirit, the Lord and life-giver, who proceeds from the Father and the Son, who together with the Father and Son is worshiped and glorified, who spoke by the prophets.

We believe in one holy, catholic, and apostolic Church.

We acknowledge one baptism for the forgiveness of sin, and we look for the resurrection of the dead and the life of the age to come. Amen.

Appendix 26

The Nicene Creed
With Biblical Support
The Urban Ministry Institute

We believe in one God, *(Deut. 6.4-5; Mark 12.29; 1 Cor. 8.6)*
    the Father Almighty, *(Gen. 17.1; Dan. 4.35; Matt. 6.9; Eph. 4.6; Rev. 1.8)*
    Maker of heaven and earth *(Gen. 1.1; Isa. 40.28; Rev. 10.6)*
    and of all things visible and invisible. *(Ps. 148; Rom. 11.36; Rev. 4.11)*

We believe in one Lord Jesus Christ, the only Begotten Son of God, begotten of the Father
    before all ages, God from God, Light from Light, True God from True God, begotten not
    created, of the same essence as the Father,
        (John 1.1-2; 3.18; 8.58; 14.9-10; 20.28; Col. 1.15, 17; Heb. 1.3-6)
    through whom all things were made. *(John 1.3; Col. 1.16)*

Who for us men and for our salvation came down from heaven and was incarnate by the
    Holy Spirit and the Virgin Mary and became human.
        (Matt. 1.20-23; John 1.14; 6.38; Luke 19.10)
    Who for us too, was crucified under Pontius Pilate, suffered and was buried.
        (Matt. 27.1-2; Mark 15.24-39, 43-47; Acts 13.29; Rom. 5.8; Heb. 2.10; 13.12)
    The third day he rose again according to the Scriptures,
        (Mark 16.5-7; Luke 24.6-8; Acts 1.3; Rom. 6.9; 10.9; 2 Tim. 2.8)
    ascended into heaven, and is seated at the right hand of the Father.
        (Mark 16.19; Eph. 1.19-20)
    He will come again in glory to judge the living and the dead, and his Kingdom will have
    no end. *(Isa. 9.7; Matt. 24.30; John 5.22; Acts 1.11; 17.31; Rom. 14.9; 2 Cor. 5.10; 2 Tim. 4.1)*

We believe in the Holy Spirit, the Lord and life-giver, *(Gen. 1.1-2; Job 33.4; Ps. 104.30; 139.7-8;*
        Luke 4.18-19; John 3.5-6; Acts 1.1-2; 1 Cor. 2.11; Rev. 3.22)
    who proceeds from the Father and the Son, *(John 14.16-18, 26; 15.26; 20.22)*
    who together with the Father and Son is worshiped and glorified,
        (Isa. 6.3; Matt. 28.19; 2 Cor. 13.14; Rev. 4.8)
    who spoke by the prophets. *(Num. 11.29; Mic. 3.8; Acts 2.17-18; 2 Pet. 1.21)*

We believe in one holy, catholic, and apostolic Church.
        (Matt. 16.18; Eph. 5.25-28; 1 Cor. 1.2; 10.17; 1 Tim. 3.15; Rev. 7.9)

We acknowledge one baptism for the forgiveness of sin, *(Acts 22.16; 1 Pet. 3.21; Eph. 4.4-5)*
    And we look for the resurrection of the dead and the life of the age to come.
        (Isa. 11.6-10; Mic. 4.1-7; Luke 18.29-30; Rev. 21.1-5; 21.22-22.5)
    Amen.

The Nicene Creed with Biblical Support

The Nicene Creed with Biblical Support

Memory Verses

Below are suggested memory verses, one for each section of the Creed.

The Father

Rev. 4.11 (ESV) – Worthy are you, our Lord and God, to receive glory and honor and power, for you created all things, and by your will they existed and were created.

The Son

John 1.1 (ESV) – In the beginning was the Word, and the Word was with God, and the Word was God.

The Son's Mission

1 Cor. 15.3-5 (ESV) – For what I received I passed on to you as of first importance: that Christ died for our sins according to the Scriptures, that he was buried, that he was raised on the third day according to the Scriptures, and that he appeared to Peter, and then to the Twelve.

The Holy Spirit

Rom. 8.11 (ESV) – If the Spirit of him who raised Jesus from the dead dwells in you, he who raised Christ Jesus from the dead will also give life to your mortal bodies through his Spirit who dwells in you.

The Church

1 Pet. 2.9 (ESV) – But you are a chosen race, a royal priesthood, a holy nation, a people for his own possession, that you may proclaim the excellencies of him who called you out of darkness into his marvelous light.

Our Hope

1 Thess. 4.16-17 (ESV) – For the Lord himself will descend from heaven with a cry of command, with the voice of an archangel, and with the sound of the trumpet of God. And the dead in Christ will rise first. Then we who are alive, who are left, will be caught up together with them in the clouds to meet the Lord in the air, and so we will always be with the Lord.

Appendix 27

We Believe: Confession of the Nicene Creed
(Common Meter)*

Rev. Dr. Don L. Davis, 2007

* This song is adapted from the Nicene Creed, and set to common meter (8.6.8.6.), meaning it can be sung to tunes of the same meter, such as:
O, for a Thousand Tongues to Sing;
Alas, and Did My Savior Bleed;
Amazing Grace;
All Hail the Power of Jesus' Name;
There Is a Fountain;
Joy to the World

The Father God Almighty rules, Maker of earth and heav'n.
Yes, all things seen and those unseen, by him were made, and given!

We hold to one Lord Jesus Christ, God's one and only Son,
Begotten, not created, too, he and our Lord are one!

Begotten from the Father, same, in essence, God and Light;
Through him all things were made by God, in him were given life.

Who for us all, for salvation, came down from heav'n to earth,
Was incarnate by the Spirit's pow'r, and the Virgin Mary's birth.

Who for us too, was crucified, by Pontius Pilate's hand,
Suffered, was buried in the tomb, on third day rose again.

According to the Sacred text all this was meant to be.
Ascended to heav'n, to God's right hand, now seated high in glory.

He'll come again in glory to judge all those alive and dead.
His Kingdom rule shall never end, for he will reign as Head.

We worship God, the Holy Spirit, our Lord, Life-giver known,
With Fath'r and Son is glorified, Who by the prophets spoke.

And we believe in one true Church, God's people for all time,
Cath'lic in scope, and built upon the apostolic line.

Acknowledging one baptism, for forgiv'ness of our sin,
We look for Resurrection day–the dead shall live again.

We look for those unending days, life of the Age to come,
When Christ's great Reign shall come to earth, and God's will shall
    be done!

*The Nicene Creed
(Common Meter)*

Appendix 28

We Believe: Confession of the Nicene Creed
(8.7.8.7. Meter*)

Rev. Dr. Don L. Davis, 2007

* This song is adapted from the Nicene Creed, and set to 8.7.8.7. meter, meaning it can be sung to tunes of the same meter, such as: Joyful, Joyful, We Adore Thee; I Will Sing of My Redeemer; What a Friend We Have in Jesus; Come, Thou Long Expected Jesus

Father God Almighty rules, the Maker of both earth and heav'n.
All things seen and those unseen, by him were made, by him
    were giv'n!
We believe in Jesus Christ, the Lord, God's one and only Son,
Begotten, not created, too, he and our Father God are one!

Begotten from the Father, same, in essence, as both God and Light;
Through him by God all things were made, in him all things were
    giv'n life.
Who for us all, for our salvation, did come down from heav'n to earth,
Incarnate by the Spirit's pow'r, and through the Virgin Mary's birth.

Who for us too, was crucified, by Pontius Pilate's rule and hand,
Suffered, and was buried, yet on the third day, he rose again.
According to the Sacred Scriptures all that happ'ned was meant to be.
Ascended high to God's right hand, in heav'n he sits in glory.

Christ will come again in glory to judge all those alive and dead.
His Kingdom rule shall never end, for he will rule and reign as Head.
We worship God, the Holy Spirit, Lord and the Life-giver known;
With Fath'r and Son is glorified, Who by the prophets ever spoke.

And we believe in one true Church, God's holy people for all time,
Cath'lic in its scope and broadness, built on the Apostles' line!
Acknowledging that one baptism, for forgiv'ness of our sin,
And we look for Resurrection, for the dead shall live again.

Looking for unending days, the life of the bright Age to come,
When Christ's Reign shall come to earth, the will of God shall then
    be done!
Praise to God, and to Christ Jesus, to the Spirit–triune Lord!
We confess the ancient teachings, clinging to God's holy Word!

Appendix 29

The Apostles' and Nicene Creed Bibliography

The following is a selected, scholarly listing on the origin and meaning of the Apostles' and Nicene Creeds, and early Christian belief:

Bethune-Baker, J. F. *An Introduction to the Early History of Christian Doctrine*. London: Methuen & Co., 1933.

Bloesch, Donald. *Essentials of Evangelical Theology*. San Francisco: Harper and Row, 1978.

Burnaby, John. *The Belief of Christendom : A Commentary on the Nicene Creed*.

Chadwick, Henry. *The Early Church, Penguin History of the Church 1*, rev. ed. New York: Penguin, 1994. (One scholar says of this book, "Chadwick has a gift for making complex matters clear and understandable. Though the basic text was written in the late 60s and is dated in some ways, it remains a great introduction.")

Davis, Don. *Sacred Roots: A Primer on Retrieving the Great Tradition*. Wichtia, KS, Los Angeles: World Impact Press, 2010.

Ferguson, Everett, Michael P. McHugh, and Frederick W. Norris, eds., *Encyclopedia of Early Christianity*, 2nd ed. New York: Garland Publishing, 1998. (Award-winning with articles by leading experts on topics)

Frend, W. H. C. *The Rise of Christianity*. Philadelphia: Fortress Press, 1984. (Called by some the most thorough and up-to-date of the one-volume surveys of the early Church)

Gonzalez, Justo. *A History of Christian Thought*. Nashville: Abingdon, 1975.

Heim, Mark S. ed. *Faith to Creed: Toward a Common Historical Approach to the Affirmation of the Apostolic Faith in the Fourth Century*.

Howell, James C. *The Life We Claim: The Apostles' Creed for Preaching, Teaching, and Worship*. Nashville: Abingdon Press, 2005.

Leith, John H. Ed. *Creeds of the Churches: A Reader in Christian Doctrine from the Bible to Present*. 3rd Edition. Atlanta: John Knox Press, 1982.

Little, Paul. E. *Know Why You Believe: Connecting Faith and Reason*. Downers Grove, IL: InterVarsity, 2000. isbn # 0-8308-2250-X

------. *Know What You Believe: Connecting Faith and Truth*. Colorado Springs, CO: Victor Cook Communications, 2003.

Kelly, J. N. D. *Early Christian Creeds*. London: Longman, 1972.

------. *Early Christian Doctrines*. 5th ed. London: A & C Black, 1985.

McGrath, Allister. *"I Believe": Exploring the Apostles' Creed*. Downers Grove: InterVarsity Press, 1991, 1997.

Pelikan, Jaroslav. *The Christian Tradition: A History of the Development of Doctrine*, vol. 1: the Emergence of the Catholic Tradition (100-600) Chicago: The University of Chicago Press, 1971.

Seitz, Christopher R. ed. *Nicene Christianity: The Future for a New Ecumenism*. Grand Rapids: Brazos Press, 2001. (A good beginning, a fairly easy read, and a must-have book!)

Simpson, Gregory. *The Nicene Creed for Today*.

Torrance, Thomas J. *The Incarnation-Ecumenical Studies in the Nicene- Constantinopolitan Creed A.D. 381.* (April 1981).

------. The Trinitarian Faith: the Evangelical Theology of the Ancient Catholic Church. Edinburgh: T & T Clark, 1988.

Webber, Robert E. *Common Roots: A Call to Evangelical Maturity*. Grand Rapids, MI: Zondervan, 1979.

The Apostles' and Nicene Creed Bibliography

------. Ancient Future Time: Forming Spirituality through the
Christian Year. Grand Rapids, MI: Baker Books, 2004.

------. *Ancient Future Faith: Rethinking Evangelicalism for a
Postmodern World*. Grand Rapids: Baker Books, 1999/2006.

Willis, David. *Clues to the Nicene Creed: A Brief Outline of the Faith*.
Grand Rapids: Eerdmans Publishing, 2005.

World Council of Churches. *Confessing the One Faith: An Ecumenical
Explication of the Apostolic Faith As It Is Confessed in the Nicene-
Constantinopolitan Creed*. (Interesting read from the mainline [or
is it "sideline"] Christian vantage point)

*The Apostles' and Nicene
Creed Bibliography*

Appendix 30

An Abridged Bibliography on Becoming an Effective Mentor and Teacher

The following is a resource list that may aid in class prep, or books you can refer to on the craft of teaching.

Christensen, C. Roland, David A. Garvin, and Ann Sweet, eds. *Education for Judgment: The Artistry of Discussion Leadership.* Boston, MA: Harvard Business School Press, 1991.

Collins, Marva and Civia Tamarkin. *Marva Collins' Way: Return to Excellence in Education and Quality in Our Classroom.* Los Angeles: J.P. Tarcher, Inc., 1982.

Fink, L. Dee. *Creating Significant Learning Experience.*

Freire, Paulo. *Pedagogy of the Oppressed.* New York: The Continuum Publishing Corporation, 1988.

Grant, Reg and Jon Reed. *Telling Stories to Touch the Heart* (Not so much on pedagogy per se, but on the craft of using story to teach)

Gregory, John Milton. *The Seven Laws of Teaching.*

Hendricks, Howard. *Teaching to Change Lives.*

Isaacs, William. *Dialogue and the Art of Thinking Together.* New York. Doubleday, A Division of Random House, 1999.

LeFever, Marlene. *Creative Teaching Methods.*

Mager, Robert F. *Developing Attitude Toward Learning.* Belmont, CA: Fearon Pitman Publishers, Inc., 1968.

McKeachie, Wilbert. *McKeachie's Teaching Tips.*

Yount, William. *Called to Teach.*

Appendix 31

At-a-Glance Responsibilities Checklist for Site Coordinators and Mentors

In order to organize and manage your Institute, you will have to give serious attention to the role of administration. The goal here is to steward your resources carefully, maintain excellence in procedures and record keeping, and strive for an overall accuracy and quality in the way you run your courses and programs. This is a service to the Lord, done on behalf of the students, staff, and faculty. Give the proper time and planning to your responsibilities in order to ensure that your Institute glorifies God in this dimension as well as the training and teaching portions of your program. Listed below is the division of labor between the Site Coordinator and the Mentor. These are integral to each other and their strong interworkings will be key to the success of your satellite and the equipping of leaders for the Church.

I. Site Coordinator Responsibilities

A. In establishing your site:

1. Clarify and communicate your vision for your training center.
2. Organize and set up all records (see *Multiplying Laborers* guidebook for details).
3. Raise any necessary funds for your site.
4. Establish and maintain a library.

B. In recruiting and training your Mentors:

1. Send mentor application(s). *The right mentor for your satellite will be committed to the church, culturally aware, and have a heart for the urban poor.*
2. Order *For the Next Generation: TUMI's Mentor Manual* and Mentor Guide (for the *Capstone* module that is being taught) for the Mentor
3. Give the mentor a copy of *For the Next Generation: TUMI's Mentor Manual* and ask them to read it through in its entirety.
4. Review briefly our understanding of *Sacred Roots* and how that shapes all of our training; the Nicene Creed and

its role in leadership development and dealing with theological diversity in the classroom

5. Review Mentor Responsibilities with the Mentor, ensuring they understand what they need to do before teaching the module, as well as on a weekly basis.

6. Copy and have them sign the "Mentor Sign-Off Form" in the back of the Mentor Manual.

C. In recruiting TUMI students:

1. Send student application(s) and pastor reference forms. *The right students for your satellite will be: solid, faithful Christians who have a church home; known by their church leaders, and/or under close pastoral supervision; burdened for the city and the poor; currently leading in some dimension in their church, or emerging as leaders; anxious for training, and willing to study hard.*

2. Announce upcoming class: e.g., send introductory letters or email newsletters, print flyers, take out an ad in local Christian newspaper, network with local churches.

3. Update list of prospective students and roster.

4. Send financial aid forms.

5. Process student applications and pastor references.

6. Update addresses in database.

7. Record and send invoices.

8. Send acceptance letters and confirmation letters (include class start date in acceptance/confirmation letters).

9. Finalize class roster and give to Mentor.

10. Pray for students.

D. In hosting your classes:

1. Plan budget.

2. Determine if you want to host courses at other sites.

3. Set academic calendar (work out time frame with your mentor – day and time of classes).

4. Select course curricula (types of classes – e.g. Independent Study, *Capstone Curriculum* and/or *Foundations for Ministry Series*).

5. Order curriculum from TUMI National three weeks before class starts.

6. Order textbooks two-to-three weeks prior to class start (if you pay for an Amazon Prime annual account);

otherwise allow four-to-six weeks prior to class start for ordered books to arrive.

7. Purchase any necessary supplies (paper, whiteboard supplies, snacks?).

E. In closing your teaching sessions:

1. Sign up existing students for next class and encourage them to invite *Oikos*.
2. Receive and record grades.
3. Record and send transcripts in a timely fashion.
4. File records (always!).
5. Maintain ongoing relationships with students and mentors.

II. Mentor Responsibilities

A. Managing the class schedule:

1. Coordinate class schedule with the Site Coordinator selecting the dates and times for the course you will be teaching.
2. Select class format (e.g. weekend, four-week, eight-week, etc.).
3. Create a course schedule (with days and dates for class, along with key subjects covered in each class, quiz dates, assignments due).
4. Establish a weekly class schedule (a template that you can use to guide your student learning on a weekly basis).

B. Studying and planning – your personal preparation:

1. Review the overall scope of the lesson:
   a. Course title and overview
   b. Objectives
   c. Devotional material
   d. Contact questions
   e. Response to the video segment questions
   f. Mentor notes

g. Case studies

h. Assignments

2. Preview video segments, three times.

3. Read and study textbooks and workbook lessons.

4. Review key theological themes associated with the course by using Bible dictionaries, theological dictionaries, and commentaries to refresh your familiarity with major topics covered in the course.

C. Preparing class paperwork (all forms can be found at *www.tumi.org/mentor*):

1. Create documents related to information on students (i.e., Attendance Sheet, Student Information Sheet, Grade Recording Sheet).

2. Access required textbooks and reading assignments.

3. Inform students: Draft and print handouts for your students (i.e., Class Schedule with Notes, Reading Assignments and Reading Assignment Forms; Scripture Memory Grading Form; Holding Fast the Good; Assignment Submission envelope).

4. Copy appropriate number of quizzes and the final exam.

D. Readying your facilities and classroom:

1. Facilities: Clean (sweep or vacuum, clean floor, touch up walls).

2. Classroom: Set up (arrange and wipe off chairs and tables for the number of students registered; check/set room temperature).

3. Equipment: Ready (set up laptop/DVD with projector; screen; prepare video and check everything to ensure working).

4. Supplies: Prepare (whiteboard, markers, and eraser; stapler, extra pens/pencils; quiz basket, etc).

5. Snacks: Set up area to serve snacks if you decide to provide them.

E. Facilitating your class session:

1. Review video segment again for that class period.
2. Read and summarize reading assignments that are due that class period.
3. Lead students through class session (refer to *Leading a Capstone Curriculum or Foundations for Ministry Class Session* in this manual).

F. Guiding students through their assignments (see *Handling Projects and Student Assignments* in this manual for additional help):

1. At the mid-point of your class, please review the details for both your Exegetical and Ministry Projects.
2. Review Scripture Memory forms with students during first class session, show them where the verse memory assignments are found in the student workbook.
3. Go over the Reading Assignment (remind students that they are never quizzed on the reading assignments, only on what is viewed on the video).

G. Assigning, recording and processing student grades:

1. Receive completed assignments from students.
2. Grade paperwork.
3. Calculate and record final grades.
4. Submit final grades to Site Coordinator.

H. Wrapping up final details:

1. Turn in extra workbooks, textbooks, Mentor Manual and DVD to Site Coordinator.
2. Maintain regular contact with Site Coordinator.

At-a-Glance Checklist for Site Coordinators and Mentors

Appendix 32
The Role of Women in Ministry
Rev. Dr. Don L. Davis

While it is clear that God has established a clearly designed order of responsibility within the home, it is equally clear that women are called and gifted by God, led by his own Spirit to bear fruit worthy of their calling in Christ. Throughout the NT, commands are directed specifically to women to submit, with the particular Greek verb hupotasso, occurring frequently which means "to place under" or "to submit" (cf. 1 Tim. 2.11). The word also translated into our English word "subjection" is from the same root. In such contexts these Greek renderings ought not to be understood in any way except as positive admonitions towards God's designed framework for the home, where women are charged to learn quietly and submissively, trusting and working within the Lord's own plan.

This ordering of the woman's submission in the home, however, must not be misinterpreted to mean that women are disallowed from ministering their gifts under the Spirit's direction. Indeed, it is the Holy Spirit through Christ's gracious endowment who assigns the gifts as he wills, for the edification of the Church (1 Cor. 12.1-27; Eph. 4.1-16). The gifts are not given to believers on the criteria of gender; in other words, there is no indication from the Scriptures that some gifts are for men only, and the others reserved for women. On the contrary, Paul affirms that Christ provided gifts as a direct result of his own personal victory over the devil and his minions (cf. Eph. 4.6ff). This was his own personal choice, given by his Spirit to whomever he wills (cf. 1 Cor. 12.1-11). In affirming the ministry of women we affirm the right of the Spirit to be creative in all saints for the well-being of all and the expansion of his Kingdom, as he sees fit, and not necessarily as we determine (Rom. 12.4-8; 1 Pet. 4.10-11).

Furthermore, a careful study of the Scriptures as a whole indicates that God's ordering of the home in no way undermines his intention for men and women to serve Christ as disciples and laborers together, under Christ's leading. The clear NT teaching of Christ as head of the man, and the man of the woman (see 1 Cor. 11.4) shows God's esteem for godly spiritual representation within the home. The apparent forbidding of women to hold teaching/ruling positions appears to be an admonition to protect God's assigned lines of responsibility and authority within the home. For instance, the particular Greek term in the highly debated passage in 1 Tim. 2.12, andros, which has often times been translated "man," may also be translated "husband." With such a translation, then, the teaching would be that a wife ought not to rule over her husband.

This doctrine of a woman who, in choosing to marry, makes herself voluntarily submissive to "line up under" her husband is entirely consistent with the gist of the NT teaching on the role of authority in the Christian home. The Greek word hupotasso, which means to "line up under" refers to a wife's voluntary submission to her own husband (cf. Eph. 5.22, 23; Col. 3.18; Titus 2.5; 1 Pet. 3.1). This has nothing to do with any supposed superior status or capacity of the husband; rather, this refers to God's design of godly headship, authority which is given for comfort, protection, and care, not for destruction or domination (cf. Gen. 2.15-17; 3.16; 1 Cor. 11.3). Indeed, that this headship is interpreted in light of Christ's headship over the church signifies the kind of godly headship that must be given, that sense of tireless care, service, and protection required from godly leadership.

Of course, such an admonition for a wife to submit to a husband would not in any way rule out that women be involved in a teaching ministry (e.g., Titus 2.4), but, rather, that in the particular case of married women, that their own ministries would come under the protection and direction of their respective husbands (Acts 18.26). This would assert that a married woman's ministry in the church would be given serving, protective oversight by her husband, not due to any notion of inferior capacity or defective spirituality, but for the sake of, as one commentator has put it, "avoiding confusion and maintaining orderliness" (cf. 1 Cor. 14.40).

In both Corinth and Ephesus (which represent the contested Corinthian and Timothy epistolary comments), it appears that Paul's restriction upon women's participation was prompted by occasional happenings, issues which grew particularly out of these contexts, and therefore are meant to be understood in those lights. For instance, the hotly contested test of a women's "silence" in the church (see both 1 Cor. 14 and 1 Tim. 2) does not appear in any way to undermine the prominent role women played in the expansion of the Kingdom and development of the church in the first century. Women were involved in the ministries of prophecy and prayer (1 Cor. 11.5), personal instruction (Acts 18.26), teaching

(Titus 2.4,5), giving testimony (John 4.28,29), offering hospitality (Acts 12.12), and serving as co-laborers with the apostles in the cause of the Gospel (Phil. 4.2-3). Paul did not relegate women to an inferior role or hidden status but served side-by-side with women for the sake of Christ "I urge Euodia and I urge Syntyche to live in harmony in the Lord. Indeed, true companion, I ask you also to help these women who have shared my struggle in the cause of the gospel, together with Clement also and the rest of my fellow workers, whose names are in the book of life" (Phil. 4.2-3).

Furthermore, we must be careful in subordinating the personage of women per se (that is, their nature as women) versus their subordinated role in the marriage relationship. Notwithstanding the clear description of the role of women as heirs together of the grace of life in the marriage relationship (1 Pet. 3.7), it is equally plain that the Kingdom of God has created a dramatic shift in how women are to be viewed, understood, and embraced in the Kingdom community. It is plain that in Christ there is now no difference between rich and poor, Jew and Gentile, barbarian, Scythian, bondman and freemen, as well as man and woman (cf. Gal. 3.28; Col. 3.11). Women were allowed to be disciples of a Rabbi (which was foreign and disallowed at the time of Jesus), and played prominent roles in the NT church, including being fellow laborers side by side with the apostles in ministry (e.g., see Euodia and Syntyche in Phil. 4.1ff), as well as hosting a church in their houses (cf. Phoebe in Rom. 16.1-2, and Apphia in Philem. 1).

In regards to the issue of pastoral authority, I am convinced that Paul's understanding of the role of equippers (of which the pastor-teacher is one such role, cf. Eph. 4.9-15) is not gender specific. In other words, the decisive and seminal text for me on the operation of gifts and the status and function of offices are those NT texts which deal with the gifts (1 Cor. 12.1-27; Rom. 12.4-8; 1 Pet. 4.10-11, and Eph. 4.9-15). There is no indication in any of these formative texts that gifts are gender-specific. In other words, for the argument to hold decisively that women were never to be in roles that were pastoral or equipping in nature, the simplest and most effective argument would be to show that the Spirit simply would never even consider giving a woman a gift which was not suited to the range of callings which she felt a calling towards. Women would be forbidden from leadership because the Holy Spirit would never grant to a woman a calling and its requisite gifts because she was a woman. Some gifts would be reserved for men, and women would never receive those gifts.

A careful reading of these and other related texts show no such prohibition. It appears that it is up to the Holy Spirit to give any person, man or woman, any gift that suits him for any ministry he wishes them to do, as he wills (1 Cor. 12.11 "But one and the same Spirit works all these things, distributing to each one individually as he wills"). Building upon this point, Terry Cornett has even written a fine theological essay showing how the NT Greek for the word "apostle" is unequivocally applied to women, most clearly shown in the rendering of the female noun, "Junia" applied to "apostle" in Romans 16.7, as well as allusions to co-laboring, for instance, with the twins, Tryphena and Tryphosa, who "labored" with Paul in the Lord (16.12).

Believing that every God-called, Christ-endowed, and Spirit-gifted and led Christian ought to fulfill their role in the body, we affirm the role of women to lead and instruct under godly authority that submits to the Holy Spirit, the Word of God, and is informed by the tradition of the Church and spiritual reasoning. We ought to expect God to give women supernatural endowments of grace to carry out his bidding on behalf of his Church, and his reign in the Kingdom of God. Since both men and women both reflect the *Imago Dei* (i.e., image of God), and both stand as heirs together of God's grace (cf. Gen. 1.27; 5.2; Matt. 19.4; Gal. 3.28; 1 Pet. 3.7), they are given the high privilege of representing Christ together as his ambassadors (2 Cor. 5.20), and through their partnership to bring to completion our obedience to Christ's Great Commission of making disciples of all nations (Matt. 28.18-20).

Appendix 33

Capstone Student Educational Learning Hours

The Urban Ministry Institute

Question

How many educational or learning hours does the typical TUMI student engage in during the *Capstone Curriculum*? I know that there are 192 (total) hours of video/classroom work. However, I'm wondering about an estimate for the following:

1. Student application and implications discussion
2. Case studies and problems
3. Assignments
4. Ministry projects
5. Counseling & prayer

I'm needing an estimate of the total hours that the typical student will spend in the teaching/learning process with the TUMI *Capstone Curriculum*. (Note: This would not include personal study or home-work time. Instead, it would be any formal group or individually guided learning, discussion, and study time that meets the learning objectives of the *Capstone Curriculum*.)

Answer

We have given our best estimate of the breakdown of video classroom work, student prep and study time, and student ministry.

Although our pedagogical structure is also structured in terms of broad areas of student work (e.g., class time, personal preparation to fulfill assignments, and ministry planning and outreach), we use the modular structure to figure student investment. In other words, the following estimates are based on what we have seen to be our average student time investments per module. The overall numbers, therefore, will be found by multiplying these numbers by our total module count (16).

Our categories (for the modular structure) are as follows:

> *Class time:* Total 192 hours (roughly 16% of time on task in module). While this number may vary, usually with more hours being given at many sites for additional coverage, this is a

reasonable estimate of our students' classroom presence hours. (3 hours per lesson, 4 lessons per module, 16 modules)

Personal preparation: Total 640 hours (roughly 56% of time on task in module). This number reflects the time our students must give to our broad range of ongoing classroom assignments. On average, our students give 40 hours per module to fulfill our reading assignments, quiz preparation and examination, Scripture memorization projects, final examination preparation and take-home exam, and in-class assignments based on module requirements (40 hours per module, 16 modules).

Student Ministry Activity and Practicum (i.e., Exegetical and Ministry Projects): Total 320 hours (roughly 28% of time on task in module). Typically, the exegetical projects and ministry projects are done in tandem; students select a given text and must write an exegetical essay/term paper covering the central ideas of the module, and then arrange a venue/event in conjunction with their church or ministry situation/assignment to 1) present the gist, outline, or main teaching included within their project, 2) receive and evaluate the feedback from the presentation that summarized their major insights in the module, and 3) write a brief summary explaining the overall presentation, its impact, and their reaction to the presentation (20 hours per module, 16 modules).

Our totals, therefore are as follows:

Capstone Student's Engagement in Curriculum	Total Hours for All 16 Modules	Percentage Breakdown
Class Time	192	16%
Personal Preparation	640	56%
Student Ministry Activity and Practicum	320	28%

Frankly, in filling out these percentages we sought to neither over-inflate the number of hours our students give to their modular instruction, nor deflate the number of hours our students invest per class. Honestly, although we submit these numbers eagerly and believe they (by and large) are accurate, we know that these numbers underestimate the number of hours that TUMI students have given to our instruction over the course of our history. Because of the nature of the students (adult learners whose culture is both urban and oral), the prospect of doing this kind of work has been challenging for many, and their time-on-task has understandably needed to be more generous in comparison to other schools that our faculty have taught at. This says nothing of their quality of work nor their seriousness as students, only that our best students are vintage "work-aholics," balancing family, ministry, and job responsibilities as they have pursued ministry education at the Institute.

Appendix 34
Mentor Sign-Off Form

A printable copy of this form can be found at *www.tumi.org/mentor*

As you consider serving as a Mentor, it is important that you familiarize yourself with the overall TUMI purpose, strategy, and pedagogy contained in this manual. Please read this manual through before you begin your work as a Mentor.

After you have read this manual, please read carefully and check the boxes below, indicating you both understand and support the Institute's doctrine, programming, and strategy. Sign the document, and turn in your signed sheet to your Site Coordinator. Feel free to discuss and review key aspects of our training purposes and philosophy covered herein, and be sure to dialogue regarding any questions that may impact your mentoring of courses at your TUMI satellite.

On behalf of our TUMI National staff, we praise God for your service to Christ as you help equip servant leaders for the Church. May God's Kingdom be advanced as you leverage your gifts to equip others, for God's glory!

❑ I have read, understand, and support the statements concerning the identity and mission of World Impact, Inc., and of its research organization, *The Urban Ministry Institute.*

❑ I have read, understand, and support *The Urban Ministry Institute's* commitment to the Great Tradition, and its goal to retrieve those roots for the renewal and revival of the urban church.

❑ I have read, understand, and support TUMI's statement on its specific calling to advance the Kingdom among the urban poor (cf. *Our Distinctives: Advancing the Kingdom of God among the Urban Poor*)

❑ I have read, understand, and am committed to fulfilling the responsibilities in the job description of a Mentor of *The Urban Ministry Institute.*

❑ I have read, understand, support, and will teach in a manner consistent with World Impact's *Affirmation of Faith* statement.

_____   _____
Signature   Date

Mentor Sign-Off Form

Made in the USA
Coppell, TX
23 March 2022